DICTIONARY OF
THE AMERICAN INDIAN

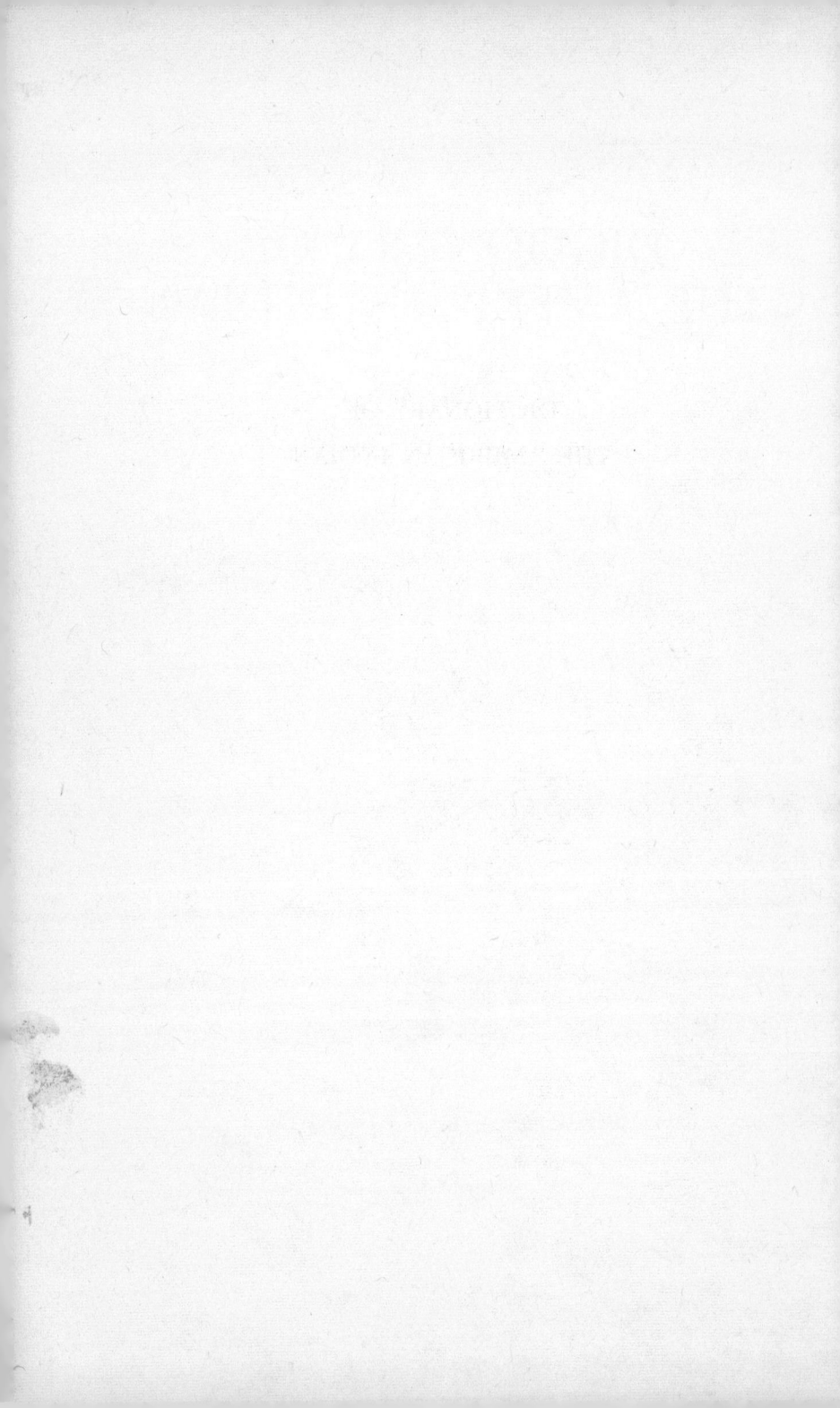

DICTIONARY OF
THE AMERICAN INDIAN

by JOHN L. STOUTENBURGH, JR.

Executive Director

MARATHON COUNTY HISTORICAL SOCIETY

Wisconsin

PHILOSOPHICAL LIBRARY

New York

DICTIONARY OF
THE AMERICAN INDIAN

A

Aatsosni

This is one of the clans of the Navajo, meaning "narrow gorge."

Ababco

A tribe or sub-tribe of the Algonquian Indians. Were possibly a division of the Choptank. In 1741, the Colonial government officially recorded their possession of the land on the south bank of the Choptank River in Maryland. In 1837, there were but a few members of the tribe left and all were of mixed blood.

Abayca

Mentioned by Ponce de Leon in 1512. This Tequesta village was situated on the southern end of Florida.

Aberginian

This was a term used by the early settlers of Massachusetts when talking about the Indians of that area. These Indians are possibly the Wippanap, which was an Abnaki tribe. The name may be a corruption of Abnaki or aborigines.

Abihka

A Creek town, the exact location is unknown but is supposed to be along the upper part of the Coosa River in Alabama.

Abikudshi

An early Creek town on the right bank of the Tallahatchee Creek near the Coosa River in Talladega County, Alabama. These were Abihka Indians and spoke the dialect of the Chickasaw to some extent.

1

Abiquiu
This was a pueblo founded by the Spanish around 1747. It was raided by the Ute in that same year and was abandoned for about a year. In 1748 there were about twenty families living at Abiquiu. It was again raided by the Ute and Navajo and was again abandoned until 1754. In 1765, the name of this town was changed to Santo Tomás and was located on the Río Chama in Río Arriba County, New Mexico.

Abmoctac
This was an early Costanoan village near the Dolores mission in San Francisco, California.

Abnaki
An Algonquian tribe. The name was used by the Colonial English and French to designate the tribes which were situated in what is now the state of Maine. In 1604 Champlain visited a small village of bark huts situated near the mouth of the Penobscot River, near what is now Bangor, Maine. These Indians fought on the side of the French until the decline of the French power in America.

Accomac
Accomac, Virginia, see Powhatan; one of the villages of this tribe.

Accomac
A tribe of the Virginia Confederacy. In the Algonquian dialects, means "land" or "land beyond," "the other side place." After 1812 they lost their identity as a tribe.

Acconoc
A Powhatan village around 1608. Situated between the Chickahominy and Pamunkey Rivers in New Kent County, Virginia.

Accoondews
Powhatan for large blueberries.

2

Acela

A small Indian village in west central Florida. This village was visited by De Soto in 1539. A corruption of the name is given to the Ocilla River.

Achillimo

A Chumashan village which was near the Santa Inez mission in what is now Santa Barbara County, California.

Achois

An Indian village in Encina valley in southern California. This is the area where the mission of San Fernando was established on September 8, 1797.

Achougoula

From the Choctaw "ashunga" meaning pipe. Known as the pipe people. One of the villages of the Natchez confederacy. There were nine villages in 1699.

Achsinnink

A village of the Delawares. This village existed about 1770 on the Hocking River in Ohio. The Chippewa meaning for the word meant "at the place of the rough rock." Literally, a place with many rocks and difficult to travel over or through.

Achusi

In the year 1539 De Soto spent the winter in this port. This is in the Muskhogean area and is now known as Pensacola in the state of Florida.

Acoma Pueblo

This is a large, mostly unchanged pueblo, now known for their pottery. Their name "akóme," means "people of the white rock." This pueblo was situated on a rock mesa 357 feet high about 60 miles west of the Rio Grande in Valencia County in New Mexico. About 1540 it was visited by Coronado's army who called the town Acuco. This is the oldest inhabited settlement in the United States. The Indians of

3

Acoma irrigated their crops and raised corn, melons, etc. They also had large flocks of domesticated turkeys. Acoma is located about 12 miles south of U.S. Highway 66 and about 60 miles west of Albuquerque, New Mexico.

Acorn
See anafkimmens.

Acoti
This Indian site, west of Taos in New Mexico, was indicated as the "birth place of Montezuma." This was stated on an Indian map in 1856.

Actinea
This plant is used in its entirety by the Navajo for the making of a light greenish yellow dye.

Adai
A tribe with a dialect similar to that of the Anadarko. They were members of the Caddo confederacy. In 1529, they were visited by Cabeza de Vaca. The tribe was very helpful to the French around 1719. The trail connecting the villages was known as the "contraband trail." This trail was used by traders who went between the French and Spanish provinces. One of their cities was near the Spanish fort at San Antonio, Texas. This tribe was under Spanish and French control and suffered at the hands of both.

Adario
A Tionontate chief, known also by the names of Sastaretsi and the rat. In 1688, he made a treaty with the French to attack the Iroquois. When his war party was well on its way, he heard that the French were making peace with the Iroquois. The French were about to send envoys to Montreal. Adario made out as if he had decided to return and not fight. He then returned and ambushed the envoys. His men told the French envoy that the French had told him to do it. He then set the Iroquois free and told them he hoped

4

that they would repay the French for their bad faith. . . .
On August 25, 1689, the Iroquois attacked Montreal and
hundreds of settlers were killed. Following this, Adario
came forth and made the peace and for this the French
honored him. Adario died in Montreal in 1701 and was
buried with honors . . . by the French.

Adirondack

A Mohawk term meaning "they eat trees." This refers to
their habit of eating the bark of trees when there is a great
lack of food. This was one of the Algonquian tribes that lived
north of the St. Lawrence river.

Adobe

A type of sun dried brick made of mud and straw. The
brick is made 18 inches long by 5 by 8 inches. The size
varies but this is the usual size. The word was known in
ancient Egypt and was called "brick" on the ancient hiero-
glyphics. From there it went to Arabic "at-tob" and then
Spanish "adobar," meaning to daub or plaster. Wooden
molds were not used until the Spanish influence in the 16th
century. Early adobe bricks were made round and were
mixed with burned brush and sticks. The bricks were stuck
together with a mixture of adobe mud. Adobe bricks had to
be made near a water supply and the bricks are packed in
slanting rows so that they will shed water if it should rain
while they are curing. The base of a wall made with adobe
brick is the part that wears first and this should be watched
and repaired. Adobe brick houses are cool because of their
thick walls. The walls are usually plastered or smoothed
over with more adobe mud. Present day houses in the Southwest constructed of adobe bricks are far superior to other
materials in this area.

Adoeette

This was a Kiowa chief, known as "Big Tree." Living in
what is now the southwestern part of Oklahoma, this chief

and his men made many raids into Texas, even though the government put Fort Sill right in his midst. For attacking a wagon train and for his part in the attack, Adoeette was confined to the penitentiary at Fort Sill. He was released with the understanding that he and his tribe would live at peace. He became a Christian and settled down on his reservation.

Adzes
The adz was primarily a woodworking tool. The blade resembles that of the celt. The adz was usually made of stone, but was also made of bone, shell and copper. Used to scrape charred wood, the point was not very sharp. The adz was used a great deal by the Indians of the Pacific Northwest.

Aegakotcheising
A village of the Ottawa, situated in the present state of Michigan. This village was active around 1851.

Aepjin
The name of the resident chief of a small Indian village in Rensselaer County in New York. The name is Dutch and means "little ape."

Afsinimins
The Powhatan Indian word for walnut.

Agacay
An old Timucuanan town about 150 miles from the mouth of the St. Johns River in Florida.

Agaihtikara
Known as the "fish eaters." These Indians were a division of the Paviotso, living near the Walker and Carson Rivers in Nevada. The tribe, numbering about 1500 Indians, was under the rule of Chief Oderie. This tribe was active around 1866.

Agawam

The name generally meant "the place to cure fish." Agawam was found in New England around the areas of Ipswich in Massachusetts and also near Springfield and Wareham, both of Massachusetts. These sites were disposed of in the late 1600's.

Agawano

Situated in the mountains about seven miles east of the Rio Grande, this was a prehistoric pueblo of the Nambe of New Mexico.

Agriculture

Many Indian tribes practiced agriculture in some form or other. Their tools were simple and so their farms were not large as compared to present day standards. Their tools were simple pointed sticks, bone or stone. The work usually was done by the women. The various types of plants will be found under their common names and will be described more fully.

Aguacay

This large village was visited by De Soto in 1542. Situated along the Washita River in Arkansas, this village was important because of its salt manufacture and was an important trading area for this product.

Ahapopka

An old Seminole Indian town near the head of the Ocklawaha River in the north central part of Florida. The name referred to the "bog potato."

Ahone

The word for God used by the Powhatan Indians of Virginia.

Ahosulga
A Seminole town probably in Lafayette County in Florida.

Ahpewk
Virginia Indian word for feathers.

Ahqwohhooc
This is the word for drum in the Virginia Indian language.

Ahuamhoue
A former village of the Chumashan people near the mission Santa Inéz in Santa Barbara County, California.

Ais
A tribe of unknown connections who lived along the east coast of Florida. They planted nothing and lived entirely on fish and wild fruits and berries.

Akasquy
This now extinct tribe was visited by La Salle in January of 1687. This tribe lived near the Brazos River in Texas. They made their clothes of bison hair and were adorned with the feathers of birds.

Akonye
A band of the Apache of the San Carlos and Ft. Apache agency in Arizona. The name means "the people of the canyon."

Alachua
Formerly a Seminole town. It was settled by the Creeks in 1710. The Indians of this town took an active part in the Seminole war of 1835 to 1842. The principal town was Cuscowilla.

Alafiers
This was a Seminole town near the Alafia river in Flor-

8

ida. This tribe was led by Chief Alligator. These Indians took an active part in the Seminole war of 1835.

Alawahku
This was the elk clan of the Pecos Indians of New Mexico.

Albemarle Sound
Albemarle Sound, North Carolina, see Pasquotank.

Alder
See the Navajo, g'ish.

Alexandria
Alexandria, Virginia, see Pamacocack.

Algic
A term used by H. R. Schoolcraft and other later writers. The term was used to describe the Algonquian tribes and their languages.

Algonkian
This term is used to describe the rocks found in the region of Lake Superior. This is a formation found between the Paleozoic and Archean formations. This name was given to this formation because it is found in the same territory in which the Algonquian tribes were located.

Algonkin
This term was originally applied to a small Algonquian tribe known as the Weskarini. This small tribe lived along a tributary of the Ottawa river, east of the present city of Ottawa, Canada. These Indians formed a close alliance with the French but were soon forced to scatter because of the attacks of the Iroquois.

Algonquian
A linguistic stock. The name is from the Algonkin tribe. The Algonquian family occupied more territory than any

9

other in North America. The tribes were mainly agricultural and sedentary, with the exception of the tribes of the north in Canada. The typical lodge of the Algonquian was oval and made from the bark of the birch tree. The Virginia Indians built long houses. In the north the houses were made of logs. In the south and the west the houses were made of small saplings and twigs. A form of picture writing was done by the Delawares and the Chippewa. The design was scratched or painted on bark. The eastern Algonquian were intelligent and brave but they lacked organization. Under the leadership of Pontiac, Tecumseh, Philip, Powhatan and Opechancanough and many others the Algonquians went far, but with difficulty because they would not work together. The exception to the rule came with the Virginia Indians under the rule of Powhatan; they resisted the whites until they almost became extinct.

Alipconk
A village of the Wecquaesgeeks (q.v.), meaning the "place of elms." It was located on what is now the present town of Tarrytown, New York. This town was destroyed by the Dutch in 1644.

Alive
See kekewh.

Alki
A word found on the official seal of the state of Washington. This is a word from the Chinook Indian dialect, meaning "In the future."

Alle
A pueblo near Salinas in New Mexico. Occupied by the Piros around the year 1589.

Allegheny
An Iroquois reservation under the jurisdiction of the State of New York.

Allu
This was the Antelope clan of the Pecos tribe, found in New Mexico.

Alouko
An old Seminole town situated on the east side of the St. Marks River in Wakulla County, Florida.

Alpincha
A town of the Chumashan. Located in the center of what is now Santa Barbara, California.

Alsea
A Yakonan or Chinookan tribe living on the Alsea River in Oregon.

Altar
An Indian altar was one of many things. It could be a simple affair of just an animal skull such as a bison, or it could be a pile of rocks. Certain springs and other areas were used and visited on special occasions. Some altars were very complicated, such as the Hopi. These had many parts such as altar bowls, prayer sticks, pipes, rattles, feathers and the skins of animals. Some altars were directional and pointed north, east, south and west. Altars were used for special reasons, for example to pray for rain, good crops, good hunting, etc.

Alton
Alton, Illinois, see Piasa, also pictographs.

Alum
Raw alum is used as a mordant by the Navajo Indians during the dyeing process.

Amador
Amador, California, see Yuloni.

Amaye

A town that was visited by De Soto in 1542 in the southwestern part of what is now Arkansas.

American Horse

An Oglala Sioux chief. . . . Fought with Sitting Bull in the Sioux war. He was killed at Slim Buttes in South Dakota on September 29, 1875. He was a signer of the treaty which was secured by the Crook commission.

Amerind

This word was suggested in 1899 by an American lexicographer as a word to be used when talking about the races of man that lived in the New World before the arrival of the Europeans. The name is used from time to time in scientific and lay literature.

Amherst

Amherst, New Hampshire, see Souhegan.

Amkonnmg

The Powhatan Indian word for the poisonous blossom of the black cherry.

Amofens

The Powhatan Indian word for daughter.

Amonsoquath

The Powhatan word for bear, used by the Indians of Virginia.

Amoque

A ranchería of the Maricopa. Formerly of the Gila river in southern Arizona.

Ampkone

This is the Powhatan word for frying pan.

Amu

The "Ant Clan" of the Pecos tribe of New Mexico.

Anadarko
A tribe of Caddo Indians living on the Trinity and Brazos Rivers in Texas.

Anafkimmens
The Powhatan for acorn.

Analco
An ancient pueblo of the Tewa, next to the San Miguel chapel located in what is now Santa Fe, New Mexico. The original building was found to have been built by the Spanish, the foundation being built by the Pueblos.

Anaskenoans
A former village of the Powhatan of Virginia. Located on the Rappahannock River in Caroline County.

Anath
The Powhatan Indian word for farewell.

Anchor stones
These were crudely shaped stones which were used as anchors for Indian boats. They were usually smoothed and had a groove pecked around them so that a cord could be fastened around it. These anchor stones were rarely more than 40 pounds in weight.

Andesite
A rock found mainly in the west. Light grey to black, found in and around volcanos. Used by the Indians for the making of utensils and other implements.

Aomataŭ
The Powhatan Indian word for a boat.

Apache
The Apache are divided into many groups or clans. Their names were taken from natural features, never from animals. The Apache were a rather nomadic people and were

always on the move. They have a rather high skill in the making of baskets. They lived on the plains of New Mexico and west Texas, were very warlike and raided whites and Indians alike. Such leaders as Cochise, Geronimo, Victorio, Nana and others are well known.

Apaches del Perrillo

This band of Apaches was located near the Rio Grande in southern New Mexico, so named by the Spanish, "Apaches of the Little Dog." So called because a dog found a spring and thus saved the Spanish who were in dire need of water.

Apishamore

A word of the Algonquian and Chippewa dialects, meaning "to lie down upon," to lie on. Usually meant to indicate a saddle blanket made from the skin of the bison calf. Used on the Great Plains.

Apoanocanosutck

The Virginia Indian term for bread.

Apokan

The Powhatan Indian word for a tobacco pipe.

Apome

This is the term used for the thigh, used by the Powhatan Indians of Virginia.

Apones

The Powhatan word for bread.

Apooke

This is the word for tobacco as used by the Powhatan Indians of Virginia.

Aposoum

This is the Powhatan word for an opossum.

Apple

See maracah.

Aquile
A village in the northwestern part of Florida. Visited by De Soto in 1539.

Aquixo
An Indian village situated near the St. Francis River in Arkansas, near the west bank of the Mississippi River. Visited by De Soto in 1541.

Aragaritka
A name given by the Iroquois tribes to the Huron and the Tionontati who were driven out of the area between Lake Huron and Lake Erie, and also from lower Michigan.

Arapaho
An important Plains tribe of the Algonquian family. They divided themselves into about five divisions: The Northern Arapaho, the Southern Arapaho, the Atsina or Gros Ventres, "The wood lodge people or big lodge pole people," and the "rock men." Many names were given for the smaller groups or bands such as the "bad faces," "greasy faces," "bad pipes," "forks of the river men," the "watchers," the "wolves."

Arawakan
A settlement in southern Florida of tribes from the West Indies.

Archaeology
This is the scientific study of the works of ancient man during recent or pre-historic times, dealing mainly with man.

Architecture
Building materials and construction varied with the locale. Materials and the climate had a great deal to do with the type of house that was built. Skin tents were made by the tribes that moved around a great deal. Adobe houses were built in dry hot areas. Wooden houses were built in

areas where there was an abundance of wood. Bark was used. Defense also played a big part in construction, many tribes of the Southwest built high up on cliffs.

Aridian

The arts and other works of the Indians of southern Arizona. They were similar to those of the Zuñi. Also applied to those Indians who lived in the other desert areas of the Southwest.

Arikara

A plains tribe which split off from the Pawnee in northern Nebraska.

Arm

See mackatahone.

Arrow

An Indian arrow was made from a variety of materials. The Indians of the California area used hardwood for the shafts. Some areas used a hardwood foreshaft and the shaft of a lighter or pithy wood. The Indian arrow had six parts: The head, shaft, foreshaft, shaftment, the feathering and the nock. The head was the point of the arrow. The shaft was the main, rod-like part, which sometimes had a piece of a harder material attached to it at the front end, called the foreshaft. The shaftment was the other end of the shaft, and the nock the end which was grooved for the bowstring. The feathering was the feathers attached at the end. Length varied with the individual and materials at hand. Usually the shaft was plain. The west coast area arrows were painted with stripes for identification. The Plains Indians cut grooves lengthwise, these were sometimes called "lightning marks" or "blood grooves." Some arrows had no feathers, others had either two or three feathers. The feathers were from a great variety of birds.

Arrow

See asqweowan.

Arrow feathers
    See assaconcawh.

Arrowhead
    An arrowhead or arrowpoint was used on the end of an arrowshaft. The points were usually made of flint; however, many other materials were used such as bone, antlers, wood, shell and copper. Copper was used by the tribes in the region of the Great Lakes and up into Canada. With the coming of the whites, arrowpoints were made of iron. An arrowhead was usually smaller than two inches in length. Spearheads were longer. The shapes varied, but they generally were made in the shapes of leaves, such as the willow. Some points had no barbs and were made for easy withdrawal. Other points were barbed and were used in warfare. They were made to inflict a jagged wound and were difficult to remove. The points were usually fastened to the shaft with sinew, rawhide. Warpoints were sometimes fastened rather loosely so that they would come off when they struck an enemy.
    See raputtak.

Artifact
    This is a term used by the archaeologist and others for the manufactured works of man, such as tools, etc.

Asapan
    This is the Powhatan Indian word for hasty pudding.

Ashamomuck
    A village of the Corchaug, located in Suffolk County on Long Island, New York.

Ashes
    See pungwe.

Ashes of juniper
    See the Navajo term for their use, gad bididze' doo bilatxahi bileeshch' iih bixtoo.'

Ashkanena
A band of the Crow Indians, meaning "Blackfoot lodges."

Asomoches
A group of the Delaware Indians. Formerly living on the east bank of the Delaware River between Salem and Camden.

Aspinet
A leader of the Nauset. He was well known to the colonists in Plymouth, Massachusetts, in 1621. In the winter of 1622 it was Aspinet and his tribe who came and saved the colonists who were starving. He brought corn and beans. However, Standish and others were rather against Aspinet and eventually drove the Indians into the swamps. Aspinet died possibly in 1623.

Asqweowan
The Powhatan Indian word for arrow.

Assaconcawh
This is the Virginia Indian term which is used to describe the feathers on an arrow.

Assahampehooke
The Powhatan Indian term for the lobster.

Assimoest
This is the word for fox in the language of the Powhatan Indians of Virginia.

Assiniboin
A large Siouan tribe. They lived in the general area of Lake Superior, Lake Winnipeg to the Lake of the Woods. The Assiniboin were also found in Missouri and west to the Rockies. They continually fought with the Dakotas. Bison was used as a main part of their diet and the tribe spent a great deal of time making pemmican. They were great

traders and used the pemmican for barter with the whites. Burial consisted of a circular grave about five feet deep, lined with bark or skins. The corpse was placed in a sitting position. The grave was then covered with logs and then dirt. If death occurred at a distance from the tribal burial area, the corpse was carried along with the tribe and placed on a high scaffold until the burial place was reached. Many of the tribe now live on the Fort Belknap and Fort Peck reservations in Montana.

Assumption

A mission, established at the Wyandot village in 1728. Located near the present site of the city of Detroit. Later moved to the opposite shore and continued until 1781.

Assuti

A band of the Nez Percé. They lived on the Assuti River in Idaho. They joined with Chief Joseph in the Nez Percé war of 1877.

Assuweska

A village of the Powhatan confederacy. Located on the Rappahannock River, 1608.

Astialakwa

A pueblo of the Jemez. Located on the top of the mesa that separates the San Diego and Guadelupe canyons. This was the possible seat of the Franciscan mission of San Juan which was established early in the 17th century.

Atepua

A pueblo in the region of the lower Rio Grande River in New Mexico. Built around 1598.

Athabasca

The tribe is regarded as Chipewyan, a northern Athapascan tribe (q.v.). The name means generally "grass and reeds here and there."

Athapascan

A widely distributed linguistic Indian family, considered by some to be the most widely distributed in North America. This linguistic stock extended from the Arctic coast to northern Mexico and from the Pacific to Hudson Bay and from the Rio Colorado to the mouth of the Rio Grande in the south.

Athens

Athens, Pennsylvania, see Tioga.

Atlatl

This is a device used to aid in throwing a spear. It is a short stick which has a notch or cup in one end in which the spear end is placed. The atlatl gives the thrower added leverage. The atlatl is not thrown with the spear but is retained in the hand.

Atripuy

The country occupied by the Piros. Mentioned by Oñate in 1589. Located in the lower region of the Rio Grande valley in New Mexico.

Atsina

A branch of the Arapaho (q.v.). Known variously as the "white clay people," "gut people," "beggars," "spongers," "belly people." Sometimes confused with the Gros Ventres of the Missouri and the Hidatsa. They were placed on the Fort Belknap reservation.

Attacapa

A tribe and a linguistic family. They lived in southern Louisiana. They were good buffalo hunters, the buffalo coming into their territory in the fall.

Attomoys

The Powhatan word for dog.

Attucks

Crispus Attucks, part Indian and part Negro. A well known leader who was the first person killed in the Boston massacre of March 5, 1770. This battle is considered by most historians as the opening battle of the American Revolution. On March 5th Attucks was said to have led a group of sailors to the Old State House at Framingham, Massachusetts. It was here that the first encounter between British and American troops was fought. It is generally believed that Attucks was a sailor. His mother was Indian and his name was taken from her, meaning "small deer," however, he was a very large man.

Aucutgagwafsun

The Virginia Indian word for a copper kettle.

Auhtab

Powhatan Indian for a bow, as in bow and arrow. See bow.

Auppes

This is the Powhatan word for the bow string.

Avavares

A tribe that was visited by Cabeza de Vaca in 1527 to 1534. A possible Caddoan group, living in Texas. This tribe traded bows and bone to the Mariames, the latter was ground up by the Mariames and used for food.

Avon

Avon, New York, see Skaniadariio.

Avoyelles

Meaning "the vipers," this tribe was located near the Red River in Louisiana. The tribe belonged to the Caddoan family. The tribe lived in villages. Very little is known of their beliefs and ceremonies. The Biloxi Indians settled in their territory and when the whites came to the Gulf States

21

area, the tribe started on its way down. Through war and new diseases the tribe all but disappeared and only three women were left in 1805.

Awani

A tribe living in the Yosemite Valley in Mariposa County in California. There were nine villages in this valley.

Awatobi

A pueblo of the Hopi on a mesa about nine miles southeast of Walpi in northeastern Arizona. This was one of the original villages that was visited by Tobar and Cardenas of Coronado's expedition in 1540. In 1629 it became the seat of the Franciscan mission under Father Porras. In 1700 Awatobi was attacked by the Indians of Walpi and Mashongnovi and the mission was never again inhabited.

Awl

Awls were made from a variety of materials. Thorns, cactus needles, agave, splinters of flint, wood, bone, antlers. Bear and turkey bones were also used extensively. The awl was generally used to make holes or perforations. Used mainly in the sewing crafts, they were also used to hold wounds shut as a pin. Used for scratching, etching, pipe picks and in pottery making.

Axes

Indian axes vary in size from an ounce to 30 pounds. Usually they are from one to six pounds. In general, the ax is rather heavy and wedge shaped. Made from granite or other hard rock, although sandstones and slates were used when harder material was not available. One groove was usually cut around the thick part of the ax. In the areas of the pueblos, axes generally had two or more grooves. The haft was usually fastened with sinew or rawhide. The ax was used for many things; it was not very well suited for the cutting of trees but was useful when cutting the charred wood in a dugout canoe. The ax was used in warfare. Iron axes brought by the whites were much sought after by the Indians.

Axol

A pueblo of the Tewa in New Mexico. Visited by Oñate in 1598.

Ayanabi

A neutral town of the Choctaw on the Yannubbee creek in Mississippi. It was here that the Creeks and the Choctaws met to make peace in the early 18th century.

Aycate

An old Maricopa ranchería located on the Gila River in the southwestern part of Arizona.

Aztec National Monument

These pueblo ruins are located a few miles from Aztec, New Mexico, on U.S. highway 550. They represent the Anasazi people who lived in the area around 1100 A.D. There is also a small museum near the ruins.

B

Babiche
A word taken from an Algonquian dialect, used by the Canadian French. The original word possibly came from the Micmac "ababich," meaning cord. Used when talking about a thong, especially one made from the skin of the eel.

Babisi
A ranchería near the southern border of Arizona.

Backhook
A small tribe living along the Pee Dee River in South Carolina. The Hook tribe lived around 1700 and were the foes of the Santee tribes of the Carolinas.

Bacuvia
An early settlement in the area known as Apalachee, Florida. Known about the early part of 1700.

Badwisha
A tribe of the Mariposa of California. This tribe lived near the Wikchamni.

Bagaduce
A peninsula in Hancock County, Maine. Formerly occupied by the Abnaki around 1602.

Bagiopa
The name, meaning "people," is of a possible Piman origin. This tribe was located along the reaches of the Colorado River and probably belonged to the Shoshone group.

Baguiburisac

This tribe was located on the Colorado River in Arizona near the Gila and Williams fork. The tribe lived in houses which were low, with a wood roof which was covered with dirt. They were visited by Oñate in 1604.

Bahekhube

A village occupied by the Kansa who lived along the Blue River and the Kansas River in Kansas.

Bakihon

A band of the Upper Yanktonai Sioux. The name means "gash themselves with knives."

Baking stone

A rectangular stone, rarely over a foot long and about an inch thick. Usually made of soapstone. An interesting feature of the baking stone is the hole in the center of one end. This hole was used to enable its user to move it in and out of a fire. It is possible that the hole was used to enable the stone to be lowered into a pot for the purpose of boiling liquids. The stone resembled a huge pendant. This particular type of stone was used mainly in southern California. Flat stones were also used by the Pueblos to bake their bread and served in much the same way as our present day griddle.

Balcony House

Located in Mesa Verde in Southern Colorado. A cliff dwelling of about 25 rooms. The name is derived from the fact that the floor beams of one of the dwellings extend out and form a balcony along the front.

Bald Eagle's Nest

An Indian town situated on the right bank of Bald Eagle Creek, near Milesburg, Pennsylvania.

Ballokai Pomo

A division of the Pomo which formerly lived in Potter Valley, Mendocino County, California.

Ball playing

In the eastern part of America, ball playing was a favorite man's game. It was also played in California. Generally in the west other games were played. Ball playing was done by eight or ten men, however, there were times when there were hundreds of men playing at one time. Before each game there were special ceremonies and feasts. Usually the game was played on a large field with a goal at each end. Rackets were used and the ball was made of deerskin which was stuffed with hair or moss. The game was adapted by the whites and in Canada the game is now known by the name of la crosse and is played with 12 men on each side. In the north, the Indians used only one racket. In the south the tribes used two rackets.

Bandelier National Monument

This monument is open to the public from May to October. It is located south of Los Alamos and west of Santa Fe, New Mexico. It has large unusual cliff houses in Frijoles Canyon.

Banner stones

Also called "butterfly stones." The term is applied to a group of stone objects of varied form. Usually look somewhat like a double headed ax only much smaller. Sometimes made of shell, these being found in Florida. They were also occasionally made of clay, slate or steatite. They were perforated through the center such as is seen in a double bladed ax. The use of the banner stone is not known. Many theories have been given for their use. Such uses are given when a general idea of the tribe is known and it is then possible to have an idea of their use. Such uses could be, fastened to a ceremonial wand, hung around the neck, fastened to the headdress or used as a ceremonial weapon. Usually made of selected materials which have a fine grain and pleasing color.

Bannock

A Shoshonean tribe who lived in southern Idaho and western Wyoming. The failure of the government to provide sufficient food when they were put on a reservation led to an outbreak in 1878. Many Bannock women and children were killed in the resulting campaign.

Baptiste

Jean Baptiste, a Christianized Indian of the Onondagas, see Ochionagueras.

Baraboo

Baraboo, Wisconsin, see Yellow Thunder.

Bark

The bark of trees was used by many American Indians in many ways. In the spring when food was rather scarce, the bark of trees was eaten. Certain Algonquian tribes ate a great deal of bark and the name of Adirondack was applied to them, meaning "they eat trees." The inner bark of certain spruce and hemlock was made into cakes by certain Pacific and southwestern tribes. Other barks were used with tobacco for smoking. The barks of pine, cedar, birch and elm were used for the making of boxes and baskets for cooking, storing and for the covering of food supplies. Bark was also used for the covering of houses and for the making of beds and for the construction of coffins by the Iroquois tribes. Dyes were made from the bark of certain trees as well as torches, padding, ropes, baskets and many uses in ceremonies.

Basal grinding

This is the method of grinding the base of a stone tool to prevent it from cutting through its binding.

Basin sagebrush
See the Navajo ds'ah.

Basketry
The craft of making baskets was practiced by the American Indians. There were many uses and types. Baskets were mainly made by the coil method or they were woven. The materials were as varied as the kinds of baskets. Roots, fibers of plants, the barks of trees and many other materials were used. The same types of techniques were used in the making of nets, traps, etc., as were used in the making of baskets. Designs were often copied from nature and dyes were secured from plants and minerals.

Batawat
A tribe of the Wishosk who lived in the area of the mouth of the Mad River in northwest California.

Bat House
A pueblo of the Hopi. Located on the northwest side of the Jeditoh valley in northeastern Arizona. It was built and occupied by the "Bat clan."

Batista
A village of the Koasati. Located on the lower Trinity River in Texas.

Batni
A sacred location used for special offerings by the Snake People of the Hopi tribe. Also the name given to a gourd container in which sacred water is carried for the ceremonies. Also considered to be the site of the first pueblo built by the Hopi, located near Tusayan in northeastern Arizona.

Baton
Usually a ceremonial staff of authority. Carried by the chief or shaman. They were made of bone, deer antlers and sometimes of flint.

Bauka

A village of the Maidu, located on the Feather River in California.

Bayberry

A plant used by the Indians, especially of the New England area. Used in the making of bayberry candles. The small grey berries were collected by the Indians and were boiled in water. The wax floated to the surface and was skimmed off and made into candles. This method was taught to the early settlers in New England. Also known as the "wax myrtle."

Bayfield

Bayfield, Wisconsin, see Shaugawaumikong.

Bayogoula

A tribe of the Muskhogean who lived several miles from the mouth of the Mississippi River. The name Bayogoula is a Choctaw word and means "the bayou people." In 1706 most of the tribe was killed in a battle with the Tonica. In the year 1721 smallpox killed the rest of the tribe.

Bayu

A village of the Maidu located on Sandy Gulch in Butte County, California.

Beads

Beads were made of innumerable materials, shells, wood, teeth, claws, seeds, clay, bird beaks, bone, minerals. Glass beads were brought by the settlers and formed a big item of trade. Wampum used in the northeast was made from the clam shell, both the white and purple part being used, the purple part having more value.

Beans

See peketawas, and peccataas.

Bear
See amonsoquath, also monnonfacqueo.

Beaver
Beaver, Pennsylvania, see Sawcunk.

Beaver
See cuttak, also pohkewh.

Beaver Island Indians
A tribe of the Chippewa formerly living on the Beaver Islands of Michigan near Lake Michigan.

Beavertown
A village of the Delawares, located at the head of the Hocking River in Morgan County, Ohio.

Bed
See cawwaivuh, petaocawin.

Bedalpago
See race.

Bedford
Bedford, Pennsylvania, see Shawnee Cabins.

Beech Creek
A Seminole town located on Beech Creek in Florida. It was settled by the Indians from the Chattahoochee River in Georgia.

Bee plant
The Rocky Mountain bee plant has long been used as a food and as a plant from which a dye is made by the Navajo Indians.

Bejuituuy
Located on the Rio Grande River in New Mexico, this was a pueblo of the Tigua.

Bellacoola

A group of northwest coast Salish tribes who lived along the Bellacoola River and in British Columbia.

Bells

Early American Indian tribes made bells of clay which were fired. Copper bells were found in the mounds of some Southern states, however, it is thought that these are trade bells which came from Mexico and Central America. Metal bells were brought in by the whites as a trade item and were widely distributed.

Below

See noufvmon.

Benson

Benson, Arizona, see Quiburi.

Beothuk

A name given to the Indians of the Newfoundland area, meaning "Indian" or "red Indian." Given this name by the Europeans because they painted themselves with red clay continually. They are generally to be considered as a separate and distinct linguistic stock.

Bernalillo

Bernalillo, New Mexico, see Puaray. Also see Sia.

Bethlehem

A center of Indian conversion. This was a Moravian settlement started in 1740, located in Pennsylvania. See Tatemy.

Betty's Neck

A village of Indians located near Middleboro in Massachusetts. The name is derived from one of the Indian women in the village.

Bible

The language of the Massachusetts Indians was the first Indian language into which the bible was translated. This translation was made by John Eliot in 1661 and was finished in 1663. The Bible was later translated many times to fit the needs of the various tribes and missionaries.

Big Bear

Big Bear, a Cherokee Chief, see Yanegua.

Big Bill

A chief of the Paiute. In September 11, 1857, Big Bill joined forces with the Mormon John D. Lee in the Mountain Meadow massacre in the southwestern part of Utah.

Big Canoe

A chief of the Kalispel. Born in 1799, he died on the Flathead Reservation in Montana in 1882.

Big Foot

In 1890, Big Foot and a tribe of the Hunkpapa Sioux were captured at Wounded Knee Creek in South Dakota and all but a few were wiped out by American troops. There were about three hundred in the band at the time, including men, women and children.

Big Hammock

A large Seminole settlement in the central part of Florida, north of Tampa Bay.

Big Island

A Cherokee town situated on the Little Tennessee River near the Tellico River in Monroe County, Tennessee.

Big Jim

Born in Texas in 1834, Big Jim was a full blooded Shawnee, and was the grandson of Tecumseh. He and members of the tribe went to Mexico to become free. However, while he was in Mexico he caught smallpox and died in 1900. He had one son named Tonomo who was born in 1875.

Bird
See tihehip.

Bird stones
Many of these stones were found in the Ohio area. They are carefully shaped stones and resembled the shape of a bird. Their exact use is not known. It is possible that they were used in a ceremony or used by women in connection with marriage or pregnancy.

Birdtown
The town of Birdtown, North Carolina, was formerly an Indian village. See Oconaluftee.

Birmingham
See Old Mad Town, a village of the Upper Creeks.

Bison
First described by a European in 1530, in reports of Alvar Nuñez Cabeza de Vaca. The bison, also known as the buffalo, was known generally as far east as the Allegheny Mountains. Various methods were used to catch the bison. They were caught in large traps made of trees, they were driven off cliffs, they were circled by fire and were also killed with spears, bows and arrows. In the summer, the animals were hunted by the whole tribe and severe penalties were placed on those who hunted alone and scared the herd away. Certain parts of the buffalo or bison were given the various tribal members and thus even the old and weak were assured of food. The hides were used for blankets, tents and many other items of manufacture.

Bissasha
A Choctaw town in Newton County, Georgia. The name means "the blackberries are ripe there."

Bithahotshi

The Navaho word for "the red place." This is a mesa near Holbrook, Arizona. Also used to designate the Hopi villages and an ancient pueblo ruin in the same area.

Bitterball

A sacred plant to the Navajo which was also used as a medicine. The plant was also used for the making of a green dye.

Black

See mahcatawaiuwh.

Black Beaver

A valued scout and guide. Black Beaver was also an interpreter between the whites and the Kiowa, Comanche and Wichita tribes. He died in Anadarko, Oklahoma, May 8, 1880.

Blackbird village

A village of the Chippewa, located in Saginaw County, Michigan.

Black drink

A drink made by the Catawba Indians of South Carolina. Also known as "Carolina Tea," made from the leaves of the Ilex cassine. The action of this tea was as a purgative and diuretic. The plant contains caffeine similar to tea and coffee. Used by many other Southern tribes. The name of the Seminole chief Osceola means "black drink singer."

Black Hawk

Born in Illinois in 1767, Black Hawk was a great Indian leader. In the war of 1812, he joined the British. In the treaty of 1804, he surrendered all of the tribal lands east of the Mississippi. In October 3, 1838, he died. His remains were eventually placed in the Burlington Historical Society in Illinois. The building burned down in 1855 and so his remains were also lost in the fire.

Black Indians

These were Indians who traded with the Dutch along the Schuylkill River in New York. They were called "Black Indians" because they were of a darker color than the general local Indians. Known around the year 1656.

Blacksnake

A chief of the Seneca Indians, born possibly in 1760, although the exact date is not known. He fought on the side of the Americans in the battle of Ft. George on August 17, 1813. He died in 1859.

Black Tortoise

This was a tribe of mythical Indians who are supposed to have lived in the Mississippi Valley area. They are supposed to have been driven away by the Elk Indians.

Blade

A term used for a number of cutting tools, usually made of stone.

Blank

This term is used to describe those artifacts (q.v.) that have been roughly shaped but are not yet completed articles. Many blanks are made at a time and are sometimes stored for later completion.

Blankets

The Indian blanket is almost as well known as the Indian feather bonnet. The Indian blanket so often now seen hanging on a wall or used as a rug, had far more uses than modern man has dreamed of. The use as a covering of the body is well known; however, the Indian used the blanket as a bed, cover, door covering, partition, sunshades, for babies, as bag to carry articles and as a surface for the drying of foods. The blankets became a vital part of the Indian life. Today as in the past the blankets are woven from the hair of animals such as the sheep. The bark of trees was also used. Designs were woven directly into the blanket. Some blankets are trimmed with fur or feathers. In 1831 a factory was established in Buffalo, New York, making a blanket known as the "Mackinaw blanket." Indians who in the late 19th century refused to dress in the "modern" way were called "blanket Indians." When the Spanish explorers came to the Southwest, they brought with them the sheep. The Navaho soon learned the value of their wool and even the present day Navaho is well known for his "Navaho blankets."

Blood grooves
See arrow.

Bloomingsburg
Bloomingsburg, Indiana, see Toisa.

Blount Indians
This was a tribe of the Seminole Indians. Formerly living along the Apalachicola River in Florida, they were moved to the Chattahoochee River area in Alabama and finally moved to the Polk County area of Texas in 1870.

Blowgun
Usually associated with the Pygmy of Africa and the Indian of South America, the blowgun is not as well known in connection with the Indians of North America. The darts were usually made of thin splints of wood or reed. The butt end was wrapped in cotton or the down from the thistle. The Iroquois, Cherokee and the Muskhogean tribes made great use of the blowgun.

Blowout
This is a depression caused by wind and erosion; sometimes houses were built over the hollow spot.

Blueberries
See accoondews.

Boalkea

A village of the Pomo in the upper Clear Lake area in California.

Boat

See aomataú.

Boats

The Indian boat is often thought of as the birch bark canoe or the dugout. However, there were many other kinds of boats. The particular area and the materials at hand had a great deal to do with the kind of boat that would be made. The birchbark canoe was a general northeastern type. Where trees were plentiful the dugout was used. Other types were made from the skin of animals. On the western plains area, the boats were known as "bull-boats," due to the lack of wood and the use of animal skins for a covering; they were rather like a large skin-covered wash-tub.

Boat stones

These stone objects are found east of the Mississippi. Their use is not known. They are considered to be charms which are worn around the neck.

Boca del Arroyo

A village of the Papago, located in Pima County in southern Arizona. The name means "mouth of the wash."

Boguechito

This was a group of Choctaw Indians that lived in Neshoba County in Mississippi. The name means "big bayou."

Bohnapobatin

This was the name given to the Pomo who lived in the region of Clear Lake, California.

Boketawgh

The Powhatan Indian word for fire.

Bolbone

A subdivision of the Cholovone living near the San Joaquin River in California.

Bone

The American Indian made use of the bones from many animals. He made musical instruments and other objects. Many tribes used the leg bones of birds to make flutes. Fish hooks were also made from bone.

Bosomworth

Mary Bosomworth, a Creek Indian, was the interpreter for Governor Oglethorpe of Georgia. She had a fine command of the English language and married the Reverend Thomas Bosomworth, who was her third white husband. She was also known as Mary Musgrove and Mary Mathews.

Bow

See auhtab.

Bow string

See auppes.

Boxelder Indians

A tribe of the Shoshoni Indians who formerly lived in the northwestern part of Utah.

Boxes

Indian tribes that were sedentary generally made boxes of wood. These were mainly tribes that lived in wooded areas. Such tribes as the Northwest Coast Indians, who made boxes of cedar, and those on the east coast made boxes and containers of the bark of the birch tree. The Plains Indians had little or no wood and so made containers from the hides of animals, which were known as parfleches. The California Indians made many round wooden cases for the holding of feathers. Many boxes and containers were made especially for the holding and storage of food and feathers.

Boy
See aomatau.

Bramble
See cawmdgus.

Brant
Joseph Brant, see Thayendanegea.

Brantford
Brantford, Ontario, see Thayendanegea.

Brass
See ofawas.

Bread
See apoanocanosutck.

Breccia
A type of rock made up of many small rocks of one age cemented together by minerals of another age.

Brewerton
Brewerton, New York, see Touenho.

Brewster
Brewster, Massachusetts, see Satucket.

Briertown
A village of the Cherokee, situated along the Nantahala River, Macon County, North Carolina.

Bring into a boat
See paakfetowee.

Bristol
Bristol, Maine, see Samoset.

Broken Arm
Broken Arm, a chief of the Winnebago, see Spotted Arm.

Brother
See kemotte. Also see nemat.

Brulé
The Brulé were a sub-tribe of the Teton, a division of the Dakotas. They were known by Lewis and Clark (1804) as the Tetons of the Burnt Woods. This sub-tribe lived along the Missouri River from the White to the Teton rivers.

Bruneau Shoshoni
A band of the Shoshoni who lived along the Bruneau Creek in the southeastern part of Idaho.

Bryson City
Bryson City, North Carolina, see Yonaguska, a chief of the Cherokee. Also see Tikwalitsi.

Bucker Woman's Town
A village of the Seminole located near Long Swamp in the central part of Florida.

Buckongahelas
The head chief of the Delaware Indians who lived in Ohio. He joined the side of the English who were fighting the Colonists. In 1794 he became disgusted with the conduct of the English at the battle of Presque Isle, Ohio, and changed sides and fought for the Americans. He was a signer of various treaties such as, Ft. Wayne, Indiana, 1803, Greenville, Ohio, 1795, and one at Vincennes, Indiana, in 1804. He died soon after, possibly in the same year (1804).

Buena Vista
The name means "good view." The name was given to a prehistoric pueblo on the Gila River in Graham County in southeastern Arizona.

Buffalo

See bison.

Buffalo

Buffalo, New York, see Red Jacket.

Buli

This was known as the butterfly clan of the Hopi Indians.

Bullets Town

Located in Coshocton County in Ohio. This was possibly a Delaware village, located on both sides of the Walhonding River.

Bullroarer

Generally speaking, the bullroarer is a sacred instrument and is associated with rain, wind and thunder and lightning. This instrument consists of a rectangular slat of wood from six inches to two feet long and from a half an inch to two inches thick. The instrument has a cord attached to one end. The cord is held at one end and the wooden part is twirled above the head. The resulting sound is supposed to represent wind, thunder and lightning. The cord is usually measured from the heart to the outstretched right hand of the user. The wood used is mainly pine or fir and is collected from trees that have been struck by lightning. Also known as the rhombus, whizzer, lightning stick.

Burden strap

See tump line.

Bureau of American Ethnology

Organized in 1879 and at that time placed under the supervision of the Smithsonian Institution in Washington, D. C. The Bureau was founded and organized by Major J. W. Powell. Major Powell died September 23, 1902, and was succeeded by W. H. Holmes.

Bushyhead

Dennis W. Bushyhead, see Unaduti.

Busk

Sometimes called the "green corn dance." This was a celebration done by the Creeks. It was an annual and very solemn affair. The ceremony lasted from four to eight days. Special foods were prepared and drunk and strong emetics were taken. A new fire was lit with four logs pointing in the four cardinal points. This was a period of cleaning and forgiveness and gave a new moral and physical life to all. Everything was made new, even clothes.

Butterfly stones

These disk-shaped stones were also known by the name of banner stones (q.v.).

Buzzard Roost

Two towns of the Creeks were known by this name, one along the Flint River in Georgia and the other one along the Chattahoochee River west of Atlanta, Georgia.

Byengeahtein

A village of the Nanticoke, located in Lancaster County, Pennsylvania.

C

Caacat

A village of the Chumashan located near Point Conception in California.

Cabusto

A possible town of the Chickasaw in the northeastern part of Mississippi. Visited by De Soto in 1540.

Caca Chimir

A village of the Papago located in Pima County in southern Arizona.

Cachanila

A village of the Pima, located along the Gila River in Arizona.

Cache

A term used by the archaeologist to denote a deposit of implements. These implements are usually made of flint or other stone. The objects are usually made in the form of flaked disks or blades which are leaf shaped. These caches are generally found in the Mississippi Valley and the Atlantic States. One cache contained over 8,000 disks and many of these caches have over 5,000 blades. The use or reason for such large accumulations is not known definitely. The caches are usually found in connection with burial sites.

Caching

The caching or hiding of supplies was a common thing among the Indian as he couldn't always carry everything, and if he expected to return to the same spot articles were buried and fires built over the spot to hide the location.

Sand, rocks, water, hollow trees all were used as materials to hide articles.

Caddo

A confederacy of tribes that belonged to the Caddoan linguistic family. The tribes of this group were visited by La Salle in 1687. They lived along the Red River and its tributaries in what are now the states of Arkansas, Louisiana and over into Texas along the Brazos, Sabine and Colorado rivers.

Cadecha

A tribe of the Timucuan in the Utina confederacy, located in the middle part of Florida.

Cahawba Town

A settlement of Choctaw towns in Perry County along the Cahawba River in Alabama.

Cahelejyu

A ranchería located in the lower part of California. The name means "brackish water."

Cahiague

A village of the Hurons, located on Lake Ontario. This is the site of the Jesuit mission of St. John the Baptist (1640).

Cahinnio

A tribe closely related to the Caddo (q.v.). They lived on the southwestern part of the Arkansas and the Red River in Texas. They were visited by Cavelier de la Salle in 1687. By the end of the 18th Century, the tribe became extinct.

Cahokia

A tribe of the Illinois.

Cahokia mound

This mound, located about six miles from St. Louis, Missouri, is the largest prehistoric earthwork in the United

States so far discovered. Also known as Monk's mound, this mound is 998 feet by 721 feet and is 99 feet high. The name of the mound is derived from the Cahokia, a tribe that formerly lived in that area. There are over 45 mounds smaller in size in the same area.

Cahuilla
A Shoshonean tribe of California.

Cajats
A Chumashan village located near what is now Santa Barbara, California.

Cajuenche
A tribe of the Yuma, speaking the Cocopa dialect. This group lived in and around the California area. By 1851, only ten members of this tribe were known to exist.

Calapooya
A division of the Kalapooian family. However, this term is used to mean all of the tribes or bands of the Ampishtna, Tsanklightemifa and the Tsawokot.

Calaveras Man
In 1866 a skull was "discovered" in Bald Hill, California, and was known as the Calaveras Man. This skull was reported to have been found 130 feet below the surface in Tertiary deposits. However, this has never really been proved and so it is doubtful that this skull has come from a very ancient man.

Caliche
This is the crust of calcium carbonate that forms on the soil in semiarid regions, especially in the southwest.

California Indians
The California Indians include a great many different peoples. There are three large linguistic groups, the Athapascan, the Shoshonean, and the Yuman, and eighteen smaller

linguistic divisions which are distinctively Californian. Their culture did not reach a high stage of development, and agriculture was not practiced except among the Yuman. Acorns were an important source of food. Some important tribes were the Pomo, Chumash, Miwok, Yokut, Yuma and Maidu. Many California Indians were called Mission Indians (q.v.).

Calcium carbonate
Also known as limestone, a natural cement found in breccia (q.v.).

Caloucha
A tribe located near St. Augustine, Florida.

Calumet
The calumet is also known as the "peace pipe" and the "war pipe." However, strictly speaking, the calumet is the stem of the pipe. It is the stem that is significant. This is decorated with feathers or carved for the occasion; there are calumets for sacred as well as for public arrangements. For example, if a calumet is to be used for war and is smoked at a meeting of both sides, the feathers and the carving of the calumet will at once show what the intentions are. Another example to show what power the Indian felt was contained in a calumet: A band of Sioux were trying to destroy an enemy band of Indians and their French leaders. The Sioux presented twelve calumet pipes, all of the pipes but one were feathered and designed for peace but one had a carved viper on its stem. This denoted that the Sioux would not live up to their bargain but would instead attack. It was thought that the calumet power was so great that it would be wrong to attack if all pipes were of peace, but with one pipe showing treachery, this would give the Sioux an excuse to attack. However, the enemy, instead of missing this little "loop-hole" in the agreement, discovered the one different pipe and so were not caught.

Calusa

The Calusa were an important tribe living in the south-western part of Florida and inland to Lake Okeechobee. In 1513 the Calusa attacked Ponce de Leon with a fleet of about eighty canoes. The battle lasted all day and the Spanish had to withdraw. The Calusa had much gold which they had taken from Spanish wrecks. The tribes had made human sacrifices and all enemies were killed. The early Calusa are supposed to have been cannibals. Little or nothing is known of the Calusa language connections.

Cambujos

This was an imaginary Indian "province" which was supposed to have been visited by the abbess María de Jesus of Agreda, Spain, in the 17th century.

Camden

Camden, South Carolina, see Wateree.

Camitria

A former pueblo of the Tewa, located in Rio Arriba County in New Mexico. It was visited by Oñate around 1598.

Camp circles

It was no simple matter for a large group of Indians to move about and to be able to set up camp, so many rules and social orders were observed. When camping, the tribe would camp in a large circle. Each member had a set place to erect his tent. Most of the property, save personal articles, belonged to the women. The men guarded the camp and thus had only their weapons to care for. Most tribes had concentric circles of about three or four lines. These camps sometimes extended for over a quarter of a mile. The camps were a living picture of the tribal organization. They showed where the leaders were, religious tents, etc. Each had its own place in the circle.

Campti

A village of the Natchitoches Indians located along the Red River in Louisiana. It was abandoned in 1792 because of great sickness in the tribe and was later occupied by the French.

Canada

A term used by early writers to designate the Indians who lived north of the St. Lawrence River. The Huron name Canada means "village."

Canadasaga

A town of the Seneca Indians, located near the town of Geneva, New York. In 1732, most of the tribe died of small-pox and they moved to an area known as New Castle. In 1779 their town was destroyed by Sullivan.

Canajoharie

An important village of the Mohawk Indians of New York. Their village was located along the banks of the Mohawk River.

Canandaigua

This was a rather important town of the Senecas, located near the present town of Canandaigua, New York.

Canarsee

One of the thirteen tribes of Indians that lived on Long Island, New York. The tribe was located in and around what is now Jamaica Bay. All of the Long Island tribes had to pay tribute to the Iroquois. They also lived near Maspeth and Hempstead. It is interesting to note that the present land upon which Brooklyn is situated was land which was secured from the Canarsee Indians.

Caneadea

An old Seneca village located in Allegany County in New York. It was the most southerly of the Seneca towns. It was from here that their war parties departed toward the south and west.

Cannetquot

A small group of Indians that lived near what is now Patchogue, Long Island, New York. They lived in this area about 1683.

Cannibalism

Another word which is sometimes used is anthropophagy. The practice of eating human flesh seems to interest many people and so in the early records it is often written about and sometimes the truth is stretched. However, human flesh was eaten, especially under stress such as starvation, or as part of a ceremony where certain parts were eaten either raw or cooked. The heart, bone marrow and brains were eaten. Sometimes a prisoner was made to eat his own flesh as part of a torture, this was done by the upper New York tribes and those in Canada. Other tribes that are known to use human flesh at various times are the Algonkin groups, Cree, Foxes, Iroquois, Micmac, Chippewa, Kiowa, Caddo, Sioux and some of the California tribes, as well as the Northwest Coast Indians.

Canocan

A pueblo visited by Oñate in 1598. Located along the lower Rio Grande River in New Mexico.

Canoga

Canoga, New York, see Red Jacket.

Cañogacola

An ancient tribe that was visited by Fontaneda in 1575. The tribe was located on the northwestern coast of Florida.

Canonicus

In 1622, this chief of the Narraganset sent the Indian challenge to the colonists. However, he later made friends with Roger Williams and signed over his land to the latter.

Canopus
A chief of the Wappinger Indians, see Nochpeem.

Canopus
The main village of the Nochpeem, located in Putnam County in New York State.

Cant
A ranchería, possibly of the Maricopa. Located near the mouth of the Salt River in southern Arizona.

Cantaunkack
A village of the Powhatan Indians of Virginia. They lived along the York River around 1608.

Cantico
A word used by the Dutch and the English for a dance, lively gathering, a noisy ceremony, used to describe Indian demonstrations. It was spelled in many other ways: kantico, kanticoy, kinticka, kantikanti, antico.

Canton
Canton, Georgia, see Red Bank.

Canuga
A ceremonial comb made of bone, used to "scratch" ballplayers. Also the name of two Cherokee towns in South Carolina.

Canyon De Chelly
Located about a hundred miles from Gallup, New Mexico, this National Monument is located near Chinle, Arizona, on the Navajo Reservation. It was occupied about 349 A.D. by the Navajo.

Capahowasic
A village of the Powhatan confederacy, located in Gloucester County, Virginia.

Capasi

A village in northern Florida, possibly belonging to the Apalachee. It was visited by De Soto in 1539.

Cape Breton

A village of the Micmac about 1760. Located on Cape Breton Island, north of Nova Scotia.

Cape Fear Indians

The name was given to the Indians that lived near the mouth of the Cape Fear River in North Carolina. The colonists were English and in 1661 they started a small settlement here. They took some of the local Indian children and are supposed to have sent them to England for schooling; however, the Indians did not like this and they drove the colonists away.

Cape Magdalen

This was a mission established on the St. Lawrence River in 1670 for the Algonkins.

Cape Sable Indians

A group of Micmac Indians who lived near Cape Sable in Nova Scotia. They were very active in the wars against the early settlements.

Capola

A Seminole Indian village on the eastern side of the St. Marks River in Florida, one of the many Indian towns that were visited by Bartram during his trip through Florida in 1791.

Carises

The name for a group of tribes that formerly lived along the Sierra Nevada and Coast ranges of California. They were possibly Shoshonean or Mariposan.

Carlisle School

This was the first non-reservation Indian school established in the United States. Located in Carlisle, Pennsylvania. The school was formerly opened November 1, 1879.

Carolina tea
A ceremonial drink. See "black drink."

Casa Blanca
The Spanish words for "white house." This name was given to several places, including the Laguna pueblo in Valencia County in New Mexico, and a Pima village along the Gila River in Arizona. Also given to a ruined pueblo in the Canyon de Chelly in the northeastern part of Arizona.

Casa Grande National Monument
This large pueblo was built by the Salado in the 14th century. It is located on state highway 87, near Coolidge, Arizona.

Cashaw
This word was used for the crooked necked squash which was used by many of the American Indians. Sometimes spelled kershaw, ecushaw, cushaw.

Cashong
A small Seneca village located near the present site of the city of Geneva, New York. Occupied about 1779.

Casitoa
A village of the Calusa on the southwestern coast of Florida.

Cassapecock
One of the Powhatan tribes that lived along the York River in Virginia about 1616.

Cassville
Cassville, Wisconsin, a city in Grant County, see Penah.

Castahana
A group of hunters mentioned by Lewis and Clark, also

known as the "Snake band." They were closely related to the Arapaho.

Casti
A Timuquanan village on the St. Johns River in Florida.

Castleton
Castleton, New York, see Schodac.

Catahecassa
A strong chief of the Shawnee, born about 1740. He fought the whites and not until 1795 did he stop the warfare. He was defeated by General Anthony Wayne. From that time on he became a staunch supporter of the whites and kept the Shawnee peaceful, even when the British tried to stir up trouble.

Catalpa
Also known as the Indian bean and the candle tree, an ornamental tree.

Catatoga
A former Cherokee settlement, meaning "the new settlement place." Located in Macon County in North Carolina.

Catawba
An important eastern Siouan tribe, located in South Carolina. Also known as Esaw or river people. In the early days, the Catawba were very warlike and made many raids on their neighbors to the north. They were friendly to the Colonial government and tried to get them to fight against the French. Between wars and smallpox, as well as the dealings of the whites, the Catawba were talked and written away from their land. In 1841 the state of South Carolina "bought" all of their reservation but one square mile. This act further reduced the tribe. They still live on their small reservation and are known for their pottery making, which is still done in the old way. They are also being taught to

raise cattle as well as farming. As on many reservations, they live a rather difficult and poor life.

Catawba grape
This is the cultivated variety of the northern fox grape. This grape was named by Major Adlum in 1825, after the Catawba Indian tribe of South Carolina.

Catfish Lake
A settlement of the Seminole. Also a small lake in Polk County, Florida.

Catherine's Town
A village of the Seneca Indians of the Catherine, New York, area. Named after a woman who was captured by the Indians and later became a power in the tribe.

Catholic
First full-blooded Indian to become a Roman Catholic Priest was Negahnquet (q.v.).

Catlinite
This was the red claystone used by the Indians, especially in Minnesota. Used for the making of pipe bowls. The stone was named for the man who called attention to the stone, George Catlin, who was a famous traveler and painter of Indian life in general. The quarries where this stone was collected were considered sacred and so even enemies could come there without fear to renew their pipestone supplies for the making of ceremonial pipes.

Catoking
A village of the Chowanoc located in Gates County, North Carolina.

Catskill
This was a division of the Munsee tribes and was also a part of the Esopus. The Dutch name "Catskill" was given to the totem of the band, however, it was a wolf!

Cattachiptico

A small village of the Powhatan confederacy of Virginia.

Cattaraugus

An Iroquois reservation under the State of New York.

Caughnawaga

This was the seat of the Mohawk tribe in New York; it was here that the Jesuits maintained a mission (St. Pierre). The town was raided and destroyed by the French in 1693.

Cauwaih

The Virginia Indian term for the oyster.

Cawmdgus

This is the Powhatan word for the bramble or briar.

Cawruuoc

A village of the Neusiok on the northern side of the Neuse River in Craven County, North Carolina.

Cawwaivuh

This is the Powhatan word for bed, also sometimes petaocawin.

Cawwontoll

A small village of the Powhatan Indians, located along the Rappahannock River in Virginia.

Cayomulgi

A small town of the Creeks, located along the Coosa River in Alabama.

Cayovea

A village of the Calusa on the southwestern coast of Florida.

Cayuga

An Iroquoian confederation, one of the five nations of the Iroquois. The Cayuga lived along the shores of Cayuga Lake in New York. Some of the tribe went to Ohio soon after the Revolution and became known as the Seneca of Sandusky.

Cayuse

A tribe that lived in Oregon and Washington. They belonged to the Waiilatpuan tribe. They were very close to the Wallawalla and the Nez Percés. In 1855, the Cayuse joined in a treaty which formed the Umatilla Reservation. Smallpox and wars have caused the decline and extinction of all the pure blooded Cayuse.

Cayuse pony

Named after the Cayuse Indians who caught wild horses and bred them. The name is well-known in the northwestern part of the United States.

Cazazhita

A division of the Dakota Indians under Chief Shonka. The name meant "bad arrows" or "broken arrows."

Cazopo

A former Costanoan village near the Dolores Mission. Cazopo was built near what is now San Francisco, California.

Cebolleta

A place in the northeastern part of Valencia County in New Mexico. In 1746, it became a settlement of the Navajo under Father Juan M. Menchero. However, the following year the Navajo became tired of such a sedentary life and they moved away. The name means "tender onion."

Ceca

The word was mentioned by Oñate as being a pueblo of the Jemez (1598) in New Mexico.

Cedar

See the Powhatan Indian word, naraak. Also see moroke.

Cedar City
Cedar City, Utah, see Unkapanukuint.

Cedarhurst
Cedarhurst, Long Island, New York, see Rockaway.

Cegiha Sioux
A band of Sioux who lived along the Ohio and Wabash Rivers, then moved west.

Celt
The origin of the name celt is uncertain (Latin, celtis, meaning chisel). The celt resembles a chisel or un-grooved ax blade. Usually made of stone and varies in size up to twenty pounds. The celt is a wedge shaped object, sometimes polished smooth, others rather rough. Their distribution is greater than the grooved ax. See adzes.

Cement
Cements and glues were used by many American Indian tribes. These glues and cements were used for fastening arrow points, mending pipes and for patching canoes. The Virginia Indians made a glue from the boiled ends of the deer antlers. The only mineral cement known to the Indians was used by the Indians of southern Arizona and California . . . they used bitumen. The gum of the mesquite and greasewood was used in the southwest and in the areas of the evergreens, the pitch from these trees was used, heated and used hot.

Cepowig
A village of the Conestoga about 1608, near York County, Pennsylvania.

Chabin
A tribal division of the Assiniboin, the name means "mountain."

Chachaubunkkakowok
A village of Christianized Indians who lived in 1684 in eastern Massachusetts.

Chaco Canyon
Chaco Canyon National Park, this is a large concentration of Anasazi pueblo ruins, which include restored kivas (q.v.). Located in northwestern New Mexico about 60 miles from Thoreau, New Mexico, on U.S. highway 66, on state road 55 from Cuba to Bloomfield.

Chactoo
A group of Indians who spoke the Mobilian trade language and who were possibly related to the Attacapa of Louisiana (1753).

Chafalote
A band of the Apache who roamed into Sonora, Mexico, and into the American Southwest.

Chagee
A settlement of the Cherokee near the mouth of the Tugaloo River in the northwestern part of South Carolina.

Chagindueftei
A band of the Atfalati who lived in and around Washington County in Oregon.

Chagu
The name meaning "lungs," a division of the Yankton Sioux.

Chaguate
A village of the southern division of the Caddoan tribes. Located along the Washita River in Arkansas.

Chaikikarachada
A Winnebago gens, meaning "those who call themselves the deer."

Chaizra

This was a group of the Hopi, known as the "Elk clan."

Chakankni

A band of the Molala. They lived along the Cascade range and northwest of the Rogue River in Oregon.

Chakchiuma

A tribe of the Choctaw and Yazoo tribes. They spoke the Choctaw and Chickasaw dialects. They lived in a walled town along the Yazoo River in Mississippi.

Chakpahu

An ancient Hopi pueblo on the rim of Antelope Mesa, overlooking the Jeditoh valley in northeastern Arizona. The name means "speaking spring."

Chalawai

A band of the Atfalati. They formerly lived along the southeastern part of Wapatoo Lake in Oregon. They became extinct in 1830.

Chalowe

An ancient pueblo of the Zuñi, located about a mile and a half northwest of Hawikuh.

Chamange

The Powhatan Indian word for a tobacco bag.

Chamizo

A plant used by the Navajo, see diwozhiibaih.

Chananagi

Near the present site of Montgomery, Alabama, this was a former village of the Upper Creeks. The name means "ridge or hill of land."

Chanco

An Indian of the Powhatan of Virginia. This Indian warned the English about an intended massacre by Opechancanough and thus saved many English lives (March, 1622).

Chankaokhan

A tribe of the Hunkpapa, a division of the Teton Sioux. The name "sore back," referred to the horses.

Chankute

A division of the Sisseton Sioux. The name means to "shoot in the woods among the deciduous trees."

Channel flake

This is a long spall (q.v.) or flake which is chipped the length of an arrow or spear point, thus forming a groove.

Chanona

A division of the upper Yankton Sioux, meaning "shoot at trees."

Chanshushka

A division of the Dakota, meaning "box elder."

Chantapeta

A Hunkpapa group, a division of the Dakota. Named after their chief who was known as "Fire Heart."

Chaouacha

After the Natchez war, this small tribe came under French suspicion even though they fought on the French side. The French used Negro slaves to attack the tribe. The purpose was to make the slaves and the Indians enemies, thus they would not band together and at the same time this would weaken the Indians. The tribe lived just above the present site of New Orleans, Louisiana.

Chapana

An ancient village of the Costanoan Indians of the central part of California near the mission San Juan Bautista.

Chapant

The Powhatan Indian word for shoe.

Chapokele

A band of the Atfalati, living near Wapatoo Lake in Oregon.

Chapticon

A tribe living in Charles County, Maryland, displaced by the whites in 1652.

Chaquantie

A tribe possibly connected with the Caddo who lived on a branch of the Red River in Louisiana. This was a rather peaceful tribe.

Charleston

An Indian village site, see Otopali.

Chartierstown

A village of the Shawnee, occupied up to about 1748 on the Ohio River in Pennsylvania. The town was named after Peter Chartier, an Indian half-breed.

Chaskpe

A tribe that was visited by La Salle in 1683. They were allies of the Chickasaw. They lived in the area of the state of Illinois.

Chasta

A possible Athapascan tribe who lived on both sides of the Rogue River in Oregon.

Chatagihl

A band of the Atfalati who lived along Wapatoo Lake in Oregon. The name means "firewood bark."

Chatelaw

An old Chickasaw town in northern Mississippi. The name is said to mean "copper town."

Chatoksofki

A town of the Upper Creeks. Located in Talladega County in Alabama. A favorite meeting place for the annual busk (q.v.). The members of this town were considered to be the best ball players of the Creek nation.

Chattooka
A village of the Neuse Indians, near Newbern, North Carolina. In 1710 a German colony began there and the Neuse Indians are said to have gone to live with the Tuscarora.

Chattahoochee
A town of the Lower Creeks, located along the upper part of the Chattahoochee River in Georgia. The name means "pictured rocks" or "rock mark." The name refers to the picture writing which is found on the rocks in the area.

Chattanooga
A Cherokee name for a point along the Tennessee River where the site of the present city of Chattanooga is located. The ancient meaning of the name is "hawk hole," there is no known meaning in recent Cherokee.

Chattanooga
Chattanooga, Tennessee, see Running Water.

Chaubaqueduck
An Indian village located on Martha's Vineyard in 1698.

Chaui
A confederacy of the Pawnee who lived in what is now Nebraska. Very little is known of this group.

Chaunis Temoatan
A village of the Virginia Indians known for its salt making; it existed about 1586. The village was about 160 miles north of the Roanoke settlement.

Chaushila
A tribe of the Mariposan of central California. They lived along the Fresno River.

Chautauqua

A Seneca word meaning "one has taken out fish here," this refers to the lake in the area. Now well-known for the Chautauqua Literary and Scientific Circle which was founded in 1878 by Bishop Vincent of the Methodist Episcopal Church.

Chawakli

An ancient town of the Lower Creeks who lived in Calhoun County, Florida.

Chawopo

A village of the Powhatan Indians located near the mouth of the Chipoak Creek in Virginia.

Chayopin

A tribe that lived near the missions of San Antonio in Texas, who were a division of the Tonkawa. They also lived near the present city of Goliad, Texas.

Cheawanta

The Powhatan Indian word for the robin.

Chebacco

A word possibly derived from the Algonquian dialects. Used to describe a type of fishing boat used in the Massachusetts and Newfoundland areas, also called "pink sterns" and "tobacco boats."

Chechawkose

A chief of the Potawatomi who lived along the south side of the Tippecanoe River in Indiana.

Checopissowo

A small village of the Powhatan confederacy (1608). They lived on the Rappahannock River in Virginia.

Cheeshateaumuck

At the time, the only New England Indian to complete his studies at Harvard. He received his degree in 1666.

Cheesoheha

A Cherokee settlement located along the upper Savannah River in South Carolina. The village was destroyed during the Revolution.

Chegoli

Possibly a Creek town, along the east bank of the Tallapoosa River in Alabama. Visited by William Bartram in 1799.

Chehalis

A name for a group of several Salishan tribes living on the Chehalis River and Grays Harbor, Washington.

Cheipfni

The Virginia Indian term for the land.

Chekilli

This was the principal chief of the Creek confederacy at the time of the settlement in Georgia in 1733. He visited England in 1735.

Chemehuevi

A tribe of the Shoshonean. They are an offshoot of the Paiute and they lived along the Colorado River and over into California.

Cheraw

Cheraw, South Carolina, see Pedee.

Cheraw

A tribe of Siouan relations. They lived in the vicinity of the present city of Cheraw, South Carolina. Toward the end of 1768, they moved in with the Catawbas (q.v.).

Cheroenhaka
See Nottoway.

Cherokee
A tribe of the Iroquoian family. They formerly held all of the land from southern Virginia, North Carolina, South Carolina, Georgia and over even to Ohio. Their name variously means "the cave people," "real people," "inhabitants of the cave country." Their language, customs and other archaeological evidence points to their origin as being from the north. A well known Cherokee was Sequoya, who invented the Indian alphabet and thus advanced the lot of the Indian greatly.

Cherry blossoms
See amkonnmg.

Chesapeake
A possible tribe of the Powhatan. The name is Algonquian and means "country on a great river."

Cheskchamay
The Powhatan Indian word used to denote friendship.

Chest
See pacus.

Chestnut
See opomens, also opommins.

Chettrokettle
An important pueblo of the pueblos of the Chaco Canyon Group. Also known as the "rain pueblo." Located in New Mexico.

Cheyenne
Their name means "to speak a strange language." This is an important tribe of the Plains group and part of the Algonquian family. Before 1700, the tribes are said to have

lived in Minnesota and along the headwaters of the Mississippi. They also lived along the Missouri River and were great farmers and pottery makers. However, they were driven out to the plains where they became great hunters of the bison. They fought closely with the Sioux, Kiowa, Comanche. They were very active in the battle against General Custer. They became a typical tribe of the plains and followed the great bison herds and lived in skin tipis. The sun dance was one of their great tribal ceremonies.

Chicago
The name of a chief of the Illinois Indians. A site on the southern part of Lake Michigan called by the Sauk, Fox and Kickapoo "the place of the skunk." So called because a large skunk was killed at that site by the Fox.

Chickahominy
A tribe of the Powhatan confederacy and one of the most important of the Virginia tribes. The name means "hominy people," "coarse pounded corn people." In 1613 they joined with the English.

Chickamauga
A band of the Cherokee who helped the English in the Revolution. In 1794 they were defeated and hostilities ended for them.

Chickasaw
Related to the Choctaw, this was an important Muskhogean tribe. They lived along the Mississippi, Yazoo and Tallahatchie Rivers. One of their main towns was located at the site of the present Memphis, Tennessee.

Chickasaw trade language
See Mobile.

Chiconessex
Called "a place of small turkeys." A village of the Pow-

hatan confederacy, located near the present Accomac, Virginia.

Chicora
A name given by the Spanish to a tribe that lived along the coast of the Carolinas, especially the Edisto River region (1521). The tribe was wiped out by the Spanish and English slave traders just before the end of the 17th century.

Chief
The chief of a tribe can be considered as the political head of the group. He had certain rights and obligations. There were many grades of chiefs and various titles were given for certain distinctive reasons. The Creeks and the Iroquois had the most complex governments and there was no head chief as such. Some chiefs were made because of property ownership or deeds. In many cases the chieftainship was inherited, generally through the mother.

Chilano
A village of the Caddoan. Located in Texas along the Sabine River.

Child
See nechan, also neckaun.

Chillicothe
One of the four tribal divisions of the Shawnee in Ohio. The exact meaning of the Indian name is not definitely known.

Chillicothe
Chillicothe, Ohio, see Shawnee.

Chilocco Indian School
A government Indian school established and opened January 15, 1884, in northern Oklahoma. Mainly organized as an industrial school.

Chilula
A small group of Athapascans who lived on Redwood Creek in northern California.

Chimakuan Family
A language group of the Northwest Coast, the Quileute being the only living representatives. They were whalers.

Chinook
A northwestern tribe which lived at the mouth of the Columbia River in Oregon.

Chioro
A village of the Papago located in Pima County in Arizona.

Chippewa
One of the largest Indian tribes north of Mexico. Their name means "to pucker up" or "roast until puckered up," this term referred to the type of moccasins with the "puckered toe." They lived in the Great Lakes regions. Even though the Chippewa were large in number, very few came in contact with the whites. They at times of stress and under certain battle conditions, practiced cannibalism. They built bark houses. They also gathered wild rice and were great canoemen.

Chippewa Princess
A female warrior of the Chippewa. See Nanawonggabe.

Chippfni
This word is used by the Powhatan Indian when referring to the earth.

Chiricahua
An important division of the Apache. They were the most belligerent of the Arizona Indians. Cochise and Geronimo were their best-known leaders, but they had many others.

Chishafoka
   A Choctaw town located at the present site of the city of Jackson, Mississippi.

Chisro
   A clan of the Hopi known as the "snow bunting clan."

Chitimacha
   A tribe and a linguistic family who lived on the banks of Grand Lake in Louisiana.

Chitola
   A clan of the Zuñi, known as the "Rattlesnake Clan."

Chiutaiina
   A clan of the Taos pueblo of New Mexico, known as the "Eagle Clan."

Chiwere Sioux
   A group of Sioux tribes including the Iowa and Missouri.

Choctaw
   The name refers to the flattened head of the tribes. This is an important tribe of the Muskhogean. The Choctaw were first visited by De Soto in 1540. These Indians were the outstanding agriculturists of all the Southern tribes. Most of their warfare was on the defensive. They lived in large towns, mainly for their mutual defense against their enemies, the Creeks.

Chokatowela
   A group of the Brulé Teton Sioux.

Chokecherry
   See the Navajo word, didzedig'ozhiih.

Cholosoc
   A former village of the Chumashan, located near the present site of Santa Barbara, California.

Cholovone
A group of the Mariposan stock, living along the San Joaquin River in California. Now probably extinct.

Choromi
A village of the Costanoan near the Santa Cruz mission in California.

Chorruco
A tribe that lived along the Texas coast. Cabeza de Vaca lived with this tribe for six years (1529).

Chosro
A clan of the Hopi, known as the "Bluebird Clan."

Choyopan
A clan of the Tonkawa, means "moving the eyelids or eyebrows."

Chronology
This is the method of arranging the events of the past in a sequence or order of their happening in the past.

Chua
A clan of the Hopi, known as the "Rattlesnake Clan."

Chuah
A village of the Chumashan about six miles from the present city of Santa Barbara in California.

Chuba
A village of the Papago in southern Arizona.

Chukai
This is the mud clan of the lizard phratry of the Hopi Indians of the Southwest.

Chumashan family
Also known as the Santa Barbara Indians. This is the linguistic family on the coast of southern California. These Indians were great fishermen and depended more on sea

70

food than on plant products. They were very friendly to the Spanish at first, but as the missions were established they grew to dislike the outsiders and in 1824 the Indians threw off the mission authority. The Chumash Indians made canoes of planks which were calked and lashed together and they were skilled with the canoe in open sea.

Chumpache
A village of the Chumashan in Ventura County, California.

Chunkey
This was a man's game played by the Indians of the Mississippi area. Usually played in the larger towns where a special place was set aside for the game, known as the "chunkey yard or chunk yard." The game was played with a stone disk and a stick with a crook in one end. It was played by rolling the disk along and then throwing the stick after it in such a way that when the disk stopped rolling, it would come to rest in the curved or crooked end of the stick. See discoidal stones.

Chunsetunneta
A village of the Chastacosta located on the north side of the Rogue River in Oregon.

Chunut
A tribe of the Yokuts who lived in the plains east of Lake Tulare, California. They lived in communal houses made of tule.

Chupatak
A village of the Pima in southern Arizona, means "mortar stone."

Churehu
This was the mole clan of the Isleta pueblo in New Mexico.

Cibecue

A division of the Western Apache.

Circle

See mufsetagwaioh.

Cist

A term used for a grave or depository for storage, etc.

Clackama

A tribe of Chinook Indians that lived on the Clackamas River in Oregon.

Clallam

A tribe of the Salishan family living on Puget Sound, Washington.

Clan

The clan is a division within a tribe, and members are related theoretically and sometimes actually.

There were certain rights and privileges which were granted through clan membership, either earned or inherited. Such rights as a name of some guardian deity, representation on the tribal council, share of community property, the rights to child bearing women, tribal burial and the rights to certain songs and chants. The clan or gentile name is usually some outstanding feature of an animal, such as a clan named after the deer would be called "cloven foot" or "those whose nostrils are large and fine looking." In the clan, descent is traced through the female. See gens.

Clarksville

Clarksville, Georgia, see Soquee. Also see Wafford.

Clarksville

Clarksville, Virginia. See Occaneechi.

Clay

See pufsagwun.

72

Clayton
Clayton, Georgia, see Stikayi.

Clear Lake Indians
A name that was given rather loosely to the Indians who lived along the shore of Clear Lake in northern California. Actually they were Pomo Indians.

Cleveland
Cleveland, Ohio, see Pontiac.

Cleveland
Cleveland, Tennessee, see Unaduti.

Cliff dwellings
This is a term usually applied to those types of houses found in the Southwest. Located mainly in Arizona, New Mexico, Colorado and Utah. The houses are built high up the sides of cliffs, usually in natural rock shelters or caves. The Indian learned to build walls along the front margins and to build rooms. This was done for shelter and protection from enemies who could not attack from the top but had to come from below and thus were at a disadvantage. Food was grown on top of the mesa or down in the canyons. Water was secured from springs or hollow places in the rocks. Some well-known cliff dwellings are located at Mesa Verde in Colorado, Montezuma Castle in Arizona.

Cliff Palace
A large, rather well preserved cliff dwelling in Walnut Canyon in Mesa Verde, Colorado. This ruin has over 146 rooms.

Cliff rose
The evergreen twigs of this plant are used by the Navajo Indians for the making of a golden dye. When the plant blooms late in autumn, the Navajo believe that there will be a hard winter with much snow.

73

Clinton

Clinton, New York, see Skenandoa.

Clothing

Generally speaking, the North American Indians were rather well clothed. Of course, those in the south and hot areas wore less. The skin of the deer, known as buckskin, was used as well as the hide of the bison, elk, moose, mountain sheep and the pelts of rabbits and birds. The bark of the cedar tree was used by the Indians of the Northwest Coast. The clothes were decorated with beads, shells, scalp locks, porcupine quills, claws of animals and feathers.

Clubs

There were many varieties of clubs in use. Some were ceremonial and were highly decorated. Others were used in warfare and were held or thrown. Some were round, wrapped in skins and fastened to sticks, others were egg shaped. Clubs were also used for pounding pemmican and for driving tent stakes.

Coaque

This was the group of Indians that lived on the islands off the coast of Texas (Malhado Island). It was here that Cabeza de Vaca was shipwrecked in 1527.

Cochise

A well-known chief of the Apache. In 1861 Cochise went to the Americans under a flag of truce to deny any part in the abduction of a white child. However, the commanding officer did not hold up his end of the bargain and held all of the chiefs and later hung them all because they did not confess. Cochise escaped and even though he was shot, he made good his escape. He organized the Apache of Arizona and surrounding areas and fought the American troops for ten years. In September, 1871, he was finally defeated. He died in peace June 8, 1874. He was succeeded by his son,

Taza, who became chief. Cochise County in Arizona is named after this great chief.

Cochiti
A Keresan pueblo, both in early times and modern.

Cockenoe
A Montauk Indian. The Algonquin word means "interpreter." Cockenoe was made captive in the Pequot war of 1637. He assisted John Eliot, a missionary who translated the Bible into the Massachusetts language.

Cocopa
Part of the Yuman family who lived along the Colorado River and over into lower California. They cremated their dead. Cocopa was also a name applied to a group of Spanish rancherías.

Cocospera
A settlement of the Pima located along the headwaters of the San Ignacio River in Sonora, Mexico. The settlement was abandoned because of the attacks by the Apache.

Cod fish
See ouhshawkowh.

Coeur d'Alene
A plateau tribe now living on the Coeur d'Alene Reservation in Idaho.

Cohas
A tribe that was attacked by the Huron of New York in 1748.

Cohasset
Cohasset, Massachusetts, see Sagoquas.

Coihgwus
Virginia Indian word for the gull.

Colbert

General William Colbert was a Chickasaw chief. He fought in the Revolutionary War and in the War of 1812. He was the signer of the treaties which ceded the Chickasaw lands to the Americans in 1816.

Cold

See nonfsamats.

Columbia

Columbia, North Carolina, see Scuppernong.

Colville, Nevada

See Pagaits.

Comanche

A southern branch of the Shoshonean groups. They were the only ones of that group that lived entirely on the plains. They lived in what is now Kansas. They were friendly to the Americans in general, but were bitter enemies to the Texans who took their best hunting grounds. They fought the Texans for forty years. Most of them are now on the reservation in Oklahoma.

Combahee

A small tribe that lived along the Combahee River in South Carolina. Through disease and war they became extinct in the early days of the settlement.

Comeya

A name given in a general way to the tribes that lived from San Diego east to the Colorado River. They were very poor and had no animals. They had poor clothing and were said to sell their children for a livelihood.

Commotins

The Powhatan Indian for turtle.

Complex

As used in archaeology, this term is used to describe a

76

group of activities which when combined, make up the overall picture of a culture.

Compton
Compton, Rhode Island, see Saconnet.

Conchoidal
This term is used to describe the surface of articles that have been chipped and thus have a surface made up of concave and convex parts.

Concord
Concord, New Hampshire, see pennacook.

Conestoga wagon
This was a large wagon with a white top cover. It was pulled by six to eight horses. The name comes from the town where they were mainly made, the village of Conestoga, Pennsylvania. The village in turn got its name from the Conestoga Indians of that area (Iroquoian).

Confederation
This was a group or political organization of two or more tribes who banded together for offense or defense. These alliances when formed caused each tribe to give up some of its own rights for the good of all concerned.

Congaree
A Siouan tribe that lived in South Carolina along the Santee and Wateree Rivers. After the Yamasi war of 1715, they were so reduced in number that they moved in with the Catawba of South Carolina.

Connewango
Meaning "at the falls," a village of the Seneca located near Warren, Pennsylvania. Destroyed by Colonel Brodhead in 1781.

Conoy
A tribe related to the Delawares.

Coonti
A plant used by the Seminole of Florida from which the Indians make flour for the making of bread. Sometimes spelled kunti, koontie.

Cooperstown
Cooperstown, New York, see Uncas.

Coos
A term used to describe the Indians of Coos Bay, Oregon. They belong to the Kusan family.

Coosa
Also spelled Kussoes. A small extinct tribe that lived near the mouth of the Edisto River in South Carolina.

Copehan
A linguistic family occupying a large area in central California.

Copper
See matafsañ.

Copper
The use of copper by the Indians north of Mexico came mainly from the tribes of the Lake Superior area. Copper was used to a large extent in the Ohio region. The ore was used as it was found at first and then it was discovered that it could be pounded into various shapes. So celts, tablets, bracelets and various other blades were made.

Copper kettle
See aucutgagwafsun.

Cornplanter
A well-known Seneca chief. He was also known as John O'Bail. He is supposed to have been born about 1732 at Conewaugus, New York. His father was a white trader named John O'Bail or O'Beel. He became a friend of the whites and later on he renounced them all. However, the

State of Pennsylvania gave him a pension and a land grant where he lived until his death in 1866.

Corn pone
This was a small round flat bread, made variously of corn, seeds, corn and eggs, also sometimes made of sweet potatoes, sugar and herbs. The Powhatan word for pone means to "bake."

Correlate
Used to describe the process of finding the connections between one culture and another, to give the story a sequence of events.

Corrugated Pottery
A type of pottery that has a design from the coiling or pinching method, also from the use of a woven basket technique.

Corydon
Corydon, Pennsylvania, see Yoroonwago.

Coshocton
The name of a village, meaning "finished or completed." Named after a chief of the turtle tribe of the Delaware Indians. Located on the present site of Coshocton, Ohio.

Costanoan family
This is the linguistic family of the central coastal area of California. They built their homes of tule or grass. They made baskets but no pottery.

Cotton
De Soto's troops found the Indians of the lower Mississippi Valley using cotton blankets. These are thought to have been brought from the west from tribes in Arizona and New Mexico, especially from the Hopi.

Coups
This term is French-Canadian for a sign of victory, how-

ever, coups were counted by many American Indian tribes. There were usually three coups. First for killing an enemy, second for scalping and the third for touching a dead enemy. Stealing an enemy horse also was sometimes counted and made a fourth coup. Each coup gave a man a score in battle and so his rank and other favors would be more, depending on the number of coups he had.

Coyotero
The Western Apache. The name means "coyote men," and probably was given them because of their roving, food-hunting way of life.

Crab
See tuttafcuk.

Cradle
The Indian cradle board was made in various ways and materials varied with the locality. Generally speaking, the baby was laced into the cradle for about a year. It could be carried, hung from the back or side of a horse or leaned against a house. Cradles were handed down in a family and with some tribes they were considered sacred. They were lined with the down from birds, moss, soft animal skins, cedar bark. The cradle was sometimes notched to show how many children had used it. If the baby died, the cradle was buried with the child in it, or it was burned, broken or thrown away.

Cranberry
Cranberry, New Jersey, see Tatemy.

Cranetown
Cranetown, Ohio, see Tarhe.

Crayfish town
A town of the Cherokee, located in upper Georgia about the year 1800.

Crazy Horse

A chief of the Oglala Sioux. He was a bold and daring leader of the Sioux. His name is said to have been given him because a wild horse dashed through his camp when he was born. In 1875 Crazy Horse and the Sioux and Cheyenne fought off the army in all directions. He fought with Sitting Bull on the Little Bighorn River and in June 25, 1876, they defeated General George A. Custer. General Mackenzie followed Crazy Horse to the Bighorn Mountains and there with the help of his artillery they finally defeated Crazy Horse in the spring of that year. He was placed under arrest in September 7, 1877. It is said that Crazy Horse tried to escape and was shot, however, this has been doubted for years and the full story has not been told.

Cree

A rather important tribe of the Canadian area; they belonged to the Algonquian stock.

Creek

A small stream, see meihsutterafk.

Creeks

The largest division of the Muskhogean. Their name was given them by the English because of the numerous streams or creeks in their country. They became allies of the English in 1703, but were hostile to the Spanish in Florida. They revolted against the Americans in the Creek war in 1813 and were defeated by General Jackson. They also fought in Florida in 1835 to 1843 in what is known as the Seminole war.

Crescent City

Crescent City, California, see Tatlatunne.

Croatan Indians

A group of Indians who claimed to be descendants of

the mixture of whites and Indians of the "lost colony of Roanoke Island." For many years they were classed as "free negroes," however, they fought this and they finally were recognized officially as descendants of Raleigh's lost colony. This has not been proved.

Crooked
See okhorime.

Crook's Commission
A government commission which made a treaty with the Sioux in Dakota in 1887, providing that they give up half the lands they had held.

Crow
Formerly living along the Missouri River, they went to the vicinity of the Rocky Mountains. Known as the "bird people." They are a Siouan tribe and part of the Hidatsa group of Indians. The Crows were a wandering tribe. They have been classified as River Crows and Mountain Crows.

Crow
See the Virginia Indian word for this bird, ohawas.

Crow Dog
A chief of the Oglala Sioux. He shot and killed Spotted Tail in a brawl on the reservation in 1881. He was tried and sentenced to hang. The Supreme Court ruled, however, that it had no jurisdiction over crimes committed on the reservations. He was then released.

Crown
See cutaantaqwapifsun.

Cubac
A rancheria of the Papago. Located near what is now Tucson, Arizona.

Cuchendado

The last tribe of Texas Indians that Cabeza de Vaca met along the Gulf Coast as he started inland.

Cucheneppo

The Powhatan Indian word for woman.

Cueva pintada

The "painted cave," so named because of the many cave paintings or pictographs in the area. Located about 25 miles from Santa Fe, New Mexico.

Cujant

A Papago rancheria in northwest Sonora. Settled about 1771.

Culture

This term has come into use, meaning the activities or beliefs of a group which differs from another group of individuals. In archaeology this means the artifacts or material remains of a group of individuals which differs from another group.

Culver's black root

See Oxidoddy.

Cumaro

A village of the Papago in southern Arizona, near the Sonora border.

Cumumbah

Said to be a mixture of Ute and Shoshone who lived near Salt Lake and Ogden valley in Utah.

Cupheag

The Algonquian name for Stratford, Connecticut, meaning "shut in."

Cuppotaiv

Virginia Indian term for deaf.

Cuppotoon
The Virginia Indian term for the fish known as the sturgeon.

Cupstones
These are stones with round hollow depressions in them, some with many and others with only one. Their use is not known. It was thought that they were used for the cracking of nuts and were called "nut-stones." It is also thought that they were used for the mixing of paint, handles for drills, fire stones and other uses.

Curcye neire
The Powhatan Indian term for "I am cold."

Curdled milk
See ootun.

Curled hair
See vtchepetaiuwk.

Curly Head
This was a well-known chief of the Mississippi Chippewa. He died on his return from a meeting in August 19, 1825.

Cuscowilla
A Seminole town that was established by the Creeks on Cuscowilla Lake in Florida. It was visited by William Bartram in 1775.

Cushtusha
A Choctaw town in Mississippi. The name means "fleas are there!"

Cusick
Albert Cusick, see Sagonaquade.

Cussewago
A village of the Seneca (1750). Later the same site was

used for the building of Ft. Le Boeuf. The present site of Waterford, Pennsylvania.

Cutaantaqwapifsun
The Virginia Indian term used to describe the crown or roach of deer hair that is worn on the head.

Cutans
A name used by Rafinesque to describe a fictitious group of prehistoric people who lived in North America.

Cuttak
The Virginia Indian term for the animal known as the otter. Sometimes known as the beaver, see pohkewh.

Cuttatawomen
The name that Captain John Smith reported for the two tribes of Powhatan Indians that had villages of the same name, each on a different spot. One was on the Rappahannock River and the other on Lamb Creek, both n Virginia.

Cuvfmc
The Powhatan Indian word for sister.

Cuyamunque
A Tewa pueblo located about 15 miles northwest of Santa Fe, New Mexico. Built about 1680.

D

Daahl

This was the "earth" or "sand" clan of the Jemez pueblo of New Mexico.

Dahnohabe

A village of the Pomo located on the west side of Clear Lake in California.

Dakota

This is the largest division of the Siouan family. Commonly known as the Sioux. Their name variously means "allies," "adders," "enemies." They used the names of Dakota, Nakota and Lakota themselves. It has been said that the Dakotas are the highest type physically and mentally of any western tribe.

Dance

See kantokan.

Danokha

A village of the Pomo on the north shore of Clear Lake in California.

Dark

See pahcunnaioh.

Dasoak

Known as the "flying clan" of the Huron.

Daughter

See amofens.

Dauphin

The Lost Dauphin of France, see Williams.

Davis, John

A Creek Indian that was taken prisoner by the whites while a small boy. He became a translator and was an active worker with the missionaries.

De

This was the coyote clan of the Tewa, Tesuque and San Ildefonso of New Mexico.

Dead

See tfepaih.

Deadoses

A small tribe of Indians that lived in Texas about 150 miles from the coast, near the Brazos River. They resembled the Tonkawa. In 1777 and 1778 the whole tribe was wiped out by smallpox.

Deaf

See cuppotaiv.

Deer

See vttapantam.

Deflector

This is a slab of rock or other material which is used in a fireplace in a kiva or other structure to control the fire.

Dekanawida

An Iroquois prophet and statesman who had a large part in founding the federation of the Five Nations. Legend gives him a semidivine character.

Delaware

This was the most important confederacy of the Algonquian. The English called them Delawares from their river. The French called them loups* or "wolves." They called themselves the Lenápe or Leni-lenápe, which meant the "real men." When the whites and the Iroquois entered their country, they moved to Ohio, Wyoming and into Indiana.

Dendrochronology

This is the science of tree ring dating. Each year a tree grows it leaves another ring, dark rings for the winter and the light rings for the summer, wide rings for a fast growing season and a narrow ring for a dry season.

Deposit

This term means mainly an accumulation of rock and debris which has been laid down by the action of the elements. This action can be measured and so artifacts (q.v.) can be dated sometimes when the action and the resulting layers are measured.

Deseronto

A Mohawk chieftain, see Odiserundy.

Dest

A village visited by William Bartram in 1799. They belonged to the Timuquanan of Florida.

Destchin

A band of the Ft. Apache, Arizona, Indians who lived about 1881.

Detroit

Detroit, Michigan, see Pontiac.

Devil Town

Devil Town, Georgia, see Skeinah.

Dhiu

A pueblo of the Piros located near the Rio Grande about the year 1598. One of the many pueblos visited by Oñate in New Mexico.

Diatom

Microscopic algae found in rocks. Their presence can give an indication of climatic conditions in past ages.

Didzedig'ozhiih

The bark and roots of this small tree are used by the

Navajo for the making of a purple shaded dye. The word is Navajo for chokecherry.

Didzeh

Navajo for the wild plum. The roots of the wild plum are used for the making of a purple dye.

Diegueño

A term applied to Indians living in the area of San Diego, California, including various tribes.

Diffusion

This term is used to describe the process by which the culture of one people has spread to another culture (q.v.) and become a part of it.

Digger

First applied to a small tribe of the Paiutes, the only one of this group practicing agriculture. Later it was used for every tribe that used roots as a main part of their diet, and covered a great many western tribes from California to Idaho.

Dighton rock

A large rock eleven feet by five feet, found near the Taunton River in Massachusetts. It had one surface covered with problematic inscriptions similar to pictographs.

Directional colors

The Hopi Indians paint their kachinas (q.v.) special directional colors. These colors show the person who observes the kachina from which direction the kachina has come: Red on a kachina shows that he has come from the South or the Southeast; yellow, from the North or the Northwest; bluish-green the West or Southwest; white denotes the East or Northeast; black denotes down or the underworld. When all of the colors are used on a kachina it denotes up. These colors may be in solid forms, stripes, dots, etc.

Discoidal stones
Round stone objects whose actual use is unknown. Sometimes called "chunkey stones" (q.v.). They vary from one inch to eight inches in diameter.

Disconformity
A term used to describe a geological change where the lower bed of an area is eroded away, and the upper bed, of a different material, is deposited on the eroded surface.

Dishes
Dishes made by the American Indians varied with their needs. Some made them of clay, bark, wood, stone and other materials. The type of material on hand and the kind of food to be placed in it was the deciding factor.

Ditsakana
A division of the Comanche. Also called the Yamparika, because they ate the root of the yampa.

Diwozhiibaih
This is the Navajo word for the shrub, chamizo. This plant grows on the mesas and is used for the making of a light yellow dye.

Dl' oh' azihih
Navajo for the plant known also by the name Mormon tea. Used by the Navajo for the making of a light brown dye.

Dobbs Ferry
Dobbs Ferry, New York, see Wecquaesgeek.

Dog
See attomoys.

Dogi
A group of Indians who became extinct before 1670. They lived in the Piedmont region of Virginia.

Dokis band

A group of Indians who live in and around the Ontario area. They are Chippewas. They are mixed with French blood.

Dolores

A mission that was established on the present site of San Francisco in California. Started in October 9, 1776, called San Francisco de Assisi but better known as the Dolores mission. This first tribe to come to the mission were the Ahwaste, Altahmo, Olhon and Romonan.

Domitilde

Sister of chief Nissowaquet (q.v.).

Dooesedoowe

Known as the "plover clan" of the Iroquois.

Doustioni

A tribe that belonged to the Caddo confederacy who lived along the Red River in Louisiana.

Dover

Dover, New Hampshire, see Piscataqua.

Drills

Drills were made of stone, wood, bone and other hard materials. They were used for boring holes in many objects. There were hand held drills and drills that were held by hands and knees. Some drills were rather simple and others more complicated, such as the bow drill.

Drowning Bear

See Yonaguska.

Drum

See ahqwohhooc.

Dry-painting

An ancient art, also known as sand painting. Mainly

done by the Navajo who do them as part of special ceremonies. They are usually destroyed after the ceremony. The colored sands are collected or ground from various colored sandstones. The design is usually begun at the center, there are certain established designs that are made.

Ds'ah
Navajo for the basin sagebrush. Used by the Navajo for medicinal purposes and for the making of a light green dye.

Duck tablets
Objects of unknown use. Made in a somewhat stylized duck design. Found in Florida.

Dueztumac
A rancheria about 120 miles from the mouth of the Gila River in southwestern Arizona. Used by the Maricopa.

Dull Knife
A strong Cheyenne chief. He was a signer of the treaty at Ft. Laramie in 1868. He was killed in a battle while making his escape from Ft. Robinson in northwestern Nebraska.

Durham
Durham, North Carolina, see Shakori.

Dyami
The eagle clan of the pueblos of Laguna, Acoma, Santa Ana and San Felipe in New Mexico.

Dyes
Indian dyes were made of many materials. The materials to be dyed and the materials at hand decided what colors could be used. Lichens, roots, berries, pokeberries, bloodroot, sumac, grapes, alder, etc., provided dyes.

Dyosyowan
A village of the Seneca meaning "it is oil covered." Located in Erie County, New York.

E

Eagle

The eagle was used as a basis for many ceremonies. Its feathers were used on war bonnets, rattles, shields, pipes, baskets, prayer sticks. The clipping, coloring and special additions to the feather formed a system of ranks and deeds. It was possible to look at an Indian and be able to tell his rank and his deeds by the types of feathers and how they were worn.

Ears

See metawce.

Earth

See chippfni.

Earth lodge

The earth lodge was a type of house made by many tribes, in particular the Pawnee, Omaha, Ponca and Osage. This was a type of house that was made partly underground. First a large circle was drawn on the ground from 30 to 60 feet in diameter. This was then dug out to a depth of about three or four feet. Next a circle of crotched logs was placed around the outer edge and also a circle in the center. Next the roof was built in all directions, leaving a space of about three feet in the center which would later on serve as a smoke hole. The whole building was then laced together and covered with tightly bound grasses. This was then covered with sod which was lapped over in a shingle effect. The roof was then pounded to make it hard and waterproof. A long entrance passageway was built, which usually faced to the east. A skin was used for a door. The lodge would be about seven feet high on the outside.

Sometimes several families would live in one lodge. Skins were used to divide the house and for warmth in the winter.

East
See vtchepwoiffonna.

Eastern Shawnee
This was a division of the Seneca. They formerly lived in Ohio and later on they separated and moved to Kansas.

Eastman, Charles A.
Charles Alexander Eastman, a well known physician and author of the Santee Dakota Indians. His father was "Many Lightnings," a Sioux. A brilliant student, he graduated from Dartmouth in 1887. He worked for the Office of Indian Affairs. Among his books are "Indian Boyhood," "Red Hunters and The Animal People." In 1891 he married Elaine Goodale, they had six children.

Ebahamo
A tribe that formerly lived along Matagorda Bay in Texas. They were met by La Salle. They were friendly with the Caddo, to whom they were closely related.

Ebiamana
An Indian village which was occupied about 1565 in Florida.

Ebita Poocola Chitto
A former Choctaw town located at the head of Straight Creek in Mississippi. The name means "Fountain head or big people."

Ecatacari
A rancheria of the Nevome of northern Mexico, built about 1702.

Echantac
A Costanoan village near the San Juan mission in California.

Echilat
An old village of the Costanoan. Located about twelve miles south east of the San Carlos mission in California.

Echota
The name, meaning "unknown," was the name of several Cherokee villages. One located in Tennessee, one near Clarksville, Georgia; New Echota in Gordon County, Georgia, and one in North Carolina.

Echulit
A village of the Tolowa, located near a lagoon about five miles north of Crescent, California.

Eclauou
A village of the Utina Indians, located in the central part of Florida. Active around 1564.

Economy
Economy, Pennsylvania, see Shenango.

Edelano
A village of Indians, located along the St. Johns River in Florida. Built in the 16th century. The tribe is unknown.

Edisto
A small tribe of Indians, now extinct. They lived along the Edisto River in South Carolina.

Eeh
A division of the Iruwaitso who lived in Siskiyou County in California.

Eeksen
A tribe of the Salish who lived on the east coast of Vancouver Island. They spoke the Comox dialect.

Eel River Indians
These Indians were a part of the Miami who lived in Boone County, Indiana.

Egan

A settlement of the Algonquian located near what is now Quebec.

Eguianna-cahel

This was a rancheria which was connected with the Cadegomo mission, located in lower California.

Ehartsar

One of four divisions of the Crow Indians.

Ehressaronon

A Huron name which is used to designate any of the tribes which lived south of the St. Lawrence River, mainly Iroquoian.

Ehutewa

A village of the Liuseño near the San Luis Rey mission in southern California. Sometimes known as Hatawa.

Einake

This was a society of the Ikunuhkatsi of the Piegan tribe. The name means "soldiers" or "catchers."

Ekaentoton

This was the ancient home of the Ottawa. Located on Manitoulin Island. This is the Huron name for the island. Occupied about 1649.

Ekgiagan

A village near the Soledad mission in California. Occupied by the Chalone, which were a division of the Costanoan family.

Ekoolthat

Meaning "bushes on the hill people." A tribe of the Nootka who formerly lived on the west coast of Vancouver Island.

Ekquall

A former rancheria, located about thirty miles south of

San Diego, California. It was under the mission San Miguel de la Frontera.

Elakulsi

A settlement of the Cherokee located in Georgia in the northern part.

Elephant mound

A mound that is located in Grant County, Wisconsin. For many years this mound has been used for farming and has lost much of its original shape. However, the animal was intended to be a bear and not an elephant. The long "trunk" is supposed to be the result of erosion.

Eleunaxciay

A village of the Chumashan, located near what is now Santa Barbara, California.

Eliot Bible

The first printing and translation of the Bible into an American Indian language. See Bible.

Elks

A group of mythical people who controlled the country from the Mississippi River to the east. This is a story of the Dakota.

Ellijay

This was the name of one of several towns of the Chero- kee. Located on the Keowee River in South Carolina, Macon County in North Carolina and one located near what is now Maryville, Tennessee.

El Morro

Meaning the "castle." This was the remains of a pre- historic pueblo located on a rock mesa known as El Morro, also known as "Inscription Rock." This pueblo was located about thirty-five miles east of Zuñi in New Mexico. It was visited by Oñate in 1605.

Elochuteka
An Indian village, possibly Seminole. Located between the Big Withlacoochee and Hillsboro River in Florida.

Elogio
A settlement of the Papago, located near Pima County in Arizona.

Elothet
A Nootka town located on Vancouver Island. The chief of the town was called Wickaninish.

El Peñon
A small settlement of the Seminole, near the Mosquito River in Florida.

Elquis
A village of the Chumashan located in Ventura County in California.

Eluaxcu
A Chumashan village located near what is now Santa Barbara, ·California.

Elwha
A village of the Clallam near the mouth of the Clallam River in the state of Washington.

Emamoueta
An unidentified tribe of Indians which was placed on a map that was made by Marquette in 1673. Located on the Arkansas River, west of the Mississippi.

Emistesigo
Said to be over six feet tall, he was a chief of the Upper Creeks. He fought the British in Georgia. He attacked a large force of soldiers and succeeded in taking their cannon. He and seventeen of his warriors fell in this battle in hand to hand combat. He died at the age of thirty.

Encaquiagualcaca

A pueblo of the lower Rio Grande that was visited by Oñate in 1598.

Enekelkawa

A former village of the Luiseño, near the site of the San Luis Rey mission in southern California.

Enemy

See macherew.

English

The first English contact with the American Indians was a rather friendly one. However, in 1605, things changed. The Indian was taken advantage of and the Church became very active and with theological zeal, tried to exterminate "the accursed seed of Canaan." With only a few exceptions like John Eliot (q.v.) and Roger Williams, the rest became land hungry. In the late 1600's and late 1790's, several colleges were started and were aimed in whole or part at the education of the American Indian. Such colleges are Harvard, Dartmouth and William and Mary. The charter of Dartmouth in 1769 says in part, "for the education and instruction of youths of the Indian tribes in this land." Harvard, "the education of the English and Indian youth in knowledge and Godliness." Harvard had only one Indian graduate in the Colonial period, Cheeshateaumuck (q.v.). Other English influence has been intermarriage with the Indian as well as the introduction of certain tools and farm implements and weapons, as well as trade beads, etc.

Enmegahbowh

A Methodist Indian minister. Born in the Ottawa tribe, he was adopted by the Chippewa when he was a small boy. He was educated at the Methodist Missionary School in Jacksonville, Illinois. He was ordained as a minister and was given the name Rev. John Johnson. He assisted in establishing an Indian missionary school at Gull Lake in Minnesota in 1873.

Eno

A tribe that has been associated with the Shakori of North Carolina. They disappeared about 1720. It is thought that they joined with the Catawba of South Carolina. They were a very peaceful tribe and had great farms.

Ensenore

This was a chief of the Wingandacoa of North Carolina. He and his tribe were friendly to the English on Roanoke Island in Virginia.

Eolian

This is a term used to describe sand or silt which has been deposited on a surface, such as a grave.

Epley's Ruin

Named after the owner of the ranch upon which this large prehistoric ruin was located. In the southeastern part of Arizona.

Erie

This is a large tribe of Iroquoian Indians. They were located from the Ohio River to the Genesee River, along Lake Erie and the Allegheny River. Riqué and Gentaienton are two well-known Erie towns.

Erie

Erie, Pennsylvania, see Rique.

Erio

A tribe of the Pomo who lived along the Russian River in Sonoma County in California. The name was given by the Spanish explorers.

Eriwonec

A village of the Delaware Indians, who fought a great

deal with the Conestoga Indians. The Eriwonec lived along the Delaware River in Salem County, New Jersey.

Erner
A village of the Yurok who lived along the Klamath River in Del Norte County, California.

Erosion
This is the gradual wearing away of the land or other surface by the action of the elements of wind and water.

Ertlerger
A village of the Yurok along the lower Klamath River in Humboldt County, California.

Ervipiames
A tribe of Indians that lived in the central part of Texas, somewhat west of the Trinity River.

Escooba
A former Choctaw town located in Kemper County, Mississippi.

Escoumains
A band of the Montagnais who lived along the north shore of the St. Lawrence River in Saguenay County, Quebec.

Escumawash
A village of the Chumashan near the Santa Barbara mission in California.

Esekepkabuk
A band of the Crow Indians.

Eskimo
The scope of this dictionary does not include the Eskimo with the Indians of North America. Authorities do not agree with each other when it comes to calling the Eskimo an

"Indian." The Eskimo are a distinct linguistic stock and live in Arctic America. To all intents and purposes the American Indian, as referred to in literature and history of the United States, is thought of as those tribes who live north of Mexico and were here at the time of the settlement and who took an active part in the early history of the United States. It is for this reason that the Eskimo are not included in this dictionary.

Eskini
A village of the Maidu, located in Butte County in California. The story of the Maidu creation centers about this town.

Esksinaitupiks
A division of the Piegan Indians known as "the worm people."

Eskwaw
Narraganset for squaw (q.v.).

Esmischue
A village of the Chumashan, located near the Purísima mission, Santa Barbara, California.

Esopus
This was the old name of Kingston, New York. However, the tribe lived along the west bank of the Hudson River in Greene and Ulster Counties, New York. They were a division of the Munsee.

Esopus
Esopus, New York, see Sewackenaem.

Espachomy
A village below Poughkeepsie, New York, which was under English rule in 1664.

Esperiez

A name that was given to a Hopi Pueblo by Oñate. This name was not correct (1598).

Espopolames

A possible tribe of the Coahuiltecan who lived along the lower Rio Grande.

Esqugbaag

A rancheria near the mission of Suamca (1760 to 1767). Located near the Rio San Pedro along the southern border of Arizona.

Esquipomgole

A mixture of tobacco and bark, another name for kinnikinnick. The word is Algonkian. See kinnikinnick.

Esselen

This was a family of California Indians. This small linguistic stock soon became extinct after the Spanish settlement in 1770.

Estait

A village of the Chumashan near the Purísima mission in Santa Barbara County, California.

Estancia

A Spanish word with many meanings, in this case it is meant to be a place to stay, "a ranch." This was a Pima rancheria which was visited by Anza in 1774. It is located just south of the Arizona border.

Estatoee

This name was given to two former settlements of the Cherokee, one located near the junction of the Tallulah River and the Chattooga River, in South Carolina. The other one was in the northwestern part of Oconee County in South Carolina. Sometimes called "Old Estatoee."

Etaa

This was the "turtle clan" of the Zuñi Indians of New Mexico.

Etanie

This Seminole town was located in Putnam County, Florida. In 1823, Checota Hajo was chief.

Etarita

A village which was destroyed by the Iroquois in 1649. This village of the Wolf clan of the Tionontati was also the site of a Jesuit mission, known as St. Jean.

Etchareottine

This tribe of Athapascan Indians lived in the area of Great Slave Lake in Canada and in the area of the Rocky Mountains. The Cree Indians who attacked them and took many of the tribe away called them "awokanak," or slaves, and thus the French and the English took the name and gave it to them and the lake. The Cree were known as "enna," which meant the enemy.

Ethics

Many people in the early days did not understand the rules by which the Indian was guided and felt themselves superior to the Indian. This feeling and misunderstanding caused considerable trouble for the early settler. The Indian had a strong ethical code. Many Indians were made prisoner by the whites . . . when the Indians came under a flag of truce to talk or bargain. This word- and treaty-breaking made both sides untrustworthy. For example: The stealing of horses was approved for a war-party, however, they only took horses of the enemy. The Zuñi seal their doors with clay when they leave home and no one will enter it. The Nez Percés lean a pole across their door when they are away and no one will enter their house. The rules were followed very closely by the Indians . . . if they were not, the punishment was usually very harsh!

Ethnology

This is the scientific study of the culture (q.v.) of a group of individuals, especially primitive, exclusive of prehistoric man.

Etiwaw

A small tribe of the Cusabo group of Indians that lived in South Carolina. The name is Catawba for "pine tree."

Etotulga

This was a former town of the Seminole Indians in Florida.

Etowah mound

A large mound (in area about 56 acres). Located in Bartow County in Georgia. Built by the Cherokees.

Etsekin

A village of the Kwakiutl, along the Havannah on the west coast of British Columbia.

Ettchaottine

Because of their warlike habits, these people were given their name Ettchaottine, which means "people who act in a contrary way." This tribe of the Nahane lived along Francis Lake in British Columbia.

Etuck chukke

This was a former Choctaw town, located in Kemper County in Mississippi.

Eufauia

Eufaula, Oklahoma, see Tchataksofka.

Eufaula

A town of the Upper Creek, located near Talladega, Alabama.

Eulachon

This word from the Chinook dialect is used for the

"candle-fish." This fish is caught by the Indians along the Northwest Coast. It is used for food and for its grease and oil.

Eushtat

This was the main settlement of the Klamath Indians, located along Klamath Lake in Oregon.

Evea

A chief of the Comanche Indians. He was chief from the year 1772. He had a great deal to do with the treaty that was signed at San Antonio, Texas, in June, 1772.

Exeter

Exeter, Wisconsin, see Spotted Arm.

Eyeish

One of the tribes of the Caddo confederacy. They lived along the Sabine and Neches Rivers in Texas, they were spread over a much larger area, however.

Eyes

See mufknis.

F

Fairfield
Fairfield, Connecticut, see Parker.

Family
The Indian family varied in size and general relationships. Each tribe had its rules and regulations with regard to position and some were very complex, certain property and rank going to certain members of a family. The social organization of a family of a primitive people is a most vital part of their life. The rules of families concerned adoption, marriage, births, death, prisoners. Outlaws were usually denied family rights.

Faraon
A tribe of Apaches that lived from the Rio Grande to the Pecos River in New Mexico. Known by the early Spanish explorers as "the Apache hordes of the Pharaoh."

Farewell
See anath.

Farmers band
A division of the Dakotas who lived below Lake Traverse in Minnesota.

Farmer's Brother
A chief of the Seneca, born around 1719. He died in 1814. Farmer's Brother is sometimes mentioned along with Red Jacket. He fought at Ft. George, New York, when he was over 80 years old. Even though he was a great war chief, he tried always to first have a settlement by peaceful means.

Farmington

Farmington, Connecticut, see Sukiaug.

Fast

To fast meant to do without food or water for a certain specified time. This was done on such occasions as puberty rites and special war parties. It was a spiritual thing, occult things could be seen and told while a person was fasting. A fast was sometimes used as a means of saving food, to make it last longer and at the same time invoke special spirit help.

Father

See kowfe, also see nows.

Fauna

This term is used for the animal life of an area, past or present.

Fawn

See monattecow.

Feasts

A feast was usually held at a certain specified time, such as the opening of a big hunt, or the ending, as a political tool, to impress others. Most feasts were preceded by an offering to the various points of the compass as an offering of thanksgiving.

Feather cape

See puttawus.

Feathers

See ahpewk.

Fermentation

Purposeful fermentation for production of a particular food or drink was rare. Tiswin, made by the Apache but probably not of Apache invention, is one example. It was made by soaking corn until it sprouted, then drying and

108

grinding it. It was then soaked in water in a warm place until it fermented and made a type of beer. The Zuñi chewed cornmeal and held it in the mouth for over an hour, the saliva and corn forming a yeast-producing mixture which was used in the making of bread. The Zuñi also found a means of preserving this mixture with salt and lime so that it could be saved for future use.

Fesere

A pueblo of the Tewa who lived on the mesa near the Chama River in Arriba County, New Mexico.

Fetish

It is the belief of Indians that all objects are incarnate and animate. So because of an all-powerful spirit, it is not possible for a stream to do more than go in a certain direction or course. Mountains must stay where they are and animals, plants, clouds and, in fact, all things are under the control of certain spirits. A fetish is a means of securing the help of these spirits. They may be parts of the objects, such as bones, wood, or other parts. A fetish may be loaned or sold. If a fetish loses its power, it may become a sacred object and placed with other special objects. A fetish may be the result of the owner's imagination and be made by him in a special way. For example: A fetish might be charcoal and the dried blood of an enemy, ground and mixed together. Usually a fetish must be small enough to be carried in a small bag or on a cord. The construction and use of a fetish is usually kept secret by the owner and is only disclosed to the one who inherits it from its owner.

Fife's Village

A town of the Upper Creeks, located near Talladega, Alabama.

Fightingtown

A village of the Cherokee, located on Fightingtown Creek in Fannin County, Georgia.

Filthy
See moich.

Finhalui
A lower Creek town, located in Georgia.

Fire
See boketawgh.

Fire Heart
See chantapeta.

Fire lodge
A clan of the Dakota, located near Traverse River in Minnesota.

Fire making
There were two methods used by the Indians at the time of the settlement. One was the use of flint and pyrites, which was later replaced by flint and steel. The method was to strike one against the other and this would cause a spark which started a fire in dry material. The other method was to rub sticks together between the palms, one end was placed in dry tinder and the friction would cause the tinder to ignite.

Fish
See nammais.

Fishhooks
A gorge fishhook was made by sharpening a bone on each end and fastening it in the center and using bait. The hooks evolved to the shape of the present day hook.

Fishing
When the settlers arrived in America, they found large numbers of all kinds of fish along the Atlantic Coast. Almost anything that could be caught in the sea was eaten. Many fish and their eggs were caught and dried for use in the winter. The Cherokee and Iroquois Indians sometimes used

110

drugs to poison the fish. In California, the "soap root" was used for this purpose.

Five civilized tribes

This term was used to describe those tribes that had made great advances toward absorbing or taking on the ways and means of the white settlers. They were the Cherokee, Chickasaw, Choctaw, Creek and the Seminoles.

Flagstaff

Flagstaff, Arizona, see Palatki.

Flakes

The flake is a term used by the archaeologist when he talks about the long thin "flakes" or chips which are the result of the making of spear or arrow points. Sometimes these flakes are large enough to be used by the Indian for scrapers and other tools. They were sometimes set in handles because all edges were sharp.

Flandreau Indians

This was a group of Indians that separated from the Santee and who formerly lived in Nebraska.

Flathead

The Indians known officially as Flatheads do not flatten their heads, they are known as the Salish. The Indians that bound the heads of their children were the Chinook in the Northwest, Catawba and the Choctaw and many of the Muskhogean tribes such as the Natchez and Tonika.

Flint

A variety of chalcedony. Used by the Indians for the making of a variety of implements such as arrowpoints, spearheads, knives, scrapers, etc.

Flint discs

The most perfect flint disc was found in Tennessee and is nine inches across. The uses of these discs are not known.

Florida Indians
A term used when talking about the Indians of Florida, usually applied to the Appalachian group of Indians.

Flowing water
See tammufcamcuwh.

Flunmuda
A former Costanoan village located near the San Francisco Mission in California.

Fluted
A term used to describe the surface of grooved axes, etc.

Fond du Lac
A group of Chippewa Indians who lived near Fond du Lac in eastern Minnesota.

Food
Like us all . . . the Indian had to eat. The food varied with the type of country and the knowledge and weapons that were at the disposal of the Indian. Of course, some taboos were observed by certain tribes but in extreme cases even food which was not usually eaten could then be used.

Foolish Dogs
This was a band of the Hidatsa of the Northwest Coast Indians.

Foot
See mefscate.

Foreman, Stephen
This was a well-known Cherokee Indian who worked with the Presbyterian missionaries. His work was carried out mainly in Tennessee.

Fort Ancient
A famous Indian fort in Warren County, Ohio. The fort

extends for 18,712 feet and varies from 6 to 19 feet high. The fort was along the Little Miami River.

Fort Hunter
Fort Hunter, New York, a site of a former Indian settlement; see Onekagoncka.

Fort Wayne
Fort Wayne, Indiana, see Peshewah.

Fotshou's Village
A summer village of the Tlingit of the Northwest Coast Indians.

Four Creek Tribes
A name given to the tribes of the Yokuts that lived along the four streams that ran into the Tulare Lake in California.

Fowl Town
A Seminole town in the northwestern part of Florida. This differs from Tutalosi, which has also been called "Fowl Town."

Fox
The clan of the red fox of the Algonquian tribe. The Indians identified themselves by the name of their clan to the French while they were out hunting and so the whole tribe is known as the Foxes. They lived in Wisconsin. They did not get along well with the French, and were very warlike. They had a very primitive society.

Fox
See assimoest, see also ouxe.

Francisco
A chief of the Yuma. A member of the Apache attacked the family of Royse Oatman who lived in Gila Bend in Arizona. He took the two youngest children, Olive and Mary. He sold them into slavery to the Mohave Indians. Francisco

was in Ft. Yuma when a searching party went out looking for the children, he decided to return them and made a speech which persuaded the Mohave to release Olive. (Mary had died.) Because of this he was made chief of his tribe. However, he did not last long and lost heavily in a battle and was killed by his own men.

Franklin

Franklin, North Carolina, see Tessuntee.

Frankstown

A village of the Delawares. Near the site of the present Frankstown, Pennsylvania.

French

The French did a large business with the Algonquian tribes. Early in history they were sympathetic with the Hurons and others and helped them to fight against the Iroquois . . . at the same time they were holding back the English. They made great strides with Indian languages and by mixing with the Indians they came to have great understanding of their life. For a time the French even tried to prohibit the sale of liquor to the Indians. This did not work, however, because the Indians could get it from the English and the Dutch and so they had to give a half-hearted approval to its sale.

Fresnal

A village of the Papago, located near Pima County in Arizona.

Friedenshuetten

A village of converted Indians, located along the Susquehanna River a few miles below Wyalusing in Pennsylvania.

Friendship

See the Powhatan word, cheskchamay.

Frost

Captain Frost was an Onondaga Indian, see Ossahinta.

Frying pan

See ampkone.

Fuller

William Fuller, a hereditary chief of the Miwuk Indians of California, was the last of his tribe to speak the native language. His now-extinct language had been recorded by Columbia University before Chief Fuller died (1958) at the age of 85. He was born at Bald Rock where the town of Twain Harte, California, now stands.

Furniture

The furniture of the Indian house was very simple. His beds were made of skins which were laid over a slat frame. The bed posts were driven into the ground. Stools made of wood, stone and clay were used. Sometimes the bed had a storage place on top, used by the owner for his personal things.

Fur trading

The forts and fur-trading stations of the early settlers were all the idea of these newcomers that most Indians had. The single trapper was to be feared, his idea was to work alone and exterminate the Indian. The large fur companies such as the Hudson's Bay Company, the Missouri Fur Company and others, considered it essential to work with the Indians and that they needed their help. With the animal migrations and the extensive fur gathering, the Indian was forced to make concessions. Many tribes banded together so that they could get food and furs, forming alliances that often lasted for years. Those tribes who lived along the rivers and streams became powerful because they controlled these routes.

115

Fusihatchi

A town of the Upper Creek. Located along the Talla-poosa River in Macon County, Georgia.

Fwaha

This was the fire clan of the old pueblo at Pecos, New Mexico.

G

Gaandowanang

A village of the Seneca Indians, located on the Genesee River near Cuylerville, New York. The name means "it is a great tree."

Gabrieleño

A division of the Shoshone. This division occupied most of Los Angeles County, California, south to the San Bernardino Mountains. The name was applied in a general sort of way by the Spanish missionaries.

Gachigundae

A village of the Haida, located on the northeastern shore of Alliford Bay in the Queen Charlotte Islands.

Gad

Navajo for the one-seeded juniper. Used in the making of a mordant for the dyeing of fabrics. Also used to produce a rather orange-brown dye.

Gad bididze' doo bilatxahi bileeshch' iih bixtoo'

This is a type of Navajo mordant, which was made from the ashes of the juniper. Only the green needles were used. These were placed in a pan and burned until only the ash remained. This was mixed with water and then strained. The liquid was used as the mordant.

Gado

A town of the Haida, located on the south shore of De la Beche Inlet, British Columbia.

Gahato

A village in Chemung County, New York. Thought to

be a village of the Seneca. It was destroyed by Sullivan in 1779.

Gaibaniptea

A village located on the west bank of the Rio San Pedro. Visited by Father Kino in 1697. This was a settlement of the Pima or possibly of the Sobaipuri.

Galena

A lead ore used by the Indians, especially in Illinois and Missouri. The bright cubical shapes were used in their natural form for ceremonial purposes and were placed on altars and in the mounds.

Galisto

A former pueblo, also the seat of a Franciscan mission. This Tano pueblo is located about 22 miles south of Santa Fe, New Mexico.

Gall

This was a chief of the Hunkpapa Teton Sioux. He was a war chief and assisted Sitting Bull at the battle of Little Bighorn, June 25, 1876. Chief Gall later on became a friend of the whites and is said to have denounced Sitting Bull. In 1889 he became a judge in the Indian Court on the Standing Rock Reservation.

Gamacaamanc

A rancheria, possibly of the Cochimi, located near the Cadegomo mission in lower California.

Gambel's oak

The bark of this tree is used by the Navajo for the making of a dull brown dye.

Gamchines

A possible Costanoan village near the Dolores mission, San Francisco, California.

118

Games

Indian games are generally of two kinds, games of chance and games of skill. Games of chance are played in a similar manner to dice with sticks, pebbles, etc. being used. Certain games are played only at certain seasons and involve many people, sometimes whole tribes.

Ganadoga

The name that was given to a village of the Iroquois on the shores of Lake Ontario, near the present site of the city of Toronto. The same name was also given to a village of the Oneida who lived in Oneida County, New York.

Ganagweh

A village of the Seneca, located near the site of Palmyra, New York.

Ganahadi

A division of the Tlingit who lived in British Columbia. The group divided into several branches, and settled at Tongas, Taku, Chilkat and at Yakutat. There was supposed to be a fifth at Klawak.

Ganasarage

A former Tuscarora village site, now known as Sullivan, New York.

Ganawagus

A village of the Seneca near the present city of Avon, New York. The name means "it has a swampy smell."

Ganedontwan

A village of the Seneca. The present site of Moscow, New York.

Ganeraske

A village of the Iroquois about 1670. Located along the Trent River near the northeastern end of Lake Ontario.

Gangasco
A former village of the Powhatan confederacy, located in Northampton County, Virginia. The tribe was possibly of the Accomac.

Ganneious
A village of the Iroquois, located along the north shore of Lake Ontario.

Gannentaha
This was the Huron name for Onondaga Lake, New York. The French established a mission on the lake called Notre Dame de Ganentaa. The Hurons, Onondaga and Neutrals came to the mission. The mission was abandoned in 1658 because of the hostile Iroquois.

Ganogeh
A former Cayuga village. Means "place of floating oil." Located on the site of Canoga, New York.

Ganosgagong
A small village of the Seneca, meaning "among the milkweeds." Located near Dansville, New York.

Gaousge
A possible village of the Seneca, located along the Niagara River on the New York side.

Garakonthie
A chief of the Onondaga. He died in 1676 at Onondaga, New York.

Garfish
See tatamaho.

Garomisopona
A village of the Chumashan, located near Point Conception in California.

G'asdah bee gah
This is the Navajo term for the plant known as the owl's claw. Used by the Navajo for making a yellow dye.

Gash
The home of a clan of the Tlingit called Sanyakoan. Many of them moved to Ketchikan, Alaska.

Gaskosada
A village of the Seneca located along the Cayuga Creek west of Lancaster, New York.

Gaspesien
This was a group of Micmac Indians that lived on the Gaspé Bay of the Gulf of St. Lawrence. Also known as the "Micmacs of Gaspé."

Gawunena
This was a small band of the Arapaho.

Gay Head Indians
These Indians lived on the western end of Martha's Vineyard. In 1809 they were completely a tribe of mixed-bloods, Indian and negro.

Geguep
A village of the Chumashan Indians. Located near the Santa Inez mission, near Santa Barbara County, California.

Gelelemend
Meaning "leader," this was the name of a strong Delaware chief. Also known as Killbuck and was baptized with the name of William Henry. This chief was very friendly toward the whites and did much to promote peace. In 1782 the chief and his tribe were attacked by a band of white men and all but the chief were killed; he fled to the water and swam to safety. He later joined the Moravian Indians of Pennsylvania. He died in January, 1811.

Geliac
A former village of the Chumashan Indians, located near the present city of Santa Barbara, California.

Genega's band
A small band of the Paviotso who lived in western Nevada, named after its chief. The name means "dancer."

Geneseo
A large important village of the Seneca. Located near the present site of the city of Geneseo, New York.

Genobey
A large settlement of the Jumano who lived along the eastern side of the Rio Grande in New Mexico. In 1598 this settlement was visited by Oñate.

Gens
A gens is an intratribal group, the members being theoretically related to each other. In the gens membership, privileges, etc., are traced through the male. Otherwise the clan and the gens are similar. The same gens or clan may have members in various villages or units of a tribe. (See clan.)

German
The influence of the Germans on the Indians of North America is seen in three main regions. Among the Eskimo, the Delawares and the Iroquois in Pennsylvania and New York, and among the Cherokee of South Carolina. Many Moravian missions were established. It is thought by some that the father of Sequoya was a German from Georgia.

Geronimo
Geronimo was a well-known medicine man of the Chiricahua Apache. He was born about 1834 near the headwaters of the Gila River in New Mexico. He led an active and exciting life. He was at times very peaceful and at other times he became an active enemy of the soldiers. He fought

against General George H. Crook in the Sierra Madre Mountains. He finally made peace and was moved to Ft. Sill in Oklahoma.

Gewauga

A village of the Cayugo, near the site of Springport, New York, on the east side of Lake Cayuga. This Indian village was destroyed by Sullivan September 22, 1779.

Ghost dance

A dance that originated with the Paviotso of Nevada about 1888. The religion was begun by a Paiute Indian known as Wovoka. He was a medicine man. While he was sick with fever, an eclipse occurred which excited the Indians. During this time Wovoka had a spiritual revelation from the Indian God. The results of this revelation, that the Indian would be restored to his natural heritage and that he must practice the songs and ceremonies that were given by the prophet Wovoka, started the craze of the Ghost Dance among many Indians of the day. The dance was done by men and women who held hands and slowly walked in a large circle, no musical instruments were used.

Ghuaclahatche

A town of the Upper Creek that was visited by William Bartram in 1791. It was located along the Tallapoosa River in Alabama.

G'iiltsoih

Navajo for the plant known as the rabbit bush. The flowers of this plant are used in the making of a yellow dye.

Gila Apache

A name that was applied to the Apache settlements in the south western part of New Mexico and those who lived along the headwaters of the Gila River. Later this name was applied to those Apache who lived along the Gila River in Arizona.

Gimiels

This was a band of almost pure Yumas who lived in the northern part of Lower California.

Gipuy

The early village of Gipuy was located on the edge of the Arroyo de Galisteo in the north central part of New Mexico. About the year 1591, this village was partially destroyed by a flood and was abandoned. A new village of the same name was started about four miles west.

Girty's Town

The name of this Shawnee town was derived from the name of a trader, Simon Girty. Located in Auglaize County in Ohio.

G'ish

The Navajo word for alder, the bark of which is used to make a brown dye.

Gitins

This is an important subdivision of the Eagle Clan of the Haida who live in British Columbia.

Gitlapshoi

This was a tribe of the Chinook who lived in Pacific County in the state of Washington. The name meant "grass-land people."

Glaglahecha

Known as the "slovenly ones," this was a band of the Sihasapa Teton Sioux. The Miniconjou Teton Sioux were also known by this name.

Gleuaxcuqu

A former village of the Chumashan who lived near what is now Santa Barbara, California.

Glikhikan

This noted warrior of the Delaware tried to win back

the Indians who had become Christianized. In 1769 he challenged the Moravian missionaries to a debate. The results of the debate went the other way and he himself was converted! Glikhikan was killed and scalped by the whites at Gnadenhuetten on March 8, 1782.

Gnadenhuetten
This was the name given to several Moravian missions that were established in and around Carbon County, Pennsylvania.

Gnat town
See Punxsutawny.

Goch
This was the "wolf" phratries of the Tlingit. The name was applied to the southern half.

God
See ahone and rawottonemd.

Gohate
A rancheria of the Maricopa located along the Gila River in southern Arizona.

Gohlkahin
A division of the Jicarillas, the name meant "prairie people."

Gold
Gold in the form of nuggets was found and used by the Indians north of Mexico. However, they did not work the gold into any special shapes. The Indians of Florida had some gold and the Spanish explorers were told that it came from the north. It is supposed that the gold was taken from Spanish ships which had been wrecked on the coast of Florida on their way back to Spain from Mexico.

Good
See wingan.

Gooktlam

See race.

Goose

See kahanqoc.

Gorgets

These were usually simple ornaments that were hung around the neck and were worn for their beauty. They were sometimes worn suspended from the ears. It is not known whether they had any special significance.

Goshgoshunk

This was a settlement of three villages, located in the upper part of Venango County, Pennsylvania. Occupied by the Delaware, Munsee and some of the Seneca. In 1768 it became the center of a Moravian mission.

Gosiute

A Shoshonean tribe living west of the Great Salt Lake. The name is variously spelled Goshute, Gosha-Ute. They were industrious, practicing agriculture and working for whites when they had the opportunity.

Gouges

These are stone tools of the Indians, mainly of the north, and are rare west of the Alleghenies. They somewhat resemble a shoe-horn. Their exact use is not known, it has been suggested that they are used to tap the maple trees for its sap. The sap runs down and out in the stone groove. It was thought that they were used for the cutting of a dug-out canoe. However, the birchbark canoe was more in use in the north.

Gourds

Many species of gourds were raised by the Indians. Besides food and seeds, they raised gourds so that they could use their shells for spoons, dippers, bowls, for the carrying of water, for masks and other ornaments, rattles and for the storage of foods. They sometimes bound the gourd while it was growing so that they could get a desired shape.

Grand Bois
A village, possibly of the Potawatomi, located about six miles southeast of Geneva in Kane County, Illinois. Also known as Shaytee's Village.

Grand Canyon
See Papago.

Grand River Indians
These were the Iroquois that lived on the Grand River in Ontario.

Grand River Ute
This was a group of the Yampa who lived in the Rocky Mountains and came as far east as Denver, Colorado.

Grand Saux
This name has been given to the Indians of the Plains and the Dakotas. Used to distinguish these groups from the eastern woodland tribes of the Sioux.

Grand Traverse
This settlement of the Chippewa was located near what is now Flint, Michigan. The Grand Traverse was a name that was given by the French traders for this ford in the Flint River.

Gran Quivira Monument
This National Monument is located about 23 miles south of Mountainair, New Mexico, on U.S. Highway 60. The pueblo was abandoned about 1675.

Grape Island
A settlement of the Missisauga, located in the northern part of Minnesota.

Grapes

See marakimmins.

Grass houses

Houses built of grass were of a temporary nature and were useful only in warm climates. They were rather common on the plains because of the lack of other building materials.

Grave

See ourcar.

Graver

A term now commonly used for small tool used for marking pottery, bone or stone articles. It is a cutting tool similar to those now used in the engraving crafts. At one time the term graver was applied only to those articles made in ancient Europe.

Great Barrington

Great Barrington, Massachusetts, see Westenhuck.

Great Basin

Archaeologically speaking, this covers the inside drainage areas of eastern California, Nevada, southeastern Oregon and western Utah.

Great Falls

Great Falls, Wisconsin, see Souligny.

Green Bay

Green Bay, Wisconsin, see Tolungowon, Tomau. Also see John W. Quinney, and Spotted Arm.

Green Corn Dance

See Busk.

Greentown

A village of the Delaware, located along the Black Fork of the Mohican River in Ohio.

Greenville
Greenville, Ohio, see Secawgo.

Greenwich
Greenwich, Connecticut, see Wecquaesgeek.

Greetings
See kencuttemaun.

Grenadier Squaw Town
A village of the Shawnee located in Pickaway County in Ohio. The town was named after the sister of Cornstalk, a chief of the Shawnee (1774).

Grey Eagle Band
A group of the Dakota who lived in Minnesota near Lake Traverse.

Grigras
A small tribe which consolidated with the Natchez confederacy in 1720.

Grinding corn
See vshuccohomen.

Grosse Tête
A village of the Chitimacha, located in Louisiana. The name means "large or big head."

Gros Ventres
This was the name given to two tribes, one of the Arapaho and the other one the Hidatsa. The name is French and means "big bellies." The name is derived from the sign made to show "hungry," "beggar," done by a sweeping pass made across the stomach. Also derived from the tattooed stripes on the chest of the Hidatsa.

Groton
A village of the Mohegan, located near what is now Groton, Connecticut. See Sassacus. Also see Pequot and Weinshauks.

Ground lichen
Used by the Navajo Indians for the making of a light orange dye.

Gua
A village of the Chumashan located in Ventura County in California in 1542.

Guachoya
It was here that De Soto died, May 21, 1542. This village was located on the west bank of the Mississippi River, a short distance below the mouth of the Arkansas River.

Guaes
A group of Indians that lived in the eastern central part of Kansas around 1542. They were apparently Pawnee or Wichita.

Guaislac
A village of the Chumashan, located near what is now Santa Barbara, California.

Guaxulè
A possible village of the Creeks that was visited by De Soto in 1540. Located near Cartersville, Georgia. Because of the good treatment that the Spanish soldiers received here, the name became synonymous with good luck.

Guayotri
A possible pueblo of the Tigua. Located in New Mexico in 1598 and visited by Oñate.

Guevu
A village of the Calusa, located on the southwest coast of Florida in 1570.

Gueza
A settlement of Indians located in the western part of South Carolina in what is now Edgefield County. Visited by Juan Pardo in 1565.

Guhlaniyi

A village of the Cherokee and the Natchez Indians. Located near a junction of the Brasstown Creek and Hiwassee River in Cherokee County in North Carolina.

Guhlkainde

A division of the Mescalero Apache. This group considered their original origin east of the Pecos River in Texas and into New Mexico.

Guia

A pueblo located near Albuquerque, New Mexico.

Guias

A ranchería of the Maricopa, located on the Gila River in southern Arizona (1744).

Guilitoy

A division of the Copehan family. This tribe of the Patwin lived in what is now Napa County in California.

Guima

A village of the Chumashan located near what is now Santa Barbara, California.

Guiomaer

An Indian village visited by Juan Pardo in 1566. Located in what is now Barnwell County, South Carolina.

Gull

See coiahgwus.

Gull Lake Band

This was a band of the Chippewa Indians that lived along the upper Mississippi River in Cass County, Minnesota.

Gun

See pocosack.

Gunakhe
A village of the Lakweip, located along the upper part of the Stikine River in British Columbia.

Gunasquamekook
A village of the Passamaquoddy located in St. Andrews, New Brunswick. This tribe was later moved to Pleasant Point, Maine.

Gunghet-kegawai
This is a sub-division of the Eagle Clan of the Haida. This group belongs to the Gunghet group, also known as the "Ninstints," for the name of the main village.

Gupa
A village located near the headwaters of the San Luis Rey River in California. Known also by the name of Agua Caliente.

Gusti
A village of the Cherokee, located on the Tennessee River in Roane County, Tennessee.

Gutheni
A town of the Tlingit. Located north of Dry Bay in Alaska. The name means "salmon creek."

Gwaeskun
Considered to be the northernmost town of the Haida Indians of the Queen Charlotte Islands of British Columbia. The name means "end of the island."

Gwalgahi
This was the village of a band of Natchez Indians and later on a Baptist mission. Located in Cherokee County, North Carolina, 1755.

Gwaugweh
A possible village of the Seneca who lived along the Niagara River in New York State.

Gweundus

A low social order of the Eagle Clan of the Haida.

Gwinwah

A former village of the Niska, located along the Nass River in British Columbia.

Gyaushk

Meaning "gull," this was one of the gens of the Chippewa.

Gyazru

This is the parrot clan of the Hopi Indians.

Gyilaktsaoks

A family of the Tsimshian who lived on the northern side of the Skeena River in British Columbia. The name means "the people of the canoe planks."

Gyusiwa

A large group of pueblos of the Jemez. Located in the eastern part of Sandoval County in New Mexico. In 1622 this pueblo was abandoned because of attacks by the Navajo.

H

Ha'altsedih
Navajo for the wild walnut tree. The leaves and the nuts of this tree are used for the making of a full brown dye.

Haanatlenok
This gens was a subdivision of the Kwakiutl. The name means "the archers."

Haanka Ullah
A town of the Choctaw. Located in Kemper County, Mississippi. The town received its name from the fact that it was near a large pond which had many water fowl. The name means in a sense "there cries the wild goose."

Haatze
An ancient pueblo of the Cochiti located near the foot of the San Miguel mountains in New Mexico.

Habachaca
This was a clan of the Timucua who formerly lived in Florida.

Hackensack
This was a division of the Delaware Indians. The lands of the tribe covered roughly Staten Island, Hoboken, Newark, Passaic and the valleys of the Hackensack and Passaic Rivers. The name means, "The stream that unites in low or level ground."

Hackensack
Hackensack, New Jersey, see Peckwes.

Hadley Indians
A possible band of the Nipmuc. This band had a fort on the western side of the Connecticut River in Hampshire County, Massachusetts.

Hadsapoke
A band of the Paviotso who formerly lived near the Gold Canyon and along the Carson River in western Nevada.

Hadtuitazhi
This is a group of the sub-gens of the Hanga gens of the Omaha.

Haena
A town of the Haida, located on the eastern end of Maude Island in British Columbia.

Hagonchenda
A town of the Iroquois, located along the junction of the St. Lawrence River and the Cartier River.

Hahamatses
This was a sub-division of the Lekwiltok which was a tribe of the Kwakiutl. This group were under the control of the Wiwekae and were considered to be slaves. Their name means "old mats."

Hahas
A village of the Chumashan located on Santa Cruz Island in California.

Hahatonwanna
A village of the Sioux, located near the falls of the St. Anthony in Minnesota. Mentioned by Lewis and Clark in 1804 as a sub-division of the Yankton Sioux. The name has also been used in connection with a band of the Chippewa.

Hahuamis
A tribe of the Kwakiutl who lived on Wakeman Sound in British Columbia.

Haida

This is the native name and the most popular name given to the peoples of the Queen Charlotte Islands in British Columbia. Also applied to anyone who speaks the Haida dialects. According to language and physical traits, they are grouped with the Tlingit and Tsimshian. These Indians of the Northwest coast are fine wood carvers and house builders. They made large canoes of the cedar. They had great feasts called potlatches (q.v.). They also carved large totem poles.

Haiglar

Known also as King Haiglar by the English. This was the main chief of the Catawba Indians of South Carolina (q.v.). He became chief in 1748. Chief Haiglar offered his services to South Carolina in the war against the Cherokee in 1759. In 1762 Chief Haiglar was killed by the Shawnee.

Hair

Hair was used as a textile by the Indians of North America. Hair of such animals as the bison, mountain sheep, elk, moose, deer, dog, rabbit, beaver and also man was used in various ways for weaving and for the making of wigs.

Hair forms

The style of hair-do varied with certain tribes. For example, the name Pawnee, meaning "horn" was derived from the style of hair-do of the members of the tribe; their hair was clipped short in such a way as to leave a ridge or scalp lock in the center, this was stiffened with fat and paint to form a sort of "horn." This technique of "roaching" was done by many eastern tribes. The Dakotas parted their hair in the middle and braided the two long strands and wrapped them in cloth or skins. The tribes of Idaho, such as the Nez Percés, wore their hair in a loose way. In the southwest, the men usually wore "bangs" and the hair was knotted in the back. The Hopi women usually wore their hair in whorls over each ear which signified the squash blossom until they were married, they then wore plain braids. Hair was washed in the Southwest with soap made from the root of the yucca.

Haisla
A dialect division of the Kwakiutl of the Northwest Coast of Canada and Alaska.

Haiwal
This was the "acorn clan" of the Tonkawa.

Hakan
This is the "fire clan" of the pueblos of Acoma, Cochiti, Santa Ana, Sia and San Felipe in New Mexico. The hakan of Acoma has become inactive.

Hakkyaiwal
A village of the Yaquina, located on the southern shore of the Yaquina River in Oregon.

Halant
A village of the Shuswap located near Shuswap Lake in British Columbia.

Half King
A chief of the Seneca, born about 1700. There were other chiefs known by this name, those of the Huron and the Oneida. This chief died at the home of John Harris in 1754 (the present site of Harrisburg, Pennsylvania).

Halfway Town
A village of the Cherokee, located on the Little Tennessee River. The present area of Monroe and Loudon Counties in Tennessee.

Halona
One of the Seven Cities of Cibola. This was a pueblo of the Zuñi and occupied about 1540. The only trace of this

pueblo is a mound area near the present Zuñi pueblos in western New Mexico.

Hamanao
A gens of the Quatsino tribe of the Kwakiutl of the Northwest Coast.

Hammerstones
Hammerstones were used by many tribes and were made in various ways to suit their needs. Such stones were used to drive tent stakes, etc. Some hammers were used as weapons, others used to quarry rocks. Some were grooved so that a handle could be fastened on them, others were hand held. Some hammers were shaped and others were used in their natural shapes.

Hampasawan
A former pueblo of the Zuñi about six miles from the present Zuñi pueblos in Valencia County in New Mexico. Regarded by some to be one of the Seven Cities of Cibola.

Hamtsit
A division of the Bellacoola of Talio, British Columbia.

Han
A tribe which Cabeza de Vaca had contact with when he and his men were shipwrecked in 1528 on the coast of Texas. They were a possible band of the Attacapa.

Hanahawunena
An extinct division of the Arapaho.

Hanakwa
A pueblo mentioned in early records located in New Mexico and occupied by the Jemez.

Hanaya
A village of the Chumashan located near Mission Canyon of the mission of Santa Barbara, California.

Hand
Hee metinge.

Hangashenu
One of the two divisions of the Omaha.

Hanging maw
A chief of the Cherokee Indians, whose name means "his stomach hangs down."

Hangka
One of the three divisions of the Osage. This was the right or war side of the camp circle.

Hankutchin
Known as the "river people," this is a tribe of the Kutchin who live along the Yukon River in Alaska. They are skilled salmon fishermen.

Hano
Sometimes spoken of as a Hopi pueblo. This was the easternmost pueblo of the Tusayan in northeastern Arizona. The Hano people were closely intermarried with the Hopi.

Hanocoucouaij
An Indian village on the east coast of Florida north of what was called Cape Canaveral in the 16th century.

Hantiwi
A tribe of the Shastan who formerly lived in Modoc County, California.

Hapaluya
An Indian village that was visited by De Soto in 1539. Located in the upper or northern part of Florida.

Hapanyi
This was the "Oak Clan" of the Keresan pueblos of northern New Mexico. Now extinct.

Hapes

A tribe that was visited by the early Spanish explorers, located near what is now Eagle Pass, Texas. In 1688 they were almost wiped out by smallpox and in 1689 they were completely exterminated by the Indians of the coastal area.

Haqihana

This was a local band of the Arapaho, known as the "wolf band."

Harahey

A form of the name of a province of the New Mexico pueblos that were visited by Coronado in 1540-51. It is possible that these Indians may have been Pawnee.

Harbor Springs

Harbor Springs, Michigan, see Waganakisi.

Harris

Mary Harris, the wife of Eagle Feather, see White Woman's Town.

Harrison

General William Henry Harrison, see Tippecanoe.

Harsanykuk

A village of the Pima, located on the Sacaton Flats in southern Arizona.

Harutawaqui

A village of the Tuscarora of North Carolina. The village was active in 1701.

Haslinding

A village of the Hupa, located on the Trinity River in the southern part of the Hupa Valley.

Hassimanisco

An Indian village located on the Connecticut River in the state of Connecticut.

Hassinunga

A small tribe of the Manahoac who lived along the headwaters of the Rappahannock River in Virginia (1610).

Hasty pudding

See asapan.

Hat

See the Powhatan word, puttaiquapifson.

Hatchet

It is generally considered that the hatchet is a tool for domestic uses around camp and not used as a weapon. However, it was used as a club or tomahawk on occasion. Iron hatchets replaced the stone tools at the time of the settlements.

Hatchures

A term used by the archaeologist (q.v.) to describe a type of design on pottery, mainly closely aligned parallel lines.

Hatcheuxhau

A village of the Upper Creeks, located near the site of La Grange, Georgia.

Hatteras

Located east of Pamlico Sound, this was a settlement of the Algonquians. These Indians of the coastal area of North Carolina are sometimes referred to as the Croatan Indians of Roanoke Island.

Hauguequins

Virginia Indian term for a small stone pot.

Haukoma

A division of the Pomo, located on the western side of Clear Lake in California.

Havasupai

This small Yuman group is known as the "blue or green

141

water people." They live in the Grand Canyon and the Central Arizona area and in the San Francisco Mountains.

Haverstraw
A name given by the Dutch to a tribe of Delawares who lived along the Hudson River in Rockland County, New York.

Hayah
This was the "snake clan" of the Pecos tribes of New Mexico.

Haza'aleehtsoh
This is the Navajo term for the plant known as the wild celery. Used by the Navajo for the making of a light yellow dye.

Head
See mintabuckkam.

Head of arrow
See raputtak.

Heashkowa
This is the red corn clan of Acoma. Located about two miles southeast of the present Acoma pueblo in New Mexico.

Hehlkoan
A group of Tlingit near Wrangell, Alaska, who belonged to the wolf clan. The name means "the people of the foam."

Hekpa
This is the Fir Clan of the phratry of the Hopi Indians.

Helapoonuch
A village of the Chumashan, located about fifteen miles from the present site of Santa Barbara, California.

Helicopile
An Indian village located on the lower St. Johns River in Florida (1564).

Helikilika
This is the ancestor gens of the Kwakiutl tribe of the Nakomglisala.

Heluta
A Cholovone village located in San Joaquin County, California.

Hematite
This oxide of iron was used by the Indians for paint, also known as red ochre.

Hemptown
A settlement of the Cherokee located in Fannin County in Georgia.

Henaggi
A tribe of the Aathapascan who formerly lived along the Smith River in California. The tribe is now extinct.

Henakyalaso
An ancestor gens of the Kwakiutl, known as the Tlatla-sikoala.

Hendrick
A chief of the Mohawk, sometimes called King Hendrick. He was killed at the battle near Lake George, New York, in September 8, 1755. He fought with the English against the French.

Heniocane
A tribe that was possibly related to the Coahuiltecan. They lived in southern Texas and were visited by Fernando del Bosque in 1675.

Henry
See the name of Gelelemend, the Indian name of this Delaware Chief. He was baptized under the name of William Henry.

Henuti

This is the now extinct cloud clan of the pueblo of Sia, New Mexico.

Henya

A tribe of the Tlingit who lived on the west coast of Alaska and on the Prince of Wales Islands.

Hepowwoo

A village of the Luiseño located near the San Luis Rey mission in southern California.

Hermho

A former village of the Pima, located along the northern side of the Salt River about three miles from the mesa in Maricopa County in the southern part of Arizona.

Herring Pond

A settlement located near Herring Pond in Plymouth County in Massachusetts. This settlement was established for "Christian Indians." Started about 1655, the Indians that lived there were considered to be a distinct tribe.

Heshokta

A ruined pueblo of the Zuñi, located about five miles northwest of the present Zuñi pueblo in New Mexico.

Heshota Ayahltona

Ruins of Zuñi pueblos located in the "Thunder Mountains." Located in the southeastern area of the present Zuñi pueblo in New Mexico.

Hespatingh

A village mentioned in a deed of 1657. Located possibly near Bergen, New Jersey. The Indians were possibly Delawares.

Heuchi

A tribe of the Yokuts who lived along the Fresno River in the north central part of California.

Hewut
A village of the Umpqua along the river of the same name in Oregon.

Hiamonee
A Seminole village about five miles from Georgia, located along the Okloknee River in Florida.

Hiaqua
A term used by the Indians of the Northwest Coast, the name applies mainly to the shells known as the dentalium which were used as money.

Hiawatha
This was the hereditary name and title of the chieftainship of the turtle clan of the Mohawk Indians. The first known Indian to have this name lived around 1570. He is considered to be one of the founders of the Confederation of the Five Nations of the Iroquois. He was a great reformer. He was also regarded as a great sorcerer and many legends grew up about him. Longfellow made his name famous, however, the poem does not stick to the "facts."

Hicaranaou
This was an ancient village of the Timuquanan, located in the northern part of Florida.

Hictoba
One of the five divisions of the Dakota Indians (1722).

Hickerau
A small village of the Santee Indians of South Carolina, located along what is now the Santee River in South Carolina.

Hickory Indians
A small tribe of possible Delaware Indians who lived near what is now Lancaster, Pennsylvania.

Hidatsa

This is a Siouan tribe that lived near the junction of the Knife River and Missouri River in what is now North Dakota. Their language is rather close to the Crows. The name means "willows."

High Tower Forks

Also known as Etowah. See Etowah mounds.

Higos

A tribe that lived in southern Texas which was visited by Cabeza de Vaca in 1528. He called them the "fig people," from their habit of eating the fruit of the prickly pear.

Hill

See romutton.

Hillabi

A town of the Upper Creeks. Located near what is now Clay County in Alabama. They lived in four villages around 1799.

Hillis Hadjo

A prophet and leader of the Seminole Indians of Florida. Around 1817 he was killed by the Americans because of his actions on behalf of the English.

Himatanohis

This was the warrior society of the Cheyenne; the name means the "bowstring men."

Hirrihigua

An Indian village on the west coast of Florida, located in or near Tampa Bay. It was here that De Soto landed in May of 1539.

Hishkowits

Also known as Harvey Whiteshield. He was an interpreter of the Southern Cheyenne. He worked on a dictionary of the Cheyenne Indian language. He was born in Oklahoma in 1876.

Hitchapuksassi
A former Seminole town located in what is now Hillsboro County in Florida.

Hitschowon
A village of the Chumashan located on the Santa Cruz
Island off the coast of California.

Hitshinsuwit
A village of the Yaquina which was located on the
southern side of the Yaquina River in Oregon.

Hittoya
A small division of the Miwok who lived along the
upper part of Chowchilla River in Mariposa County in
California.

Hiwassee
This was the name that was given to several settlements
of the Cherokee Indians. These villages were located along
several parts of the Hiwassee River in what is now Polk
County, Tennessee.

Hiyayulge
A village of the Maricopa located along the Gila River
in Arizona.

Hlaphlako
This name was given to two towns of the Upper Creek
Indians who lived in what is now Macon County, Alabama. The name meant "tall cane."

Hlaphlako Town
This town of the Creek Indians was located on Alabama
Creek in Oklahoma. The same name was given to several
towns of the Upper Creek Indians who lived in Alabama.

Hlauhla

A small ruin of a Zuñi pueblo, located about ten miles north, northeast of Zuñi, New Mexico.

Hlgan

This name was given to a town of the Haida located on an island of the Queen Charlottes in British Columbia. The name was given to this village because of a large rock which jutted out of the water in front of the village and looked like the fin of a killer whale. The name means "the fin of the killer whale."

Hobnuts

Also known by the names of "hopnuts, hopnis, hobenis." This was a root that was used by the Algonquian Indians and grew in swamps, the plant is known as Orontium aquaticum.

Hoboken

Hoboken, New Jersey, see Sapohanikan.

Hobomok

This is the name of a chief of the Wampanoag of Plymouth, Massachusetts. He was a friend of the English and became a Christian and as such did not enter into any more battles.

Hochelaga

This was a former Iroquoian town with a strong palisade surrounding it. This village was near what is now Montreal, Canada, and it is said that it had a population of about 3600 around the year 1535.

Hogan

This is a type of house made by the Navajo. Usually made from logs or planks and sod or clay for a filler or adobe bricks. The roof was covered with sod. The hogan usually has eight sides. However, the name has been given to many other types of houses used by the Indians.

Hogansburg
Hogansburg, New York, see Williams.

Hog Creek
Until 1831, this was a village of the Shawnee. Located in Allen County in Ohio.

Hogologes
A village of the Creeks, located along the Flint River in Georgia. It was visited by Bartram in 1799.

Holatamico
Also known as "Billy Bowlegs." This was one of the last chiefs of the Seminoles of Florida. In 1858 he and his tribe agreed to move from Florida and go west to a reservation.

Holbrook
Holbrook, Arizona, see Shumway.

Hominy
A type of food made from corn. The kernels were soaked in water and wood ashes to remove the hull. The kernels are then cooked with meat or fish. Now known by the familiar name of "hominy grits."

Homna
Meaning "smelling like fish," this was a division of the Brulé Teton Sioux.

Hondo
Hondo, Texas, see Vánca.

Hook Indians
A small tribe of Indians that lived in South Carolina along the lower Pedee River. This tribe possibly belonged to the Sioux.

Hook stone
These are objects of from one to five inches in length and are shaped somewhat like the lowercase "l." They are

found in the burials of the Indians of California. Their use or function is not known. They are made of a soft stone, sometimes of soapstone.

Hopewell
Hopewell, New York, an Indian site, see Onaghee.

Hopi
To themselves, their name means "the peaceful ones or all peaceful." In 1540, they were first visited by the Spanish explorers, one of Coronado's men, Pedro de Tobar, visited several of their villages in what was then the province of Tusayan. It was here that the Spaniards learned of the Grand Canyon of the Colorado. This was a large and powerful tribe in the northeastern part of Arizona.

Horizon
This term is used by the archaeologist (q.v.). This means the level or stratum of a particular culture (q.v.).

Hornotlimed
A chief of the Seminole Indians of Florida. He was active in the Seminole War in 1817. He was also known by the name of "Old Red Stick."

Horse
The horse, as we know it today, was brought to the Indians by the early Spanish explorers. In 1541 Coronado brought the horse to the Plains Indians. Antonio de Espejo brought horses to the Hopi in 1583. The horse was brought to the Iroquois in the early 17th century.

House
See yohacan.

Howiri
A former pueblo of the Tewa located in Arriba County in New Mexico.

Hoya

Meaning "raven," this was a former settlement of Indians, related to the Edisto, located along the coast of South Carolina.

Huhliwahli

This was a Creek town, located near the north fork of the Canadian River in Oklahoma.

Huititnom

This was a small tribe of the Yuki who formerly lived along the Eel River in northern California.

Huma

Meaning the "red people," this Choctaw tribe lived in Louisiana around 1699. Due to war and disease, they have become extinct.

Humalija

A former village of the Chumashan, located near what is now Santa Barbara, California.

Humbo

A word used in New Hampshire, a word closely related to Algonquian and Chippewan, meaning to make or boil the sap of the maple tree, to make maple syrup.

Humboldt

The name is given to the Indians known as the Paviotso who lived around Humboldt Lake in Nevada.

Hume

A small tribe that formerly lived in southern Texas along the Rio Grande.

Humkak

A rather important village of the Chumashan, located on Point Conception, near what is now Santa Barbara, California.

Hungopavi

This is a pueblo ruin located about two miles north of the Bonito Pueblo in Chaco Canyon in the northwestern part of New Mexico.

Hunkpapa Sioux

This is a division of the Teton Sioux of North and South Dakota. The early history of the Hunkpapa is not known, the first mention of them is in 1825, although they may have been known by another name before this time.

Hunkpatina

One of the divisions of the Yankton Sioux who lived in South Dakota. They were visited by Lewis and Clark in 1804 and were then known by the name of Honetaparteen.

Hunting

In the early days, hunting was done for food and to secure hides for the making of clothing. Animals were hunted at night and caught while they slept, such as birds on nests. Clams, etc., were caught with the hands. Stones were held, thrown and fastened to spears and arrows for use in killing game for food. Fire and smoke were used to drive game in a desired direction. Traps, pits and snares were used. Drugs were used, such as the bark of the walnut root and buckeyes were used to catch fish in fresh water.

Huntingdon

Huntingdon, Pennsylvania, see Standing Stone.

Hupa

A tribe of the Athapascan who lived along the Trinity River in California. They are known for their fine basket work.

Huron

The name of this group of Indians is derived from the French "huré," this referred to the hair style which looked like a stiff bristle or ridge along the top of the head. These Indians were located in the lower Great Lakes region.

Husband
See wiowah.

Huspah
This was a band of the Yamasi who lived in what is now the state of South Carolina around the year 1700.

Huwaka
This was the sky clan of the Indians of the Acoma pueblo of New Mexico.

Hwoshntxyeeli binesd'a'
Navajo for the cactus known as the prickly pear. Used as food and also for the making of a rose colored dye.

Hyde Park
Hyde Park, New York, see Sewackenaem.

Hykehah
This was a former Chickasaw town, located near Pontotoc County in Mississippi.

I

Iana
This was the corn clan of the Indians of Taos pueblo in New Mexico.

Ichuarumpats
A tribe of the Paiute who lived in the southeastern part of Nevada.

Iebathu
This is the white corn clan of the pueblo at Isleta, New Mexico.

Iechur
This is the yellow corn clan of the Tigua of the pueblo at Isleta, New Mexico.

Iefeu
This is the red corn clan of the Tigua of the pueblo at Isleta, New Mexico.

Ieshur
This is the Blue corn clan of the Tigua pueblo of Isleta, New Mexico.

Ietan
This term had many forms and through many changes such as Eutaw, Ute, and Utah, referred to the tribes who lived along the Platte and Arkansas Rivers in the Rocky Mountains.

Ift
A village of the Karok on the Klamath River in California. This village was inhabited around the year 1860.

Iglakatekhila

This division of the Oglala Teton Sioux means "he who refuses to move his camp."

Ignacio

Ignacio, Colorado, see Ute.

Ihamba

This ancient pueblo of the Tewa is located near the San Ildefonso pueblo of northern New Mexico.

Ihasha

Meaning "red lips," this was a band of the Lower Yanktonai Sioux.

Ika

A tribe of the Cochimi who lived in lower California in the 18th century.

Ikanhatki

This was a former town of the upper Creek Indians who lived along the Tallapoosa River in Alabama.

Ikwe

The Chippewa for Squaw (q.v.).

Illinois

This was one of the confederacies of the Algonquian. They formerly lived in what is now Illinois, Wisconsin, Iowa and parts of Missouri.

Illinois nut

See pecan.

Immahal

A former village of the Chumashan located in what is now Ventura County in California.

Imnarkuan

A village of the Passamaquoddy, located in Washington

County in Maine. The name means "where we make maple sugar."

Inam
A well-known village of the Karok who lived along the Klamath River in northwestern California.

Inaqtek
A group or gens of the Menominee of Wisconsin.

Inaspetsum
One of the Nez Percé tribes who lived along the Columbia River in Washington.

Incised
This term is used to describe pottery that has a design which is cut or scratched into its surface.

Indian
The name was first used by Columbus in February, 1493, who believed that he had reached India. The name is now meant to include the aborigines of North and South America. However, the term as used in this book, is meant to include the Indians north of Mexico, not including the Eskimo (q.v.). There are experts who are for and against including the Eskimo along with the other early people of North America. This book deals with the Indians of the United States, as such, for practical intents and purposes.

Indian Events
Arranged by states, this listing has been collected from various sources . . . some dates are not available. To secure accurate dates for any Indian events such as pow wows and Indian ceremonials which are open to the public, it is suggested that such a request should be sent to the Indian Agent in the area or to the Chamber of Commerce in the area.

Arizona: Held in Flagstaff the first week of July, known as the All Indian Pow Wow; The first week in August at Prescott and the last week at the Hopi Reservation, the Snake Dance and the Smoki Ceremonials.

Colorado: Early in June at the Consolidated Ute Reservation at Ignacio the Bear Dances, and sometime in July or August the so called Sun Dance.

Idaho: The Nez Percé feast, held in May at Lewiston and in July, the Sun Dance at Fort Hall.

Kansas: The Potawatomi Fair held at Horton, Kansas, held in July and the Harvest Dance of the Kickapoo held at the end of October or the beginning of November.

Minnesota: The Chippewa Pow Wow at the White Earth Reservation in June and others held in July at Bena and the Rice Ceremonies held in September at Milaca.

Montana: The first week in May, the Flathead Bitter Root Dances at Camas. The end of June at the Rocky Boy Reservation, the Chippewa-Cree dances. In July there are several Indian events in Montana during the first week, at Browning the Blackfoot ceremonial lodge and Sun Dance, Fort Peck the Assiniboine and Sioux Sun Dances and at the Belknap agency the Assiniboine, Gros Ventre Sun Dances are held. The second week of July at the Blackfeet Reservation at Browning, the Blood Medicine Lodge ceremonies are held, and the third week the Piegan Medicine Lodge Sun Dance is held. The fourth week the Crow Agency holds its ceremonies. In January, at Arlee, the Flathead Blue Jay Dances.

Nebraska: In the first to third weeks there are three events, the Sioux Massacre Pow Wow, the Winnebago Pow Wow and the Omaha Pow Wow.

New Mexico: The first week in January at Taos, San Ildefonso and other pueblos several events are held such as the Buffalo or Deer Dance, Eagle Dance, and other ceremonial dances. The last week in January there are several other ceremonial dances as well as some religious ceremonies. In February the Candlemas Day ceremonies are held. In March at the pueblo at Laguna Indian fairs and ceremonies are held. In April about the third week, the Indian Corn Dances are held at Taos and San Felipe. In June and July the various pueblos hold dances and other fiesta type events. In July, at the Mescalero Agency during the first week the tribes hold the Devil Dance and later on in the month they hold the Corn Dance and the Corn Dance fiesta. The early part of August the Old Pecos Dances, followed by the Corn dances and the mid month affair known as the Inter Tribal Ceremonials, one of the main events which is held at Gallup. In September at Acoma and at San Ildefonso there are several ceremonies such as the Harvest Dances. In the early part of October the Navajo Indian Fair is held at Shiprock. During December several events are held at Taos, San Ildefonso, Jemez and other pueblos such as the Deer Dance, Turtle Dances and several affairs of a religious nature.

New York: During the month of September the Annual Iroquois Council is held at Lake Placid, New York.

North Carolina: During July and August a pageant or theatrical affair is presented at the Cherokee Agency at Bryson City, North Carolina. October the Cherokee Fair is held.

North Dakota: In June there are several affairs held at the Belcourt reservation, the Mother Corn ceremonies and the Sage Dance as well as the Chippewa Sun Dance. The first week in September there are several Indian Fairs held at Fort Berthold, Fort Totten and at Fort Yates of the Standing Rock Reservation. During October, the Turtle Mountain Reservation holds its Chippewa Indian Fair.

Oklahoma: Near the end of March the Shawnee Cornbread Dance is held near Norman, Oklahoma. In May the Cheyenne and Arapaho hold pageants of historical interest. The first week in June the Green Corn Dance is held near Stillwell by the Cherokee. During the early part of July there are several Indian affairs held at Gore, Quapaw, Kellyville such as Pawnee Homecoming, Kiowa Indian Fair, and other Pow Wows.

In August during the second week the Seneca and the

Cayuga hold a green corn dance at Anadarko. At the middle of the month at Ponca City the Ponca Pow Wow is held, followed by affairs at Norman and other cities with Pow Wows and dances. In September at Concho, the Indian Festival and later in the month the Osage Removal Dances. In October, about the second week, the American Indian Exposition is held at Tulsa.

Oregon: About the middle of April the Root Festival is held at Warm Springs. About the third week in May, the Wild Horse Auction and Rodeo is held. The end of July and the beginning of August are known as Chief Joseph Days. The middle of August at Warm Springs the Huckleberry Feast is held.

Pennsylvania: During the month of February the Seneca have a special ceremony which honors Chief Cornplanter.

South Dakota: The first week of August at the Pine Ridge Reservation the Sioux Indian Rodeo is held.

Utah: During April at Whiterocks the Ute Bear Dance is held, and during the second and third week of July the Ute Stampede and the Ute Sun dance are held.

Washington: The end of January several Treaty Days are held at Marietta and the Swinomish Reservation. The end of April the Muckleshoot festival is held. In June the Indian Salmon Derby is held. During July there are several Pow Wows and affairs which are held at Toppenish and Nespelem. The last week in August the War Canoe Races are held at Neah Bay.

Wisconsin: From the beginning of July to about the middle of September, ceremonial dances and other events are carried on at the Wisconsin Dells. In August at the Reservation of the Menominees, the Indian Fair is held at Keshena and a pageant is put on in an outdoor theater portraying some historical event in the tribal history.

Wyoming: During the month of July there are many Indian affairs going on at Lander. During July the Arapaho Sun Dances, Shoshoni Sun Dances. During August at Lander, the Indian Pageants and at Sheridan the All American Indian Days.

Indian names
See names.

Indian Point
An early Indian village site located in the area of what is now Lisbon, New York, and occupied by Catholic Iroquois. Also a recreation area that has been maintained by the Hudson River Day Line in New York, located along the Hudson River in New York.

Indian Reservations
In compiling the Dictionary of The American Indian, I have used information and material from the following present day Reservations in the United States: Crow-Creek Agency, Fort Thompson, South Dakota; Carson Agency, Stewart, Nevada; Catawba Agency, Rock Hill, South Carolina; Red Lake Agency, Red Lake, Minnesota; Rocky Bay Agency, Rocky Bay, Montana; Rosebud Agency, Rosebud, South Dakota; Sac and Fox Sanatorium, Toledo, Iowa; Sacramento Agency, Sacramento, California; Salem Indian School, Chemowa, Oregon; San Carlos Agency, San Carlos, Arizona; San Xavier Indian Sanatorium, Tucson, Arizona; Sells Indian Agency, Sells, Arizona; Seminole Agency, Dania, Florida; Sequoyah Indian School, Tahlequah, Oklahoma; Shawnee Agency, Shawnee, Oklahoma; Sherman Indian Institute, Riverside, California; Sioux Sanatorium, Rapid City, South Dakota; Sisseton Agency, Sisseton, South Dakota; Standing Rock Agency, Fort Yates, North Dakota; Taholah Agency, Hoquiam, Washington; Keshena Reservation, Keshena, Wisconsin; Jicarilla, Agency, Dulce, New Mexico; Kiowa Agency, Anadarko, Oklahoma; Menominee Mills Reservation, Neopit, Wisconsin; Mescalero Indian Agency, Mescalero, New Mexico; Mission Indian Agency, Riverside, California; Navajo Agency, Window Rock, Ari-

zona; New York Indian Agency, Buffalo, New York; North-ern Idaho Agency, Lapwai, Idaho; Pawnee Indian Agency, Pawnee, Oklahoma; Paiute Indian Agency, Cedar City, Utah; Osage Agency, Pawhuska, Oklahoma; Phoenix Indian Sanatorium, Phoenix, Arizona; Phoenix Indian School, Phoenix, Arizona; Pierre Indian School, Pierre, South Da-kota; Pima Indian Agency, Sacoton, Arizona; Pine Ridge Agency, Pine Ridge, South Dakota; Pipestone Indian School, Pipestone, Minnesota; Potawatomi Agency, Horton, Kan-sas; Quapaw Indian Agency, Miami, Oklahoma; Blackfeet Agency, Browning, Montana; Carson Agency, Stewart, Nev-ada; Cherokee Agency, Bryson City, North Carolina; Chey-enne and Arapaho Agency, Concho, Oklahoma; Cheyenne River Agency, Cheyenne, South Dakota; Chilocco Indian School, Chilocco, Oklahoma; Choctaw Agency, Philadel-phia, Mississippi; Colorado River Agency, Parker, Arizona; Coleville Agency, Nespelem, Washington; Consolidated Chippewa Agency, Cass Lake, Minnesota; Consolidated Ute Agency, Ignacio, Colorado; Crow Agency, Crow Reser-vation, Montana; Crow Creek Agency, Fort Thompson, South Dakota; Five Tribes Agency, Muskogee, Oklahoma; Flandreau Indian School, Flandreau, South Dakota; Flat-head Reservation, Dixon, Montana; Fort Apache Reserva-tion, Whiteriver, Arizona; Fort Belknap Agency, Harlem, Montana; Fort Berthold Agency, Elbowoods, North Dakota; Fort Hall Agency, Fort Hall, Idaho; Fort Peck Agency, Poplar, Montana; Fort Totten Agency, Poplar, Montana; Great Lakes Agency, Ashland, Wisconsin; Haskell Indian Institute, Lawrence, Kansas; Hoopa Valley Agency, Eureka, California; Hopi Agency, Keams Canon, Arizona; Wind River Agency, Fort Washakie, Wyoming; Yakima Agency, Toppenish, Washington; Winnebago Agency, Winnebago, Nebraska; Western Shoshone Agency, Owyee, Nevada; Wahpeton Indian School, Wahpeton, North Dakota; United Pueblos Agency, Albuquerque, New Mexico; Umatilla Agency, Pendleton, Oregon; Uintah and Ouray Agency,

161

Fort Duquesne, Utah; Turtle Mountain Agency, Belcourt, North Dakota; Tulalip Agency, Tulalip, Washington; Truxton Canao Agency, Valentine, Arizona; Tongue River Agency, Lame Deer Montana; Tomah Agency, Tomah, Wisconsin. See Reservations.

Indian Rights Association
An organization that was formed in Philadelphia in December 15, 1882, to promote educational and civil rights for the Indians.

Iniahico
This was the main village of Apalachee, located near the present site of Tallahassee, Florida, 1539.

Inisiguanin
A town along the South Carolina coast that was visited by Ayllon in 1520.

Inkesabe
This division of the Omaha had charge of the tribal pipes, known as the "black shoulder."

Inkillis Tamaha
This Choctaw town was located in the northwestern part of Jasper County in Mississippi. The name means "English town." The name was given because it was a center for the distribution of property by the English.

Inkpa
This was a group of Wahpeton Sioux who lived near Big Stone Lake in Minnesota.

Inojey
A village of the Chumashan which was located near the present site of Santa Barbara, California.

Inoshuochn
This was a band of the Apache who lived near Fort

Apache in Arizona about 1881. The name means "bear berry."

Inotuks
This was a former village of the Karok located along the Klamath River in California about 1860.

In situ
This is the natural position in which an object is found which has not been moved since it was placed or formed.

Intanto
An old village of the Nishinam located near the Bear River in California.

Intapupshe
This ancient Osage village was located along the Osage River just above the Sac River in Missouri.

Intatchkalgi
The name meaning "people of the beaver dams," the town was located along the Opihlako Creek above the Flint River in Georgia.

Intrusive
This term is used when describing an article which is found in a layer or stratum that differs from that in which it is usually found. This indicates that it was not originally deposited there.

Inwood
Inwood, Long Island, New York, see Rockaway.

Iowa
One of the southwestern tribes of the Sioux who came originally from Winnebago stock. In 1824, they ceded all of their land in Missouri and were moved to Kansas and later to Oklahoma.

Ipisogi

A small settlement of the Upper Creeks, located near Oakfuski in Alabama.

Ironwood

See the Navajo word, ma'iidaa' or g'iishzniniih.

Iroquoian family

This is a linguistic group. This family was made up of many tribes and tribal groups. The Iroquois were highly organized and had a strong government and military organization. They had a complex social set-up. Women had a vote and the land and its houses became the property of the women. The chief and his duties were approved or disapproved of by the women . . . with the consent of the other male members of the tribe.

Iroquois Indians

These Indians were known also by the name of the Five Nations and were composed of the Mohawk, Oneida, Cayuga, Seneca and the Onondaga. Later on they were called the "Six Nations" when the Tuscarora were added to the group. See Iroquoian family.

Isanyati

This was a group of the Brulé Sioux, related to the Santee.

Isha

A former village of the Chumashan located in Ventura County in California.

Ishipishi

A former village of the Karok located along the Klamath River in the northwestern part of California. It was destroyed by fire in 1552 by the white settlers.

Ishtunga

Meaning "right side," this name was given the group of

Kansa who had the right to camp on the right side of the tribal camp circle.

Ishwidip
A former village of the Karok who lived along the Klamath River in California about 1860.

Isleta
This pueblo of the Tigua has been on the same site since its discovery by the Spanish in 1540. The pueblo stands on a high ridge, the name is Spanish and means "little island." In 1680 it was abandoned due to attacks by the Apache Indians. It was rebuilt early in the 1700's.

Istapoga
A settlement of the Upper Creeks. Located in Talladega County, Alabama.

Itaes
A former Chumashan ranch near the Dolores mission. Located at the site of the present San Francisco, California.

Itafi
This district in Florida was one of the areas where the dialect of the Timuquanan was spoken.

Itahasiwaki
A town of the Lower Creek Indians, located along the Chattahoochee River, about three miles above Ft. Gaines, Florida. About 1820, the settlement had a population of about 100.

Itara
A small Indian village that was visited by De Soto in 1539. The village was located in the northern part of Florida.

Itazipcho
This was a group or band of the Sans Arcs Sioux who were mentioned by the Lewis and Clark expedition. Also

known as the Minishala, although they were at one time two distinct bands.

Iteghu
This was a band of the Lower Yanktonai Sioux, also known by the name of Hunkpatina. The name means "burnt faces."

Iteshicha
Meaning "bad faces," this was a band of the Oglala Sioux.

Itliok
A village of the Squawmish, located along the left bank of the Squawmish River in British Columbia.

Itrahani
This clan of the Cochiti pueblo in New Mexico was known as the Cotonwood clan.

Itsaatiaga
This band of the Paviotso formerly lived near Unionville in the western part of Nevada.

Itscheabine
This group of the Assiniboin were visited by Lewis and Clark in 1804. They were a tribe of hunters and they did a large trading business with the Hudson Bay Company. They were located about 150 miles north of Ft. Mandan.

Itseyi
A name given by the whites to several Cherokee settlements in North and South Carolina. Also known by the name of Brasstown. One settlement was known in Georgia. The name means "the green place." Often translated to mean "brass" which is the result of poor spelling in the early days and poor translation.

Ituc
A former village of the Chumashan, located near what is now Santa Barbara, California.

Itukemuk
A former village of the Luiseño, located near the San Luis Rey Mission in California.

Ivitachuco
Mentioned by Bartram, this was a former town of the Apalachee, located near the present Wacahotee in Florida.

Ivy Log
This was a Cherokee settlement. Located along the Ivy Log Creek in the northern part of Georgia. This settlement was active about the time the Cherokee were "removed" in 1839.

Iwai
A village of the Yaquina, formerly located along the Yaquina River in the state of Oregon.

Iwayusota
A former band of the Oglala Sioux, the name means "uses up by begging, or begging with the mouth."

Iyaaye
A band of the San Carlos Apache, located at the San Carlos agency and at Fort Apache in 1881.

Iyakoza
A former band of the Brulé Sioux, the name means "a wart on a horse's leg."

Iyis
A former village of the Karok, located along the Klamath River in Oregon around 1880.

Iza
A settlement, possibly a Caddoan tribe in Texas. It was

this settlement that Coronado was looking for in 1540-41. He had hoped he would be able to get supplies at this settlement for his trip to Quivira and "Copala."

Iztacans

A name used around the year 1824 for a prehistoric race of people which were supposed to have lived in the United States.

J

Jacal
This is the term used to describe a house built from adobe and wood. The poles are set in rows at intervals and then plastered with mud and adobe bricks.

Jack
Captain Jack, also known as Kintpuash (q.v.), see also Modoc.

Jackash
From the Cree dialect of the Algonquian "atchâkas," used for the American variety of mink. The term was used by the fur traders.

Jack Indians
This was a tribe of unidentified Indians who traded with the Hudson Bay Company around 1731. These Indians were different from the Moose River and Sturgeon Indians.

Jacksonville
Jacksonville, Florida, see Patica.

Jacobs
This chief of the Delawares fought against General Braddock's army and all along the frontier settlements of Pennsylvania. On September 8, 1756, Col. John Armstrong led a force against Captain Jacobs at Kittanning, Pennsylvania. After a hard battle, the Indians and their leader and his whole family were wiped out.

Jacobs Cabins
A settlement located along Jacobs Creek in Fayette County in Pennsylvania. Named for Captain Jacobs, a Chief of the Delawares.

Jacona

A small Tewa village, located on the southern side of the Pojoaque River near Santa Fe, New Mexico. The village was abandoned in 1696. In 1702 a land grant was made by Spain and the land was given to Ignacio de Roybal.

Jacuencacahel

A former ranch near the mission of San Francisco in California.

Jagavans

A small Texas tribe that was visited by Cabeza de Vaca in 1530.

Jagaya

A village located in the northwestern part of South Carolina. This village was visited by Juan Pardo in 1565.

Jamac

A rancheria, possibly of the Sobaipuri who lived in southern Arizona. Active around 1732.

Jameco

A small tribe of Indians who lived on Long Island, New York. Located on the present site of Jamaica, Long Island, about fifteen miles from New York City.

Jamesville

Jamesville, New York, see Tueadasso.

Japazaws

A chief of the Powhatan Indians. It was he who talked Pocahontas into going on board an English ship in 1611. She was then held by the English as a hostage so that her father Powhatan would behave in favor of the English.

Jappayon

A small village near the San Carlos mission in California. The village was inhabited by the Esselen.

Jaumalturgo

A former rancheria of the Pima in 1697. Located south of the Casa Grande ruins in Arizona.

Jeaga

In 1570 this was a village at the southern tip of Florida.

Jeboaltae

A possible Costanoan village located near the San Juan Bautista mission in California.

Jedakne

A village · of the Iroquis, located along the western branch of the Susquehanna River in Northumberland County, Pennsylvania.

Jemez

This is the name of a pueblo in Bandelier. Located on the Jemez River about twenty miles northwest of Bernalillo in New Mexico. The Jemez took a large and active part in the revolt of the pueblos in 1680 and fought a hard but losing battle with the Spanish. The pueblo is still in existence.

Jemison

Mary Jemison, called the "white woman," lived at Nondas (q.v.).

Jennesedaga

A former village of the Seneca, located on the Allegheny River near Warren, Pennsylvania. The well known chief, Cornplanter, lived in this village in 1816.

Jeromestown

A former village of the Delawares. Located in Ashland County in Ohio. The name was derived from Jean Baptiste Jerome, an early French trader.

Jet

A type of coal used by the Indians in various areas, Colorado, New Mexico and Ohio. Used to make small figures. Sometimes ground up to make face paint.

Jewett City
Jewett City, Connecticut, see Quinebaug.

Jicara
Spanish word for a small gourd or basket used by the Indians.

Jicarilla
A name given to the Apache. A name given by the Spanish because of the fine basket work these people did. They roamed in Colorado, New Mexico, Oklahoma and into Kansas and Texas.

John Hicks Town
A settlement in the northern part of Florida. Formerly occupied by the Mikasuki Indians.

Johnson, Rev. John
See Enmegahbowh.

Johnstown
A settlement of the Cherokee Indians, located in Hall County, Georgia, along the Chattahoochee River.

Jolee
A former Seminole town located about 60 miles above the mouth of the Apalachicola River.

Jolly, John
This Cherokee Chief was known as the adopted father of General Samuel Houston. He lived around 1818.

Joseph
A fine chief of the Nez Percés. His name was given him by missionaries. He and his people roamed Idaho. In the treaty of 1863 they were forced to move to northeastern Oregon. This was not agreeable to the Indians and they tried to get back. Under the leadership of Chief Joseph,

they moved families and belongings against great odds. They moved over 1000 miles until they were stopped on October 5, 1877. They were then moved to Kansas. Chief Joseph died September 21, 1904, at Nespelem on the Colville Reservation in Washington.

Joshua
An Oregon tribe now living on the Siletz Reservation.

Joyvan
A wandering tribe, sometimes mentioned by early explorers. They lived in the southwestern part of Arkansas about 1719.

Juajona
A former Papago settlement, located in the southern part of Arizona. Visited by the early explorers Kino and Mange in 1699.

Juan Bautista
A village of the Kawia, located in San Bernardino in California.

Judac
A large Pima ranch, one of three. Located on the southern Gila River in Arizona.

Judosa
A village of the Attacapan, located on the eastern part of the Trinity River in Texas, near its mouth. Active in the 17th century.

Juichun
A group of Costanoan people who lived in California and whose dialect was similar to that of the Mutsun.

Jumano
An unknown tribe visited by Cabeza de Vaca in 1536. They lived along the Rio Grande and in areas of New Mexico.

Junaluska

This chief of the Cherokee fought with General Jackson and in the Creek wars of 1813-14. His name means "he tries repeatedly . . . but fails." This name was given him after he said that he would wipe out the Creeks in battle. After the battle he had to admit that there were still a few Creeks alive. Junaluska died in North Carolina in 1858.

Junatca

A possible Costanoan village located near the Dolores Mission near San Francisco in California.

Junetre

A ruined pueblo of the Tewa, located in Rio Arriba County in New Mexico.

Juniper

See ashes of juniper.

Junostaca

A former Papago ranch, visited in 1699 by Kino. Located in the southern part of Arizona.

Junqueindundeh

A village of the Hurons. Located along the Sandusky River about 25 miles north of its mouth in 1756.

Juraken

These were two villages with the same name. Located on the shores of the Susquehanna River in Pennsylvania, one near what is now Sunbury and the other one on the east branch of the river.

Jurlanoca

A village located on the Alachua River, shown on a chart made in 1762. Located in northern Florida, near the St. Johns River.

Jutun

A village of the Calusa. Located on the southwestern coast of Florida in 1570.

K

Kaadnaas-hadai
A clan of the Haida who lived in southwestern Alaska. The name meant "dogfish house," this was a subdivision of the Raven clan of the Haida.

Kaana
This is the corncob clan of the pueblo at Taos in New Mexico.

Kaayu
This was a Nambe pueblo built and abandoned by these people before the Spanish arrival. It was located in the mountains about seven miles east of the Rio Grande in Santa Fé County, New Mexico.

Kabaye
A name derived from the Ebahamo Indians who lived along the Colorado River in Texas. Visited by the Spanish in 1687.

Kachina
These were sacred dancers of the Hopi Indians of the southwest. They come in many forms and sizes. They appear at certain times of the year. Small figures of the Kachina dancers are often seen carved of wood, dresses made of skins, feathers, etc.

Kachina colors
The Hopi Kachina is painted many colors. The colors have special meanings. These colors are known as directional colors (q.v.).

Kachinba
A sacred spring about six miles east of Walpi pueblo in

north eastern Arizona. This was a stopping place for the Kachina dancers of the Hopi Indians.

Kachnawaacharege

This was a former fishing place of the Onondaga Indians in New York. It was at this place that Colonel Schuyler had a meeting with the Onondaga Chiefs on April 25, 1700.

Kachyayakuch

A village of the Chumashan, located near San Buenaventura in Ventura County in California.

Kadakaman

A tribe of the Laimon who lived in the lower part of California.

Kadohadacho

A tribe of the Caddo confederacy. They were first met by De Soto near the Mississippi River in Louisiana in 1541. They became very friendly with the French.

Kaekibi

This was the traditional pueblo of the Asa people of the Hopi. They were located on the Rio Chama near what is now Albuquerque.

Kaffetalaya

A former town of the Choctaw Indians located along Owl Creek in Neshoba County in Mississippi.

Kagahanin

This was the "thunder" clan of the Caddo Indians.

Kagakwisuwug

This was the thunder gens of the Fox and Sauk Indians.

Kahabi

This was the willow clan of the Hopi.

Kahanqoc

The Virginia Indian term for the goose.

Kahesarahera
A village of the Seneca Indians of New York, about 1691.

Kahl
This was the forehead clan of the Hopi Indians.

Kahmetahwungaguma
This is the Chippewa Indian name given to their village built in Cass County in Minnesota in 1730. The name means "the lake of the sandy waters." This gave them the name of the "sandy lake band."

Kahra
Meaning "wild rice," a division of the Sisseton Sioux. They lived along the Red River and Lake Traverse in Minnesota.

Kahtai
A former Clallam village located in the State of Washington.

Kai
This was a willow clan of the Navaho Indians.

Kaiachim
A former village of the Pomo located along the Russian River in Sonoma County in California.

Kaibab
Meaning "on the mountain," this name was given to a division of the Paiute who lived in the southwestern part of Utah. The name was given to the Kaibab plateau in northwestern Arizona in 1903.

Kaidatoiabie
This name was given to six bands of the Paviotso who lived in the northeastern part of Nevada.

Kaigwu
This is the oldest division of the Kiowa Indians and it is this name from which the present spelling, Kiowa is

derived. It is this division which is entrusted with the keeping of the medicine tipi.

Kailaidshi
A former Upper Creek town, located in Elmore County in Alabama and along the Tallapoosa River.

Kailaidshi
A town of the Creek Indians located along the Canadian River near Hilabi in Oklahoma.

Kaime
A tribe of the Pomo, formerly living along the Russian River valley in California.

Kainah
A division of the Blackfoot.

Kaiyau
This was a name given to those Indians who lived around Clear Lake and Upper Lake in Lake County, California. These Indians belonged to the group known as the Pomo.

Kaka
This was the "crow band" of the Arikara.

Kakagshe
This is the "crow band" of the Potawatomi Indians.

Kakake
This was the "crow" clan of the Menominee Indians of Wisconsin.

Kakanatzatia
A former village of the Sia. Located on the Jemez River in the north central part of New Mexico. It was visited by the Spanish explorer, Espejo, in 1583. It become one of the provinces formed by him, known as Punames.

Kakegha

A division of the Brulé Teton Sioux. The name means "making a grating noise."

Kakhan

This was the wolf clan of the Keresan of the pueblo at Laguna in New Mexico.

Kakick

A possible Creek tribe that lived on an island of the same name, located in the Tennessee River and above the Chickasaw River.

Kakinonba

A tribe mentioned by the French explorers several times. Located on Marquette's map as being east of the Mississippi and in Kentucky in 1674. They have also been placed in Tennessee and Illinois.

Kaku

This was a village of the Yaquina, located on the southern side of the Yaquina River in Oregon.

Kalanunyi

This is one of the five towns that were laid out by Colonel William H. Thomas, who was the Indian Agent at the time (1838). The towns were located in Swain and Jackson Counties in North Carolina and formed part of the Cherokee Indian Reservation.

Kalapooian

This was a group of tribes formerly occupying the area around the Willamette River in Oregon.

Kalashiauu

This was the racoon clan of the Chua or snake phratry of the Hopi.

Kalawashuk

A former village of the Chumashan, connected with the Santa Inez Mission near Santa Barbara, California.

Kalbusht

A former village of the Alsea, located along the southern banks of the Alsea River in Oregon.

Kalelk

Located on the northern shores of the Tule or Rhett Lake, this was a village of Oregon Indians known as the Modoc.

Kalispel

A tribe of Indians located in northern Idaho. Visited by Lewis and Clark in 1805. Also known as the "ear drop Indians."

Kalkalya

Located in Butte County, this was a former village of the Maidu of California.

Kalokta

This is the crane clan of the Zuñi Indians of New Mexico.

Kamaiakan

The chief of the Yakima. He led his people in a war which lasted for three years. The battles were waged over the removal of the Indians to reservations. In 1858 they were finally beaten near Four Lakes on a southern branch of the Spokane River. Kamaiakan crossed the border and went to live in Canada.

Kamatukwucha

This was a former Pima village, located at Gila Crossing in southern Arizona.

Kamia

A tribe of Mission Indians of the Yuman group.

Kamiah

This was a large group of Nez Percé Indians who lived in the area of Kamiah, Idaho. They were visited by Lewis and Clark in 1805, at which time they were called a band of Chopunnish and numbered over 800.

Kamit

A former village of the Pima, located in the southern part of Arizona.

Kammatwa

This was one of the four divisions of the Shasta Indians who lived in the Klamath Valley in the northwestern part of California. Also known as the Hamburg, T-ka, Aika Indians.

Kanagaro

The name for a Seneca town, located near the town of Victor in New York. The town was the "capital" of the Seneca tribes. The town was burned in 1687.

Kanagaro

Mentioned by Megapolensis in 1644. This was a town of the Mohawk Indians, located on the northern side of the Mohawk River in Herkimer County in New York.

Kanahena

The Cherokee word for sofki (q.v.), a soft corn meal mixture used for food by the Gulf States Indians.

Kanakuk

A chief of the Kickapoo Indians who lived in Illinois. He died of smallpox in 1852.

Kanani

The Navajo clan known as the "living arrows."

Kanapima

Also known by his Christian name of Augustin Hammelin, Jr. He was a chief of his tribe of the Ottawa, born

July 12, 1813, in Michigan. At an early age he was sent to a Catholic seminary in Cincinnati and later on was sent to Rome to study. Because of deaths in his family, he returned to America where he led his tribe and assisted in making a treaty with the government in 1835.

Kanatakowa
In 1654 this was the principal village of the Onondaga and was located at a place known as Onondaga Castle in New York State.

Kanatiochtiage
A settlement of the Iroquois, located along the shores of Lake Ontario. Known as the "place of wild rice."

Kanchati
Meaning the "red earth." A village of the Alibamu along the Alabama River near what is now Montgomery, Alabama. The name has also been given to a town of the Creek Indians in Oklahoma.

Kandoucho
A village of the neutrals, located near the old Huron country near Lake Ontario.

Kang
This was the mountain lion clan of the Tewa pueblos of San Ildefonso and San Juan in New Mexico.

Kanghiyuha
This is the division of the Brulé Sioux known as the "keepers of the crow."

Kanhanghton
A village of the Delaware Indians located on the Chemung River in Bradford County, Pennsylvania. It was destroyed by the Iroquois in 1764 because they were friendly to the whites.

Kanna

This was the "eel" clan of the Tuscarora, also used by the Onondaga and Cayuga tribes of New York.

Kansa

This is the southwestern Siouan tribe. They lived in the area now known as Kansas. They were first met by Juan de Oñate in 1601, when they were largely hunters of the buffalo. They became farmers because they had to eat, not because they wanted to farm.

Kansaki

This was a name given to several Cherokee settlements in North Carolina, Georgia, and Tennessee.

Kantikantic

The Virginia Indian term meaning to sing and to dance.

Kantokan

The Virginia Indian term for dance.

Kanutaluhi

A settlement of the Cherokee, located in the northern part of Georgia about the time they were "removed" in 1839.

Kapaka

A former village of the Nishinam located along the Bear River in northern California.

Kapozha

A band of the Sisseton Sioux.

Kapulo

A former clan of the Hano pueblo of the Tewa, known as the "crane" clan. Now extinct.

Karakuka

A name given for a dialect which was spoken in the Clear Creek and Happy Valley areas of California.

Karankawa
This name was given to a small tribe which was located along the coast of Texas, near Matagorda Bay in particular. They were mentioned by Cabeza de Vaca. They did not farm, but got their food from the sea and the chase. They are said to have eaten human flesh, as did other Texas tribes. They also practiced head flattening. They were exterminated in 1858 after they were attacked by Juan Nepomuceno Cortina.

Karezi
An unidentified tribe of Indians that lived along the western shores of Lake Superior (not identical to the Cree).

Karok
This group of Indians lived along the Klamath River in California. These Indians did not make canoes from the redwoods but instead bought them from their neighbors.

Kashtok
A former village of the Chumashan, located on a tributary of the Santa Clara River in Ventura County, California.

Kasihta
A Creek town located along the east bank of the Chattahoochee River in Chattahoochee County, Georgia. This town was visited by De Soto in 1540. The people of the town believed that they were descended from the Sun. A variation of the spelling is Cusseta which is the name of a town in Georgia. A town of the Creek nation was also known as Cuseta in Oklahoma.

Kaskaskia
Meaning "he scrapes it off by means of a tool," the tribes of the Peoria who lived in the Illinois confederacy. In 1673 these Indians were visited by Marquette, which is believed to be their first contact with the whites.

Kata

This was a tribal division of the Kiowa, the name means the "biters."

Katamoonchink

A possible village of the Delawares. Located in Chester County, Pennsylvania. This is the Indian name and means "hazelnut grove."

Katearas

In 1669, this was one of the principal villages of the Tuscarora. Located along the Roanoke River in North Carolina.

Katimin

This was a village of the Karok. Located along the banks of the Klamath River about a mile from the mouth of the Salmon River. It was the belief of the Karok that this was the center of the earth and was a very sacred area to them. It was the scene of many yearly ceremonies. However, the town was burned by the whites in 1852.

Kato

A band or tribe of the Kuneste who lived in the valley of the Eel River in California. They belonged to the Athapascan stock and they closely resemble the culture of the Pomo.

Katzimo

This name was given to a mesa located about three miles northeast of Acoma. By tradition of the Acoma it was the historic site of their people in the past. During a storm it was said that part of the mesa broke away and so all of the people were cut off from the rest of the world and they perished. Archaeological research on this mesa (over 400 feet high) has shown that there are remains of ancient peoples, which bears out the story of the Acoma.

Kau

This is the corn clan of the Patki or water house phratry of the Hopi.

Kauhuk

A village of the Alsea which was visited by Lewis and Clark in 1806. The name means the high place and was located along the coast in Oregon.

Kaukhwan

Located along the north side of the Alsea River in Oregon, this was another of the villages of the Alsea Indians.

Kawaika

This is a ruined pueblo located in Hopi country near Laguna, New Mexico. This pueblo has been excavated by inexperienced people and so much has been lost to future generations.

Kawanunyi

Known as the "duck place." A former settlement of the Cherokee. Now known as Ducktown in Polk County, Tennessee.

Kawia

A division of the Shoshonean of southern California. They had their first contact with the whites in 1776 by Francisco Garcés, they then lived on the northern slopes of the San Jacinto mountains and roamed over to Colorado.

Kawita

A town visited by Bartram in 1775. He called this town of the Creeks "the bloody town" because captives were put to death here. The town was located along the Chattahoochee River in Russell County in Alabama. This was one of the main towns of the Lower Creeks.

Kayepu

This was a prehistoric pueblo, now in ruins. Located

about five miles south of Galisteo in Santa Fe County in New Mexico.

Kaygen
This village of the Seneca was located along the banks of the Chemung River in New York State.

Kaynagunti
A band of the Apache known as the "people at the mouth of the canyon," they belonged to the agency at Ft. Apache in Arizona.

Ke
This was the bear clan of the Tewa pueblo of Nambe, New Mexico and also of Hano in Arizona.

Kear
The early Virginia Indian term meaning you.

Kechepukwaiwah
A former Chippewa village located on a lake near the Chippewa River in Wisconsin.

Kecoughtan
A small group of the Powhatan confederacy who lived near the mouth of the James River, near what is now Elizabeth City, Virginia. They lived in this area about 1607.

Kefhawtewh
The Virginia Indian term for light.

Kegi
This was the house clan of the Tewa of Hano in Arizona.

Keguayo
A former pueblo of the Nambe which was abandoned before the Spanish contact. Located near a group of springs about four miles east of the Nambe pueblo in New Mexico.

Kekewh
Powhatan for alive.

Kemotte

The Virginia Indian term for brother.

Kenagh

The Virginia Indian term for thank you.

Kencuttemaun

This is the Virginia Indian greeting, such as good morning.

Kennebec

A village of the Abnaki located on the Kennebec River near Augusta, Maine. This village was mentioned by Capt. John Smith in 1616.

Kennebunker

An English word combined with the Algonquian. The Indian meaning was "at the long water"; however, as it was used in Maine by the logging men it meant a type of bag used to carry the clothes in, especially in winter. The term is derived from the Kennebunk River in Maine.

Kentahere

See race.

Kentanuska

A village of the Tuscarora, located in North Carolina in 1701.

Keokuk

This man was a leader of the Sauk. He was born about 1780 in Illinois. He was at first a guest keeper. This meant that he would entertain guests at tribal expense. He did this so well that he came to have great influence and power. After the Black Hawk War he was made a chief of the Sauk. He died in Kansas in 1848. In 1883, his remains were moved to Keokuk, Iowa. A bronze bust of Chief Keokuk was placed in Washington, D. C.

Keowee

This was a name that was given to several Cherokee towns in South Carolina, one located in Pickens County and the other in Oconee County. They became the principal towns of the Lower Cherokee.

Kerahocak

A former village of the Powhatan confederacy, located on the north bank of the Rappahannock River in Virginia in 1629.

Keresan

This was the linguistic family of the Pueblo Indians who lived on the Rio Grande and Rio Jemez, including the Acoma, Tewa and Sia. They were visited by Coronado in 1540.

Kern River Shoshonean

A small tribe of Shoshoneans living in southern California.

Keskaechquerem

In a deed of 1638 this town was mentioned as a town of the Canarsee Indians of Long Island, New York, and was located near Maspeth on Long Island.

Keskistkonk

A village of the Nochpeem, located in the highlands of Putnam County in New York State.

Kestaubuinck

Mentioned by Van der Donck in 1656, this was a former Sintsink village, located in what is now Westchester County in New York.

Ketsilind

Meaning "people of the Rio Chiquito ruins." This is a division of the Jicarilla. They claim that their former home was south of Taos pueblo in New Mexico.

Kewatsana

A division of the Comanche, now extinct, meaning "no ribs."

Keya

This is the badger clan of the Tewa of Santa Clara, San Ildefonso and San Juan pueblos of New Mexico.

Keyauwee

A small tribe that lived in North Carolina. They belonged to several Siouan tribes. A village of the tribe was shown on Jeffery's map of 1761 on the Pedee River. The tribe was finally absorbed by the Catawba tribes, located near Rock Hill, South Carolina.

Khabenapo

Meaning the "stone people." This was a division of the Pomo who lived along Clear Lake in California, about 1851.

Khahitan

This was a tribe of Indians who lived along the Rio Grande. These Indians traded with the Cheyenne. It is possible that these people were Picuris.

Khaltso

This was a clan of the Navajo known as the yellow bodies and they are said to be the descendants of two girls who had an Apache father.

Khashhlizhni

This was the "mud" clan of the Navajo Indians.

Khemnichan

This band of Sioux was visited by Pike in 1811. They were living along the shores of Lake Pepin in Minnesota. Their chief was Red Wing at that time.

Khra

This was a subgens of the Cheghita gens of the Missouri.

Kiabaha

A tribe visited by Joutel in 1687. They formerly lived along the Matagorda Bay and the Maligne River in Texas.

Kiamisha

A village of the Caddo located along the Red River in Oklahoma.

Kianusili

This was a family group of the Haida that belonged to the Raven Clan. They formerly lived along the shores of the Queen Charlotte Islands in British Columbia. They were known as the "cod people."

Kiashita

This was a former village of the Jemez who lived in Guadalupe Canyon in New Mexico.

Kiasutha

A chief of the Seneca; however, there is some doubt about this and there is a possibility that he was a chief of a band of the Iroquois. He sided with the French against the English. He was an advocate of peace with the English and had important parts in the meetings at Fort Pitt in 1768. (Now known as Pittsburgh, Pennsylvania.)

Kiawaw

A small extinct tribe who formerly lived on Kiawah Island in Charleston County in South Carolina. They were a possible part of the Cusabo group.

Kichai

A tribe whose language was closely allied with the Pawnee. This Caddoan tribe were met by the French in 1701 along the Red River in Louisiana and down along the Trinity River in Texas. They finally fled from Texas and joined the Wichita.

Kichesipirini

A typical tribe of the Algonkin. In 1650 they fled from the Iroquois and moved to the northwest. They were first met by Champlain.

Kick

The Virginia Indian term for mother.

Kickapoo

The Kickapoo were first visited by Allouez in 1667. At that time they were living near the portage of the Fox and Wisconsin Rivers in Columbia County in Wisconsin. They took part in the plan to burn Fort Detroit in 1712. Many Kickapoo fought with Tecumseh and Black Hawk.

Kicking Bear

A well-known medicine man of the Sioux. He was a leader in the Ghost Dance uprising in 1890. He organized and led the first Ghost Dance at Sitting Bull's camp in the Standing Rock Reservation.

Kicking Bird

A chief of the Kiowa. He established the first school for the Kiowa in 1873. On May 5, 1875, he died suddenly from poison according to his close friends.

Kiequotank

This was a former Powhatan village located in Accomac County in Virginia.

Kikimi

A former village of the Pima, located in southern Arizona.

Kilatika

This was a division of the Miami who lived near Fort St. Louis and in the upper Illinois in 1684.

Killbuck

See the Delaware chief called Gelelemend.

Killbuck Town

A town of the Delaware located in Wayne County in Ohio. Named for its chief. Active around 1764.

Killed Pottery

A term used to describe pottery that has been broken, especially during ceremonies which have to do with the death of an individual. It was thought that if the pottery and other objects were broken after the death of the owner, the spirit of the individual would be released and could travel too.

Killhag

This is a trap made of wood. The word is derived from the Algonquian. Used mainly in the New England states, Maine in particular.

Kinaani

A clan of the Navajo. They lived at Hano Pueblo, which they abandoned around 1680 because of a drought. They then moved to Canyon de Chelly in northeastern Arizona. They later went to Tusayan.

Kinbiniyol

This is known as the whirlwind pueblo. It is one of the best preserved pueblos in Chaco Canyon in the northwestern part of New Mexico. There are also extensive irrigation ditches in this area.

Kinchuwhikut

This large Hupa village was prominent in the folk-lore of the Hupa. The village was located on the east bank of the Trinity River in California.

Kingep

This was the largest and most important tribal division of the Kiowa.

King Philip

This was the second son of Massasoit. Known to the

English as Philip of Pokanoket. King Philip had great military ability. For nine years he plotted, forming a confederacy. King Philip's War broke out in 1675. Both sides suffered great losses, but the whites finally won in the battle in which King Philip was killed in Rhode Island on August 12, 1676.

Kings River Indians
This term is used to denote those tribes that were placed on the Tule River reservation.

Kinhlizhin
This was the Navajo clan known as the "black house," red-brown sandstone was used, however.

Kinishba
This pueblo was active around 1000 to 1400 and has been restored somewhat by the Arizona State Museum. It is located on the Apache Reservation near Fort Apache about 20 miles from U.S. Highway 60.

Kinkash
In 1832, this was a band of the Potawatomi Indians who lived along the Tippecanoe River in Indiana.

Kinkletsoi
Known as "yellow house," this is a small pueblo ruin. Located near Pueblo Bonito in Chaco Canyon in the northwestern part of New Mexico. The pueblo was made from yellow sandstone and was about 100 feet wide and 135 feet long. The walls are from 18 to 24 inches thick.

Kinnazinde
This is the Navajo name for a small round pueblo located near Kintyel in Arizona.

Kinnikinnick
This term is spelled in various ways and the mixture

varies in the different areas of the country. It is a "blend" mixed by the Indians and was used for their pipes. Tobacco, sumac leaves and the inner bark of the dogwood were used. The term means "mixed" or "what is mixed" or "he who mixes." The word is derived from the Algonquian.

Kintpuash

Also known as Captain Jack. He was a leader in the Modoc war of 1872 to 1873. He was a sub-chief of the Modoc Indians who lived in the areas between California and Oregon. When he and his people surrendered on May 22, 1873, he had 80 men against 1056 regular army of the United States.

Kio

This was the pine clan of the Jemez Indians of New Mexico.

Kiohero

This was a settlement of the Cayugas who lived on the northern end of Lake Cayuga in New York State. In 1670 the French had a mission there, named Etienne.

Kiowa

The Kiowa originally were located around the head of the Missouri River in Montana. They were first mentioned by the Spanish explorers in 1732. Lewis and Clark reported that they lived along the North Platte River. They carried on a war against the whites as far south as the Durango River in Texas. They made their first treaty with the whites in 1837.

Kiowan Family

A linguistic grouping. They were first identified as a distinct stock by Gallatin in 1853.

Kipana

An ancient pueblo of the Tanos who lived in Sandoval

County in New Mexico. They were visited by Oñate in 1598.

Kisakobi

This was a former pueblo of the Hopi and the people of Walpi. Located at the base of east mesa of Tusayan in northeastern Arizona. It was occupied between 1629 and 1680 and was then abandoned and the present Walpi pueblo was built. The name is derived from the Spanish and the Hopi.

Kishkakon

This was the bear clan of the Ottawa; the name means "those who have cut tails," denoting the short tail of the bear. In 1668 they were visited by Father Allouez, who found that there were three bands at the time who lived in a single village in La Pointe du Saint Esprit, which is located near what is now Bayfield in Wisconsin.

Kishkawbawee

A former village of the Chippewa, located along the Flint River in lower Michigan.

Kiskiminetas

This was a former village of the Delawares located along the Kiskiminetas creek, located in Westmoreland County in Pennsylvania. The name means "plenty of walnuts."

Kiskitomas

This Algonquian word has many spellings. The name refers to the shell of the walnut. This nut was common to the Long Island and New Jersey Indians.

Kispokotha

This was one of the five divisions of the Shawnee Indians.

Kitami

This was a sub-phratry of the Menominee of the Wisconsin area.

Kitchawank

Meaning "at the great mountain." This was a tribe of the Wappinger Indians who formerly lived along the east bank of the Hudson River in New York State. It is believed that their control extended from Anthony's Nose (a mountain) to Croton on the Hudson. It has also been said that they extended to the area of the present Sleepy Hollow, New York. They made a treaty of peace with the Dutch in August 30, 1645.

Kitchen middens

Kitchen middens or trash piles, see shell heap.

Kitchigami

Chippewa for "Lake Superior." This tribe lived in central Wisconsin about 1669 and were ethnically related to the Kickapoo and Mascoutens. They were first mentioned by Marquette in a letter that was written in the spring of 1670.

Kitchigumiwininiwug

This term is used to describe the tribes who lived along the Great Lakes, especially the lakes Superior and Michigan. The term was applied to the Indians of Wisconsin and Minnesota. The tribes were officially recognized as the Chippewas of Lake Superior by the treaty of Lapoint in 1854.

Kitchopataki

This was a former Upper Creek town, located along the upper Tallapoosa River in Randolph County in Alabama. The name is also used for a piece of wood which was used to grind grain. Meaning to "pound and spread out ground grain."

Kitkahta

A division of the Tsimshian who formerly lived along the Douglas Channel, British Columbia. The name means "people of the poles" and refers to the salmon weirs that they constructed in the rivers to catch the salmon.

Kitkehahki
This is one of the tribes of the Pawnee Confederacy. Also known as the Republican Pawnee because they lived along the Republican River in Nebraska.

Kittamaquindi
This village of the Piscataway was located in Maryland along the Potomac River. This village was active in 1639.

Kittanning
This was an important village located on the Allegheny River in Armstrong County in Pennsylvania. The village was composed of several tribes of Iroquois, Caughnawago and Delaware. In 1756, the village was destroyed by the settlers of Pennsylvania.

Kitteaumut
In 1674, this was a settlement of Christian Indians who lived in the southern part of Plymouth County in Massachusetts.

Kituhwa
This former Cherokee settlement was located along the Tuckasegee River near what is now Bryson City in North Carolina. The name was also given to a Cherokee secret society which was pledged to the defense of the Cherokee.

Kitunahan Family
The language group of the Kutenai of northern Montana and Idaho.

Kiva
A Hopi term, used for a chamber, usually underground. Kivas are circular and used for special ceremonies. Women are not generally allowed to enter a kiva. A kiva is usually entered from the top by means of a ladder. Villages had one or many kivas, depending on the size of the village. When the Spanish restricted their use, they were hidden in

the villages. The kivas were found in Colorado, Utah, New Mexico and Arizona.

Kivezaku
This apparent band of Yuman lived in Arizona and in California. They were later driven out and absorbed by the Mohave.

Kiyahani
A band of the Apache, located at Fort Apache in 1881.

Kiyuksa
This was a group of the Sioux who lived along the upper Iowa River. Their chief was Wabasha. Their chief village was at Winona in Minnesota.

Klahum
A village of the Okinagan located near the mouth of the Okinakane River in Washington.

Klakaamu
A former Chumashan village, located on Santa Cruz Island off the coast of California.

Klamath
This tribe of Indians lived mainly in the southwestern part of Oregon. Their main village was located on Klamath Lake. In 1864 they ceded a large part of their lands to the whites.

Klikitat
A Shahaptian tribe who formerly lived in Washington state along the Lewis and White Rivers. They were visited by Lewis and Clark in 1805 when they were living along the Yakima and Klickitat Rivers.

Klondike
The name of a river in northwestern Canada. The name is a corruption of an Athapascan dialect. Thron Duick is the correct spelling. The name now means a rich gold

strike, a fortune, etc. It came into common use in 1898 during the gold rush days.

Klumaitumsh

A name given by Lewis and Clark in 1805 to a tribe who formerly lived in the state of Washington near Grays Harbor.

Knife

The Indian knife was made from a variety of materials, bone, reeds, stone, wood, antler, shells, metals and the teeth of such animals as the beaver, bear and others. The knife was used in the Indian crafts and in war as a weapon.

Koasati

This upper Creek tribe lived along the Alabama River, near the Coosa and Tallapoosa Rivers in Alabama. Many of them were removed to Oklahoma.

Kochinish-yaka

This was the yellow corn clan of the pueblos of Acoma and Laguna in New Mexico.

Kohasaya

This was a former pueblo of the Sia, located in New Mexico.

Kohhokking

A village of the Delawares located in Steuben County in 1758, near what is now Elmira in New York.

Koi

A former village of the Pomo who lived on Lower Lake Island in Lake County, California.

Koinchush

This was the wild cat clan of the Chickasaw.

Kokob

This was the burrowing owl clan of the Hopi of Oraibi, Arizona.

Kokomo

A village of the Miami. Named after their chief, Kokomo, and was located at the present site of Kokomo, Indiana. The name means "young grandmother."

Kokop

This is the firewood clan of the Hopi who were descendants of the people of the Jemez pueblo in New Mexico.

Komertkewotche

This was a Pima name given to the Estrella mountain range. This Pima settlement was located along the Gila River in southern Arizona.

Koontie

See coonti.

Kopiwari

This ancient village of the Nambe was located about five miles north of the present site of Nambe in New Mexico.

Korusi

This group of Patwin formerly lived in Colusa County in California. Their story of the creation of the earth involved a giant turtle who dove to the bottom of the sea and brought up the land and made the mountains. When a woman of this tribe died and left a very young child, it was placed in a skin bag or blanket and was then shaken to death. In 1849, one of their villages had over a thousand people in it.

Koso

A Shoshonean tribe of California, also called Panamint.

Kostuets

This Shoshonean village was located in Oregon. The name means "where the pine trees stand."

Kosunats

Also known as the Uinta Ute. This division of the Ute was located in northeastern Utah.

Kotsoteka

This was one of the large divisions of the Comanche. Their name meant "The buffalo eaters."

Kounaouons

This tribe was located in northern Maine and in 1724 they were allies of the French.

Kouse

This plant (Peucedanum ambiguum) was used by the Indians who lived along the Columbia River in Oregon. It was used in the making of bread.

Kouyam

Also known as the Karankawa Indians. These Indians lived along the Colorado River in Texas. They were visited by Joutel in 1687.

Kowasayee

A small Tenino-speaking tribe who formerly lived on the northern side of the Columbia River in Washington. They were also included in the Yakima treaty of 1855.

Kowasikka

This was a village of the Miami Indians who lived along the Eel River in Boone County in Indiana. Also known by the name of Thorntown.

Kowfe

The Virginia Indian term for father.

Koyeti

A tribe of Yokuts who lived in the south central part of California. They became extinct about 1900.

Koyonya

This was known as the Turkey Clan of the Hopi Indians of Arizona.

Kretan

This subgens of the Missouri was also known as the "Hawk" people.

Ku

This was known as the "Stone" clan of the San Ildefonso of New Mexico. The name was also given to the Hano pueblo which later became extinct, this pueblo was located in Arizona.

Kua

This was known as the "Bear" clan of the Taos pueblo in New Mexico.

Kuakaa

This was a prehistoric pueblo, located about five miles south of Santa Fe, New Mexico. This pueblo of the Tanos people was occupied by about 800 people.

Kuapooge

This prehistoric Tewa pueblo was located at the present site of Santa Fe, New Mexico. It was at the site of old Fort Marcy on the outskirts of the town. It was occupied by United States troops in 1847.

Kuato

This was a division of the Kiowa. In the year 1780, they were all wiped out in a battle with the Sioux. It is said that in this battle they were planning to retreat when their chief said that if they did, they would not be acceptable in the hereafter. This made the tribe stand their ground and they were exterminated.

Kuchaptuvela

This Hopi ruin is located on the East Mesa of the Tusa-yan mesa in northeastern Arizona, near the present Walpi pueblo. This pueblo was occupied about the time the Spanish arrived in 1540. It was abandoned in 1629 when the tribe moved further up the mesa to Kisakobi (q.v.).

Kuchtya
This was a prehistoric pueblo of the Acoma.

Kuhaia
This was the "Bear" clan of the pueblos of San Felipe, Acoma, Laguna and Cochiti of New Mexico.

Kuhlahi
This was a former settlement of the Cherokee, located in northern Georgia. The name means "the place of the beech tree."

Kuishkoshyaka
Now extinct, this was the "Blue Corn" clan of the Acoma pueblo of New Mexico.

Kukinishyaka
Now extinct, this was the "Red Corn" clan of the Acoma pueblo in New Mexico.

Kulaiapto
This former village of the Maidu was located in Butte County in California.

Kulanapan Family
This is a name adopted by Powell for the linguistic tribes in Sonoma, Lake and Mendocino counties in California. Known generally by the name of Pomo.

Kulsetsiyi
This was a former Cherokee settlement, also known as "Sugartown" by the early settlers. The name means "The honey locust place." It was located in Oconee County in South Carolina. There was also another Sugartown in Macon County in North Carolina. The locust was used as a food for sugar.

Kungya
This was the Turquoise clan of the pueblos of Tewa, San

Ildefonso, Tesuque, Santa Clara and San Juan of New Mexico.

Kunti

See coonti.

Kusan Family

This was a small linguistic group who lived along the Coos River in Oregon. Very little is known of the customs of these people. In 1855 they lost all their lands through treaty.

Kuskuski

In 1753 this was a village of the Iroquois and Delaware who lived along Beaver Creek in Lawrence County in Pennsylvania. In 1758 it had a population of about a thousand people.

Kussoes

This name appears in the South Carolina trade regulations. See Coosa.

Kutenai

A group having a distinct language, sometimes called Kitunahan, having some similarities to Shoshonean. They lived in northern Montana and Idaho.

Kutshamakin

This was a leader of the Indians in the Dorchester, Massachusetts area. He was a signer of the treaties of 1643 and 1645.

Kwahari

This division of the Comanche roamed the Staked Plains of Texas. They were the last to surrender in 1874. Their name means the "antelopes."

Kwaituki

This was a former village of the Hopi. Located on the

western side of the Oraibi arroyo or dry wash about 14 miles from Oraibi in northeastern Arizona.

Kwakina
One of the Seven Cities of Cibola. It was possibly the Aquinsa Oñate visited in 1598. Abandoned in 1629. This was a ruined pueblo of the Zuñi located about seven miles southwest of the present Zuñi pueblo in New Mexico.

Kwaleki
A former village of the Kawia, located in the San Jacinto mountains in southern California.

Kwapa
A band of Sioux who went from the mouth of the Ohio River south along the Mississippi.

Kwapahag
Mentioned in a letter of the Abnaki to the governor of New England in 1721 as a division of their tribe.

Kwazackmash
One of the tribes that entered a treaty of Point Elliott in Washington in 1855. It is possible that these were Squamish.

Kwengyauinge
A large Tewa pueblo built on a cone-shaped hill overlooking the Chama River in Arriba County in New Mexico.

Kyatsutuma
A former Zuñi pueblo, a home of the "snail people." The name refers to the water that oozes from under the rocks in the back of the shelters. This was the source of water for many of the ancient pueblos who built along the canyon walls.

Kyunu
This was the corn clan of the Jemez pueblo in New Mexico. There was also a similar clan among the people of the Pecos pueblo in New Mexico.

L

Labrets

These were ornaments worn through the lips. They were first noticed by the Spanish explorer Cabeza de Vaca who visited Texas. The labrets were made of wood, stone, bone and sometimes shell.

Lac Court Oreilles

A band of the Chippewa who lived along the headwaters of the Chippewa River in Sawyer County in Wisconsin. In 1905 there were 1,214 members left who were living on the reservation.

Lackawanna

This name, a type of coal, is also the name of a tributary of the Susquehanna River in Pennsylvania. The name means "a stream forks." The word is derived from the Lenape or Delaware dialect.

Lackawaxen

A Lenape word, meaning "the forked road." This name was given to two villages of the Delaware, one in Northampton and the other in Wayne County in Pennsylvania.

Lacustrine

A term used to describe those objects which have been placed or deposited in inland bodies of water such as a lake or pond.

La Flesche

This was the name of a former chief of the Omaha. He was born December 25, 1857 in Thurston County in Nebraska. His full name was Francis La Flesche. In 1906 he married Rosa Bourassa who was a Chippewa.

La Fuemada
La Fuemada, California, see Shushuci.

Laguna
This was the name of a pueblo located about 45 miles from Albuquerque. This was the seat of a Spanish mission which was established in July, 1699. The word is of Spanish origin and means "lagoon," the pueblo was named because of the large pond which was located near by.

Laguna Band
This name was given to a band of Indians who lived along the shores of Clear Lake in California. This band belonged to a larger band of Pomo.

Lahanna
This name was given to large Indian settlement which was located on both sides of the Columbia River near Clarke's fork. The name was given by Lewis and Clark in 1805.

Lahoocat
A former Arikara village which was active about 1797 and was abandoned in 1800. The village was located on an island in the Missouri River in North Dakota. It was visited by Lewis and Clark.

La Jolla
This was a former Luiseño settlement which was located north of San Luis Rey in San Diego County in California.

Lajuchu
A former village of the Chumashan, located near the Purísima mission in Santa Barbara County in California.

Lake Indians
This was the name used to designate the Indians who lived around the Great Lakes regions. Such a tribe was the Chippewa.

Lakmiut

A former tribe of Kalapooian Indians who lived along the tributaries of the Willamette River in Oregon.

Lakota

A name given to themselves by the Dakota (q.v.).

Lamasconson

This was one of several bands or families that were moved from their homes in Charles County in Maryland in 1651.

Laminations

A term used to describe those fine layers of sand or clay which are deposited in an area to form beds. These can be measured and are used for dating purposes.

Lamsim

A possible Costanoan village, located near the Dolores mission near what is now San Francisco, California.

Lamtama

This was a band of the Nez Percé who lived near the Salmon River in Idaho and along White Bird creek.

Lance

A device used by the Indian for hunting and in warfare. The lance used for hunting had a shorter shaft and a broader, heavier head. The war lance was lighter and had a longer shaft. The Plains Indians made more use of the lance than did the woodland Indians. This holds true with the Indians that had the horse at the same time.

Land

See cheipfni.

Langlade

Charles de Langlade married Domitilde (q.v.), sister of Nissowaquet (q.v.).

209

Languages

The American Indian languages have a variety of structures and phonetics. Many of the languages are similar in sound to those who speak Scotch. It is difficult to estimate the number of words in the Indian languages. The differences in the noun and the verb are often very indistinct. Many influences enter into the Indian languages, such as contact with other tribes and the capture of their women who speak another dialect, which is then absorbed into the tribe, where some of each dialect is used. Through the years this is changed.

Languntennenk

This was a former village of the Moravian Delawares. The village was located in Beaver County in Pennsylvania in 1770.

Lansing Man

This name was given to a skeleton which was found in 1920 under twenty feet of silt on a bluff of the Missouri River near Lansing, Kansas.

La Pointe

La Pointe, Wisconsin, see Pizhiki. Also see Shaugawaumikong.

Lappawinze

A chief of the Delaware Indians. He was a signer of the treaty of 1737 at Philadelphia. This was known as the "walking purchase." The treaty granted the whites all the land from the Neshaming creek to as far as a man could walk in a day and a half. To comply with this agreement, the governor of Pennsylvania ordered a road built inland and then he hired a trained runner to go the distance. This did not please the Delawares, however.

Lapwai

This was a band of Nez Percé who formerly lived along the Lapwai creek in Idaho.

Laredo
    Laredo, Texas, see Tepemaca.

Larkspur
    This is a sacred plant to the Navajo and is used in special ceremonies.

Las Mulas
    This was a small ranch located along the San Antonio River in 1785. In 1785 it had only five people living there. The name for this little Texas ranch meant "the mules."

Lassik
    A chief of the people who lived along the Eel River and near the headwaters of the Mad River in California. These Athapascan people lived in conical houses made from the bark of trees. They made twined baskets. Their dialect resembles the Hupa. They hunted animals such as the deer by following the animal until it dropped from exhaustion.

Latcha Hoa
    This was a settlement shown on a map of Florida in 1775. Noted as a Chickasaw settlement on the Tombigbee River which flows through Mississippi.

Lawokla
    Established in 1769, this was a village of the Moravian Delawares who lived along the Allegheny River in Venango County in Pennsylvania.

Lawunkhannek
    This was a Choctaw clan of the Kushapokla phratry.

Laycayamu
    Located near what is now Santa Barbara, California, this was a former Chumashan village.

Leather
    See vttocais.

Leatherlips

A chief of the Huron. He was a signer of the treaty in Greenville, Ohio, in August, 1795. He was ordered killed by Tecumseh. In the summer of 1810 he was killed by a club near his camp which was situated about 14 miles north of Columbus, Ohio. The Wyandot Club of Columbus, Ohio, erected a monument to him in 1888 because of his help and friendship to the whites.

Leatherwood

A former settlement of the Cherokee, located in the northern part of Franklin County in Georgia. The name is possibly that of a chief of the tribe.

Lechauwanne

A Lenape dialect, see Lackawanna.

Leedstown

Leedstown, Virginia, see Pissacoac.

Leg

See mefcot.

Legal status

July 22, 1790, is the earliest act involving relations between the Indian and the whites. The act provided the right of the president to arrest any Indian guilty of theft, murder and other crimes.

Le Have

A village of the Micmac Indians who lived in Lunenberg County in Nova Scotia in 1760.

Lehigh

A Delaware dialect which means "fork in the river." Named for a county and a tributary of the Delaware River in Pennsylvania.

Lelengtu

This was the name given to the flute clan of the Hopi.

Leliotu
This was the tiny ant clan of the Ala Hopi Indians.

Lema
One of the older and more important villages of the Pomo Indians. Located in Knights Valley in Mendocino County in California.

Lenape
See Delaware.

Lenape Stone
This stone was found on the farm of Bernard Hansell about a half a mile from Doylestown in Bucks County, Pennsylvania. The first part was found in the spring of 1872 and the second smaller piece was found in 1881. There are figures carved on this stone of the mammoth, the sun and crude human figures. There is some doubt as to the age of this stone and who did the art work on it.

Lengyanobi
This was the legendary home of the flute clan of the Hopi. It was located on a ruined mesa about 30 miles northeast of Walpi in northeastern Arizona.

Leni-lenape
See Delaware.

Lesamaiti
A former village of the Awani, located a short distance from Notomidula in Yosemite Valley in Mariposa County, California.

Leschi
This chief of the Nisqualli and the Yakima led a war party of over a thousand men in an attack on Seattle, Washington, in January 29, 1856. They were driven off by a warship in the harbor. He was captured by his own men for a reward and was condemned and hanged on February 19, 1857.

Letaiyo

This was the Grey Fox clan of the firewood phratry of the Hopi.

Lewistown

A Shawnee and Seneca settlement in Ohio. The name was derived from the Shawnee chief, Captain Lewis. The present site of Lewistown, Ohio.

Leyva

This was a settlement which was supposed to have been reached by Francisco Leyva Bonilla in 1594 to 1596. This expedition was unauthorized and his whole party was killed. The exact location is not known but it is supposed to be in New Mexico.

Lichtenau

A former village of the Moravian Delaware Indians. It was attacked by the Hurons and was later destroyed by the Americans in 1781. The settlement was located in Muskingum County in Ohio.

Lick Town

A former village, possibly of the Shawnee, located in 1776 along the upper Scioto River in Ohio.

Lidlipa

This was a former village of the Nishinam, located along the Bear River in northern California.

Light

See kefhawtewh.

Lightning marks

See arrow.

Lightning stick

See bullroarer.

Lima

Lima, New York, see Skahasegao.

Limonite

This is a brown oxide of iron, used by the Indians for paint. Sometimes called yellow ochre.

Lincoln Island

This is an island in the Penobscot River in Maine, near Lincoln and about thirty-five miles above Oldtown, Maine, which was occupied by Penobscot Indians.

Linden

Linden, Arizona, see Pottery Hill.

Linguistic Families

There is a large and diversified variation among the American Indian languages. There are fifty-six families of speech. Grammatically, there are several resemblances between several Northwest Coast Indians and the Athapascan. Some other families are the Iroquoin, Algonquian, Siouan, Muskhogean, Athapascan and Wakashan.

Lipan

A tribe of Apache was roamed and raided in southern New Mexico and Texas.

Lisbon

Lisbon, Connecticut, see Showtucket.

Lithic

When used as a suffix it pertains to those objects made of stone at a specific age, such as Paleolithic, etc.

Littefutchi

This was a former Upper Creek town located at the head of Canoe Creek in St. Clair County in Alabama. This town was burned by Col. Dyer in October 29, 1813.

Little Crow

A former chief of the Sioux. His father was Little Crow, his grandfather was Little Thunder. In 1862 he became a leader of his people in the Indian wars. After this he and his people were removed to a reservation in Minnesota. They lived in peace until August 18, 1862, when they again rose against the whites and waged a war along a two hundred mile front. He was killed by a settler named Lampson on July 3, 1863, at about the age of 60. He left six wives and twenty-two children.

Little Munsee Town
A former village of the Munsee, located a few miles east of a town called Anderson in Indiana.

Little Osage Town
This was a town of the Osage, located on the western bank of the Neosho River in Oklahoma.

Little Raven
This former chief of the Arapaho was the first signer for the Southern Arapaho of the treaty of Fort Wise in Colorado on February 18, 1861. He died in a camp in Oklahoma during the winter of 1889.

Little Rock Village
In 1832, this was a village of the Potawatomi, located on the north bank of the Kankakee River in northeastern Illinois.

Little Thunder
A chief of the Brulé Sioux, this chief was a tall man—six feet six inches tall. He took command of the battle of the Grattan massacre which was near Fort Laramie in Wyoming when chief Singing Bear was killed in 1854.

Little Turtle
Born in 1752, this chief of the Miami of Indiana was the one credited with the defeat of General Harmar on the Miami River in a battle in October, 1790. He died in Fort Wayne July 14, 1812.

Llaneros
This Spanish term, meaning the "plainsmen," referred

to the Indians who were found on the staked plains of west Texas and eastern New Mexico.

Llano
In 1858, this was a Papago village located in southern Arizona.

Lobster
See assahampehooke.

Loess
This rather loamy clay is believed to have been deposited by the action of the wind.

Logan
This noted Iroquois chief was born in Shamokin, Pennsylvania, around the year 1725. Also known as a Cayuga chief and known too as Mingo, a term given to those Iroquois who were away from their regular territory. He was killed by one of his relatives in 1780. There is a monument to Logan in the Fair Hill Cemetery near Auburn, New York.

Logansport
Logansport, Indiana, see Spemicalaba, meaning "high."

Logstown
Originally this village was settled by the Shawnee in 1747. Later on this village was occupied by the Iroquois, Nipissing and Abnaki. The village was located on the right bank of the Ohio River in Allegheny County in Pennsylvania.

Lohim
This small band of the Shoshonean Indians formerly lived along the Columbia River in Oregon. They have never officially made peace and they have tried to remain alone.

Loka
This was the reed clan of the Navajo of New Mexico.

217

Loko

This band of Paviotso lived near the Carson River in western Nevada.

Lompoc

This former Chumashan village was located near the Purísima mission in Santa Barbara, California.

Lone Wolf

This was a chief of the Kiowa and was one of the nine signers of an agreement made at Medicine Lodge, Kansas, in 1867. This treaty was the first to place the tribe on a reservation. After his son was killed by the whites, he became hostile and fought the whites until 1875, when he was captured. He was sent to prison in Fort Marion in Florida and died in 1879. His adopted son who had the same name became the chief of his tribe.

Longe

This is a shortened name for the muskelunge, a large fish which is caught in the Great Lakes regions. The name was used mainly along the northern shores of Lake Ontario.

Long feather

See meqwance.

Long Island

This name was given particularly to an island in the Tennessee River on the Tennessee and Georgia line. It was settled by the Cherokee in 1782, and as one of the Chickamauga towns. It was destroyed in 1794.

Long Lake

This was the site of a former Chippewa village located in Bayfield County in northern Wisconsin. This village along Long Lake was occupied about 1884 by the Chippewa.

Long Sioux

A chief of the Dakota bands who roamed Montana in 1872.

Long Tail

A chief of the Shawnee who in 1854 lived at a settlement called Long Tail, located in Johnson County in Kansas.

Los Luceros

A small Spanish settlement located on the site of the pueblo of Pioge on the east bank of the Rio Grande in Arriba County, New Mexico. This was a former pueblo of the Tewa.

Los Pinos

Los Pinos, Colorado, see Tabeguache.

Lost

See nowwanus.

Lost Tribes of Israel

This is a theory which has been making the rounds of the world since 721. B.C. The ten lost tribes of Israel have been found in many parts of the world. These are supposed to be a group of people who were gathered together by Sargon who was then King of Assyria. This king is supposed to have deported ten of the twelve tribes of Israel.

These so called missing tribes were supposed to be the American Indians. Much time and money has been spent trying to prove the connection of the Indian to these people.

Lovelock

Lovelock, Nevada, see Winnemucca.

Lower Chinook

Most people use this term to define those Indians who live from the mouth of the Columbia River to the Willamette River in the States of Washington and Oregon.

Lower Creek

This term is used to describe those tribes who live on the lower Chattahoochee and Alabama Rivers in South Carolina. In 1715 there were about 1733 people known as the Lower Creeks. Also known by the name of "Cousin."

Lower Quarter

The Lower Quarter Indians were those Indians who lived in what is now Raleigh, North Carolina. These Indians were active about the year 1700.

Lower Sauratown

In 1760 this was the name given to those Indians who lived along the Neuse River in North Carolina; this village was occupied by the Cheraw.

Lowertown

This name was given to a village of the Shawnee who built along the Scioto River in Ohio. This village was wiped out by a flood and was then rebuilt on the other side of the river. About 1750 these people moved themselves up to what is now Chillicothe, Ohio. This was also known as Lowertown and known, too, as Lower Shawnee Town.

Lowrey

Also known as Major Lowrey, George Lowrey or Agili. This was a cousin of Sequoya, a well known Cherokee chief. He became chief of the council of the Cherokee in 1839.

Lowrey, John

Also known as Colonel Lowrey, this was chief of the Cherokee who fought with General Andrew Jackson in the war against the Creeks in 1813. John Lowrey was one of the signers of a treaty made at Washington, D. C. in June 7, 1806.

Luiseño

This was the southernmost division of the Shoshonean in California. They received their name from the important Spanish Mission San Luis Rey. In 1856 there were about 2700 people in the tribe.

Lumbee Indians

In May 22, 1956, the Senate voted to create a new Indian tribe to be known officially as the "Lumbee Indians." The name has been given to some 4,000 Indians who live in and around Robeson County in North Carolina. These Indians claim to be descendants of the Robeson County Indians who were in the area of Sir Walter Raleigh's "lost colony," the first English settlement in North America, which vanished in 1584.

Lummi
These are a Salish tribe that lived near Bellingham, Washington.

Lupies
A group of supposedly mythical Indians who lived on the Plains of America in the late 17th century.

Lupine
The complete plant of the blue-flowered lupine is used by the Navajo Indians for the making of a greenish-yellow dye.

Lutuamian Family
A linguistic stock composed of the Klamath and the Modoc of southwestern Oregon.

M

Maak

This was one of the gens of the Potawatomi, also known as the "loons."

Maangreet

Meaning "Big feet," this was a subclan of the Delawares.

Maawi

This is a now extinct clan of the Zuñi, this was the Antelope clan and was used by the Zuñi of New Mexico.

Macamo

Named by Cabrillo in 1542, this was a former village of the Chumashan who lived on San Lucas Island in California.

Macaque

This term was used in Canada and the Great Lakes region to denote the "Mocuck" (q.v.), or sugar container of the Indians of the northeastern part of the United States and Canada.

Maccarib

This derivation of the Algonquian was used to describe the deer and also the cariboo of the north.

Maccoa

This small group of Cusabo, now extinct, was visited by Ribault in 1562. They formerly lived along the southern coast of South Carolina.

Machapunga

Meaning "bad dust," this name was given to this Algonquian tribe who formerly lived in Hyde County in North

Carolina. In 1701 they were very few and after the Tusca-rora war, they were settled on Mattamuskeet Lake.

Macharienkonck
A village of the Minisink located on a bend in the Dela-ware River in Pike County, Pennsylvania.

Machawa
This was a former town of the Timucua, located in the northwestern part of Florida in an area known as Iola on the Wicassa River.

Machemoodus
An Indian village formerly located in Middlesex County in Connecticut. This town was known as the place of the "bad noise," located on the east bank of the Connecticut River.

Macheno
A former village of the Timuquanan in the west central part of Florida. This village was visited by Bartram in his travels.

Macherew
The Virginia Indian word for enemy.

Macheto
This was a village of the Awani, located in Indian Can-yon in the Yosemite Valley in Mariposa County, California.

Machias
This was the name given to a village of the Passama-quoddy located on the Machias River in Maine. The name means "The bad place," so named because of the swift river at this point which made early travel on this part dangerous.

Machonee
A former village of the Ottawa, located near Lake St. Clair at the mouth of the Au Vaseau River in Michigan.

The chief of this village was drowned while he was intoxicated in 1825.

MacIntosh, Chilly

A former chief of the Creek Indians. He was killed by Chief Menewa, a half-breed Indian. His death was ordered because he transferred lands to the whites.

MacIntosh, William

This chief of the Lower Creeks led the Creek allies of the Americans in the War of 1812. He was a prominent leader in the battle of Horseshoe Bend in Alabama, when nearly a thousand men were killed. For his help to the whites in giving them lands, he was sentenced to die by a council of the tribe. On May 1, 1825, he was shot by warriors who were sent to carry out the sentence.

Mackatahone

The Virginia Indian term for the arm.

Mackinaw

This was a famous trading post located between Lake Huron and Lake Michigan. The name has several meanings: A species of lake trout, a type of rather heavy blanket and also the name was used to define a large flat boat or barge. The name is a derivation of French, Algonquian, and Chippewa, meaning "big turtle."

Mackinaw

Mackinaw, Michigan, see Robinson.

Macocks

A former village of the Delawares, located near the present site of Wilmington, Delaware. The village was active about 1608.

Macombo

This was a former village of the desert people known as the Papago who lived in Pima County, Arizona, in 1865.

Mad Bear Anderson

Mad Bear is an Iroquois lawyer who, in 1959, led a group of Indians to Washington. They demanded to see President Eisenhower to present a grievance, but were turned away.

Madokawando

In 1630 this was a chief of the Penobscot. He was adopted by a Kennebec chief. At first he was friendly with the English, until they took advantage of his people. He then made war on the whites and in 1691, he attacked the village of York, Maine, and killed 77 people in the village. He was aided by the French in his efforts. He died in 1698. One of his daughters was the wife of Baron Castine.

Magnus

This was a chief of the Narragansett Indians. In 1675 she was one of the six chiefs in the area. She was killed by the English in a battle in a swamp in Warwick, Rhode Island, in 1676.

Maguaga

A former village of the Huron, located about 14 miles southwest of Detroit, Michigan. This land was ceded to the United States in a treaty made in St. Mary's, Ohio, September 20, 1818.

Maguenodon

A tribe living in Oregon.

Magunkaquog

A former village of the Christian Indians who lived in Middlesex County, Massachusetts, in 1674.

Mahackemo

This was a chief of a small band of Indians who ceded their lands along the Norwalk River in Connecticut in 1640-41.

Mahala mats

Used in California to designate the "squaw" or the

squaw's rug. The term is derived from the Yokut and possibly from the Spanish word for woman, mujer.

Mahaskahod

This was a former village of hunters of the Manahoac who lived along the Rappahannock in 1608. This Powhatan village was possibly located near the present site of Fredericksburg, Virginia.

Mahcatawaiuwh

The Powhatan Indian word for black.

Mahican

See also Mohegan. This was a large tribe that occupied the upper part of the Hudson River in New York State. They were known as the River Indians to the Dutch settlers and to the French they were known as "Loups or Wolf people." They fought the Mohawks and were forced to move east in 1664. In 1730, a large body of the tribe moved to an area along the Susquehanna River in Pennsylvania and were later moved to Ohio where they lost their identity. Their government was a democracy.

Mahoning

In 1764 this was a village of the Delawares, located near what is now Youngstown, Ohio.

Mahopa

The Siouan word for magic or mystery, see Orenda.

Mahow

A Chumashan village located in Ventura County in California. This was the site of the Las Posas ranch.

Mahtoiowa

The name of a Brulé Teton Sioux chief. Due to action taken against a white man who was killed by an Indian a great battle was started. A Lieut. Grattan approached Mahtoiowa and demanded that he point out the guilty person.

The chief pointed out the tipi but would not go in and bring out the guilty party. This caused Lieut. Grattan to order his soldier to fire a howitzer into the tipi. The tipi was in an Indian village and many were killed. This caused the warriors of the village to attack the troops, killing them all. They then attacked Fort Laramie in Wyoming. Chief Mahtoiowa was killed, but the hostilities continued by Little Thunder. The name Mahtoiowa means Whirling Bear.

Mahusquechikoken

A village of Seneca, Delaware and Munsee who were under the rule of the Iroquois. Located along the Allegheny River near Venango in Pennsylvania. The village was destroyed by the troops of Broadhead in 1779.

Maidu

This single tribe constitutes the entire linguistic family of Pujunan. The tribe formerly lived in the Sacramento Valley in California and the nearby Sierra Nevada areas.

Ma'iidaa' or g'iishzniniih

A Navajo term used to describe the plant, ironwood. Used for ceremonial purposes, this plant produces berries that are blue and when made into a dye the color is grey.

Maize

This is a cereal plant. Its true derivation is supposed to be from some form of grass. The mountains of Peru seem to be the home of this American plant. Maize, or Indian Corn as it is also called, was used at the time of the settlement and its growth was highly developed at this time. The only new thing done with corn as a food was the making of "corn flakes" in historic times.

Ma'kadawiyas

See race.

Makah

The southernmost branch of the Wakashan stock in the

227

United States. They lived near Flattery Rocks in the state of Washington.

Makisin
Chippewa word for moccasin (q.v.).

Makomitek
This group of Algonquian lived in the Green Bay area of Wisconsin in 1671.

Makoua
This division of the Fox lived in central Wisconsin near the town of St. Michel about the year 1673.

Makoukuwe
A band of the Fox who formerly lived near the Green Bay area of Wisconsin in 1673.

Makwa
This was the "Bear" gens of the Chippewa of Wisconsin.

Malacite
A tribe belonging to the Abnaki confederacy in Maine.

Malaka
This division of the Patwin of the Copehan formerly lived in the Lagoon Valley area in Solano County, California.

Maliacones
This was one of the tribes that was visited by Cabeza de Vaca in 1528-34. They lived near the Avavares in Texas.

Malica
Located on De Bry's map, this was an Indian village located inland from the mouth of the St. Johns River in Florida in the year 1564.

Mallin
A former village of the Costanoan located about ten miles from the Santa Cruz mission in California.

Mallopeme

One of the Indian tribes of west Texas. Many of these people came to the mission at San José and San Miguel de Aguayo.

Mamanahunt

This was a village of the Powhatan Confederacy located in Charles City County in Virginia in 1608.

Mamanassy

Located in King and Queen County, Virginia, this was another village of the Powhatan Confederacy of Virginia.

Mamekoting

This was one of the five Esopus tribes of New York, located near Poughkeepsie, New York, and the surrounding area.

Manahoac

This small group of Siouan tribes lived in northern Virginia in 1608. They fought the Powhatan and the Iroquois.

Manamoyik

This was a former village of the Nauset who lived in Barnstable County in Massachusetts in 1762. Also known as the Quasson tribe, named after their chief.

Mandan

This was a large Siouan tribe of the northwest area. When they were first visited by the whites they lived in North Dakota. The first recorded visit was made by Sieur de la Verendrye in 1738. Their numbers were reduced by smallpox and wars with the Assiniboin and the Dakota. These Indians lived in round huts made of logs and clay. They were always friendly to the United States.

Mangachqua

A village of the Potawatomi which was included in a tract of land in southern Michigan which was sold to the whites in 1827.

Mangas Coloradas

A well-known chief of the Apache called "red sleeves." When General S. W. Kearny took control of New Mexico in 1846, Red Sleeves killed some copper miners to avenge the killing of some Apaches who were invited to a dinner by the whites and were then killed in cold blood. In return for a whipping and other indignities he received at the hands of the whites, Red Sleeves formed an alliance with Cochise and then resisted the whites. Coloradas was wounded at Apache Pass in the southeastern part of Arizona. He was taken prisoner in January, 1863. He was killed trying to escape. It is said that his escape was caused by being jabbed by a red hot bayonet and he was shot while running.

Manhasset

This small band of Long Island Indians belonged to the Montauk group of Indians. They lived mainly on Shelter Island off the eastern end of Long Island, New York.

Manhattan

Manhattan Island was bought from tribes of the Wappinger confederacy by the Dutch (Peter Minuit) for 60 guilders' worth of articles. The villages on Manhattan Island itself were used mainly as a stopping off place for hunting and fishing. The name Manhattan means, "island of hills." The main village of the Manhattan Indians was located near what is now Yonkers, New York.

Manhattan

Manhattan, Kansas, see Tatarrax.

Maninose

Several ways of spelling this Algonquian word are found, they are used to denote the soft-shelled clam found along the east coast of the United States, especially in the northern areas.

Manito
Algonquian for magic or an unseen force, see Orenda.

Mankato
Mankato, Minnesota, see Sleepy Eyes.

Mano
A term used for the grinding stone used in the grinding of grain.

Manomet
In 1685, this was a village of Christian Indians who lived in Barnstable County, Massachusetts.

Manos de Perro
One of the tribes who were visited by the Spanish explorers in 1760. They formerly lived along the Rio Grande River in Texas.

Manuelito
A chief of the Navajo about the year 1855. He died in 1893.

Many Horses
A Piegan chief of the upper Missouri area. His name comes from the fact that he owned so many horses, more than his whole tribe. He led many war parties on the Crows and Atsina in an effort to get more horses. He was killed on one of these raiding parties in 1867, when an old man.

Maple sugar
The earliest notice regarding maple sugar was made by Philosophical Transactions of the Royal Society of 1684. The methods of syrup and sugar making were learned from the Iroquois tribes of Canada and upper New York and New England tribes. The term "sugar bush" is derived from the French. The methods of collecting and preparation have changed little since the early Indians days.

Maracah
The Powhatan Indian name for apple.

Marakimmins
The Virginia Indian word for grapes.

Marameg
This was an early division of the Chippewa. They were first noticed by the whites in 1670 when they lived along the eastern part of Lake Superior.

Maraton
A village of the Chowanoc located on the east bank of the Chowan River in Chowan County, North Carolina, in 1585.

Maratsno
The Virginia Indian term for the tongue.

Margaretsville
Margaretsville, New York, see Pakataghkon.

Mariames
This tribe formerly lived in the Matagorda Bay area of Texas. They were visited by Cabeza de Vaca in 1528-34. They became extinct in the late 1890's.

Marian
This name was given to the Indians of the Huron tribes who became Christians. The name was given by other members because they used the name of Mary so many times.

Maricopa
This large group of Pima lived along the Gila River in the southern part of Arizona.

Maringoman's Castle
Occupied in 1635, this was a palisaded village of the Waoranec. Located on Murderer's Creek in Ulster County, New York.

Mariposan

This term is used for a linguistic stock of Indians known as the Yokuts who lived in San Joaquin Valley in California. These Indians were overrun by the whites during the gold rush days and did not resist the outsiders.

Marlborough

The city of Marlborough, Massachusetts, is located on the site of an Indian village. See Okommakamesit.

Mascoutens

This term was used by the early settlers to designate those Algonquian tribes who lived on the plains of Wisconsin. The tribe was first mentioned by Champlain in 1616. Champlain used the name Asistaguerouon.

Masi

This was the "death God" clan of the Hopi Indians of Arizona.

Masilengya

This was the "Drab flute clan" of the Hopi of Arizona.

Maskegon

This Algonquian tribe was also known as the "swampy Crees" by the early settlers. These Indians lived around Lake Superior. They lived closely with the Chippewa.

Maskyag

Kickapoo Indian for swamp or mash. See Muskeg.

Maspeth

This small tribe of Algonquian Indians formerly lived on Long Island, New York, located near Queens on Long Island. Their village was attacked by the Dutch in 1644. Maspeth was used as a name as early as 1638.

Massachusetts

The name means "at the great hill, or great mountain." This was an important Algonquian tribe that lived in the

Massachusetts Bay area. The tribe became almost extinct by 1620 due to a plague.

Massassoit

This was the main chief of the Wampanoag who lived in the area of Bristol, Rhode Island. Massassoit was a friend of the English. He died in 1662. His son, King Philip, became famous as a fighter against the English.

Massikwayo

This was the chicken hawk clan of the Pakab phratry of the Hopi.

Massomuck

In 1700 this was a location known as the "great fishing place," located in Wabaquasset in the southern part of Massachusetts.

Mastic

Mastic, Long Island, New York, see Patchoag.

Matafsañ

The Powhatan Indian word for copper.

Mataughquamend

This was a former village located on the northern bank of the Potomac River in 1608, Charles County, Maryland.

Matchcoat

A term used by the English to denote a type of garment worn by the Indians, especially the Algonquians along the eastern seaboard area.

Matchotic

Meaning "bad inlet," this name was applied to a group of the Powhatan tribes of Richmond County in Virginia.

Mathomauk

This was a former village of the Powhatan confederacy, located on the western bank of the James River in Virginia, 1608.

Matoaka
See Pocahontas.

Matsaki
This is a ruined Zuñi pueblo located near the northwestern base of Thunder Mountain in Valencia County, New Mexico. It was mentioned by Coronado and became one of the Seven Cities of Cibola. The pueblo was abandoned during the Pueblo revolt of August, 1680.

Mattabesec
This was an important Algonquian tribe of Connecticut. This tribe covered all of Connecticut as far over as the Hudson River in New York.

Mattamuskeet
Located in Hyde County, North Carolina, this was the only village of the Machapunga. The village was active about the year 1700 to 1701.

Mattapony
A small tribe of the Powhatan in Virginia.

Mauston
Mauston, Wisconsin, see Tokaunee Village.

Mazakutemani
This well-known chief of the Sisseton Sioux was noted for his friendship to the whites. He was born about 1826. About 1855 he became a Christian. He was a signer of the Traverse des Sioux, July, 1851, and the treaties in Washington, June 19, 1858. He died about the year 1880.

McQueen's Village
This was a former Seminole village located in the western part of Florida on the eastern side of Tampa Bay.

McGillivray
This was a chief of the Creeks of mixed blood. Alexander McGillivray was the son of a wealthy Scotchman and a

Creek woman, born in 1739. He became a leader of the Creeks and fought against the Americans on the British side. He was beaten by General James Robertson and in 1783 a treaty of peace left McGillivray without anything. It is said that he made a secret treaty with Washington in New York. He also made agreements with the Spanish and British and received pay and officer's rank from all sides. He became a wealthy man. He died in February 17, 1793, and was buried at the garden of William Panton in Pensacola, Florida.

M'cusun
The Micmac Indian word for moccasin (q.v.).

Mdewakanton
This tribe of Dakota resembles many divisions of the Sioux in their general customs and beliefs. They originally lived in Minnesota.

Mefcot
The Virginia Indian term for the leg.

Mefkewe
The Virginia Indian term for the nose.

Mefscate
The Virginia Indian term for the foot.

Meherrin
This Iroquoian tribe formerly lived along the border of North Carolina and Virginia. This tribe was active about the year 1669.

Meihsutterafk
The Virginia Indian word for a creek.

Mekewe
This was a former village of the Chumashan which was located near Santa Inez in Santa Barbara County in California.

Meletecunk
This former tribe of the Delawares lived along the coast of New Jersey, particularly in Ocean County.

Melona
This former village of the Timucuan was located along the lower St. Johns River in Florida in the 16th century.

Menaskunt
A village of the Powhatan confederacy in 1608. It was located on the Pamunkey River in Virginia.

Menatonon
This Algonquian chief was prominent from 1585 to 1586. He gave much information and help to Ralph Layne, who was sent out to get information about the new country by Sir Walter Raleigh.

Mendica
This Texas tribe was met by Cabeza de Vaca in 1527-34. The tribe became extinct at an early date.

Menequen
This small band visited the mission of San Antonio de Valero in Texas around 1745. This band is supposed to have lived in Guadalupe County, Texas.

Menewa
Born in 1765, Menewa was a second chief of one of the Lower Creek towns located along the Tallapoosa River in Alabama. He was out front in his efforts to forestall the whites from taking over the Indian lands.

Meniolagomeka
The people of this Delaware village all became members of the Moravian sect in 1754.

Menominee
This is the Chippewa name for "wild rice." This tribe now lives in the northeastern part of Wisconsin. They were

first visited by the whites in 1671 by Nicolet who met them along the Menominee River. There is a story of spirit rock which the tribe believes holds the strength of the tribe. When this rock disappears . . . so will the tribe. The tribe now lives on a reservation in Wisconsin in the deep forests. Spirit rock is located on the reservation and is about four feet high, made of granite. One of the present villages is in Keshena and the other one is at Neopit, both in Wisconsin.

Menoquet
Named for its chief, this is a former village of the Potawatomi located in Kosciusko County in Indiana.

Mento
A name used by the early French explorers of the 17th and 18th century for the tribes along the Arkansas River. They included the Wichita, Tonkawa, Caddo, Comanche, etc. They fought the Spanish and the Apache tribes.

Meochkonck
A village of the Minisink located on the upper Delaware River in eastern New York state (1656).

Mepayaya
This tribe was mentioned by Francisco de Jesús María in 1691. This tribe of the Payaya formerly lived in the vicinity of San Antonio, Texas.

Mepit
The Virginia Indian term for the teeth.

Mequachake
This was one of the main divisions of the five Shawnee villages, located in Logan County, Ohio.

Meqwance
This is the Virginia Indian word for a long feather.

Meracouman
This village was described by Joutel, who said that it was located along the route taken by La Salle in 1687.

Merced

This was a group of Cajuenche ranches located in the northeastern part of California. These Indians were visited by Father Garcés in 1775. The name is Spanish and means "grace."

Mer, Gens de la

This name, or sometimes Gens de la Mer du Nord, was used by the French to describe the Algonquian tribes who lived around Hudson Bay in Canada. The name means "the people of the sea," or the people of the "sea of the north."

Merric

Now known as Merrick, Long Island, formerly this was a small division of the Algonquian who lived along the shores of Long Island, New York.

Mesa Grande

This was a small village of the Diegueño located in the western part of San Diego County in California. The name was later given to the Mission Tule River Indian reservation.

Mesa Verde

Mesa Verde is now a National Park, located off U.S. Highway 160 near Mancos and Cortez, Colorado. Here you may see great cliff dwellings of the Anasazi people of about 300 to 1300 A.D. There are many cliff houses, kivas, and a fine museum. The park is open to tourists from May until October.

Mescaleros

This was a tribe of the Apache who formerly lived from the Rio Grande River to Pecos, New Mexico. Their name was given them by the Spanish, it was given because of their habit of eating mescal, a species of agave cactus.

Mesquites

The Mesquites were a group of Indians that lived near San Antonio, Texas. There was another group known by the same name that lived across the Rio Grande which was composed of about 150 people. They were first mentioned by Espinosa in 1716; he met them along the Brazos River in Texas.

Mestethltun

This is a former village of the Tolowa who lived along the coast of California, near Crescent, California.

Metals

Most American Indians made articles of stone; however, metals were used before the whites arrived. Copper was the ore most used, other ores such as gold, silver and iron were also used to a lesser degree. The metals were usually hammered into the desired shape. Copper articles have been found in the mounds of Alabama, Wisconsin, Ohio and other nearby states.

Metate

This word is derived from the Spanish "hand" which is an indication of the method used. A metate is used to grind corn or grains for the purpose of making flour. The device usually consists of a flat stone with a slight depression in the center. This is used to hod the grain while a rounded or flat stone is used to grind the grain with a circular rubbing motion. This pressure between the rocks causes the grains to be broken down until they form flour.

Metate Ruins

The metate ruins are so called because of the large amount of metates that were found in conjunction with the ruins of this pueblo. They are located in Apache County in Arizona.

Metawce

The Virginia Indian term for the ears.

Metea

This was a famous chief of the Potawatomi. He was one of the leaders of a massacre of the garrison at Chicago. He was active at the council at Chicago in 1821 and again when the Wabash treaty was framed in 1826. He died in Ft. Wayne in 1827.

Metinge

The Virginia Indian term for the hand.

Métis

This was a term used by the French-speaking peoples of the Northwest to denote those who were half white and half Indian, also known commonly as a "half-breed." The word is derived from the Latin (miscere), "to mix."

Metoac

This term was used to designate all of the main tribes that lived on Long Island, New York, such as the: Shinnecock, Setauket, Secatoag, Rockaway, Patchoag, Nesaquake, Montauk, Merric, Matinecoc, Massapequa, Manhasset, Canarsee and the Corchaug. The name means "the land of the ear-shell" or the "periwinkle." These Indians made much wampum which was traded to the Iroquois of the north. The Shinnecock reservation on the eastern end of Long Island is now made up of mixed bloods with the Negro being the most outstanding.

Mettone

The Virginia Indian term for the mouth.

Metucs

Powhatan Indian word for a bridge.

Metutahanke

A Mandan village located on the Missouri River about four miles below the Knife River in North Dakota. In 1837 the village was almost wiped out by smallpox.

Miami

Known as the "people who live on the peninsula," the Miami were first met by the Frenchman Perrot in 1668 when they were living along the Fox River in Wisconsin.

Their power extended to what is now Chicago and Detroit. The men practiced tattooing. They traveled by land rather than by canoes.

Miantonomo

This noted chief of the Narragansett visited Boston in 1632. Miantonomo helped the English against the Pequot. The chief was, however, not as loyal to the English as was supposed and several times the English tried to convict him of crimes. After a battle between the Mohegan and the Narraganset, Chief Miantonomo was captured and turned over to the English at Hartford; he was sentenced to death, mainly on religious grounds, and was killed by Uncas, the enemy chief. He was buried where he was killed and in 1841 a monument was erected in his honor and the place was then known as Sachem's Plains.

Miawkinaiykis

This was a division of the Piegan tribe of the Siksika. They were known as the "topknots," because of the way that they fixed their hair.

Michahai

This was a Mariposan tribe of Yokuts who lived along the Kings River near Squaw Valley in the south central part of California.

Michigamea

The state of Michigan derives its name from this Algonquian name meaning "great or much water" or "big lake." The Michigamea were first visited by Marquette in 1673. About the end of the 17th century these people were driven from their land by the Chickasaw (q.v.). By 1818 there were only three male members of the tribe left alive.

Michilimackinac

The name means "The place of the big wounded person." This island located in Michigan was one of the chief centers of this Algonquian tribe. The village was destroyed by the Iroquois and was later occupied by the Chippewa around 1671. In 1827 the Indians who had the Catholic faith separated from the rest of the tribe and set up a new town near the old one. In 1702 the Ottawa and the Chippewa both lived in the area that is now known as Michilimackinac.

Michiyu
A village of the Chumashan, formerly located between Point Conception and Santa Barbara in California, now known as San Onofre.

Mickkesawbee
This village of the Potawatomi was formerly located near the present site of Coldwater, Michigan.

Micmac
An Algonquian tribe who lived along the Great Lakes. The name means "our allies." These people extended east to Nova Scotia and New Brunswick. It is supposed that these were the first Indians that were seen by the Europeans. They are supposed to have been met by Sebastian Cabot in 1497 and the three Indians that he took back to England were believed to be Micmac Indians. The Micmac Indians became friends with the French and it was not until 1779 that the wars with the English ceased in New England.

Microliths
These are small sharp blades which are placed in a row along a shaft to make saws, clubs and spear heads. They are usually shaped like small triangles or wedges.

Middleboro
See Pachade.

Middle-settlement Indians
A term sometimes used to describe the Cherokee who

lived in upper Georgia and in western North Carolina. The term was used to distinguish them from those Cherokees who lived in South Carolina and in Tennessee.

Middle Town
A former village of the Seneca located about three miles north of Chemung in Sullivan County in New York. This village was destroyed in 1779.

Migichihiliniou
This term was used to designate those Indians who lived along Eagle Lake, northeast of the Lake of the Woods, a group of Chippewa Indians.

Miitsr
This was the humming-bird clan of the San Felipe village located in New Mexico. In 1895 there were only two living members of this clan.

Mikanopy
A chief of the Seminole who had large herds of cattle and almost a hundred negro slaves. In 1835 Chief Mikanopy and his warriors started a war which lasted for seven years.

Mikasuki
This was a former Seminole town located in Leon County, Florida. This was also known as one of the "red towns" at the beginning of the hostilities in 1817. The red towns or the "Baton Rouges" were known by the red poles which were erected in their towns to denote war. . . . This town was known for its active part in the Seminole war of 1835 to 1842.

Mikonoh
This was the Chippewa gen of the "snapping turtle."

Milford
Milford, Connecticut, see Paugusset.

Milky Wash Ruins

This is a prehistoric village located about ¾ of a mile along the Milky Hollow Bluff, located some nine miles from the Petrified Forest in Arizona. The ruins had rather odd stove-like altars. The pottery from this area is red, grey and black.

Millbury

Millbury, Massachusetts, see Pakachoog.

Milly

Milly Hado, a daughter of a Seminole Chief, saved the life of an American named McKrimmon. She begged her father to spare his life, even to the extent of giving her own life. McKrimmon was instead sold to the Spanish. Later on Milly and her tribe were captured by the Americans and it was McKrimmon who came to the aid of Milly and finally married her.

Milwaukee

This was a former village of a mixed group of Indians, the Potawatomi, Fox and the Mascoutens. This city is located in what is now Wisconsin and the name means "fine or good land."

Mimal

Mimal, California, see Sesum.

Mimbreños

These Indians who formerly lived in the southwestern part of New Mexico were a branch of the Apache and were known as the "people of the willows." They were also known as the Coppermine Apaches.

Minas

A former village of the Micmac, located in Nova Scotia in 1760.

Minatti

A Seminole village, formerly located in Polk County in the west central part of Florida.

Mineconjou

A band of the Western Sioux.

Minemaung

A village of the Potawatomi, named after its chief. Located in Kankakee County in Illinois. In 1832 it was ceded to the United States in a treaty known as the Camp Tippecanoe treaty.

Minesetperi

This was a division of the Crow Indians, also known as the "River Crows" who separated from the mountain Crows. The name means "Those who defecate under the bank."

Mingan

An Algonquian village of the Montagnais, located along the river known as the Mingan near the north shore of the Gulf of St. Lawrence in Quebec. This village was the general area to which the Indians for several hundred miles came to trade. Soon after 1661, a mission was established near this area.

Mingo

A term used in several ways. Mingo was a term used in the early Colonial period to denote "Chief," especially in the Gulf States areas. The name itself is Algonquian and means "treacherous." It was also used to describe a detached band of the Iroquois who left their main villages before 1750.

Miniconjou

This division of the Teton Sioux, related to the Brulé and Oglala Sioux, lived on both sides of the Missouri River above the Cheyenne River. They were first mentioned by

246

Lewis and Clark in a report dated 1804. In 1850, the tribe numbered approximately 1,300.

Minisink
This was one of the main divisions of the Munsee who lived in Orange and Ulster Counties in New York and over into New Jersey and Pennsylvania. Their main village, however, was in Sussex County in New Jersey.

Minnehaha
The ancient arrowmaker's daughter is a figment of Henry Wadsworth Longfellow who wrote the famous "Song of Hiawatha." The name Minnehaha is from the Teton Sioux dialect which means literally "water laughter." The Dakota-English Dictionary states that the name denotes "cascade or cataract" and would signify "waterfall." The name Minnehaha was first used in a book called "Life & Legends of the Sioux," by Mrs. Mary Eastman, printed in 1849.

Mintabuckkam
The Virginia Indian term for the head.

Mipshuntik
A former village of the Yaquina located on the north side of the Yaquina River in Benton County, Oregon.

Miqkano
This was the "mud turtle" phratry of the Menominee of Wisconsin.

Miramichi
A village of the Micmac located along the right bank of the Miramichi River in New Brunswick where it flows into the St. Lawrence River. The French had a mission established there in the late 17th century and in 1760 there was a Micmac village located nearby.

Misesopano
A village of the Chumashan, located in Ventura County

in California. In the early 1900's it was known to have been located on the Rafael Gonzales farm. The Indian village itself was active in 1542.

Mishawum
Meaning "great spring." This was a village of the Massachusetts Indians located near Boston, Massachusetts. Also known as Sagamore John's town, named after a chief who lived there. It was settled by the English in 1628.

Mishcup
Derived from the Algonquian dialects, this was the name given to the little fish called a porgy or bream. The name means "close together" and was used to describe the scales of this small fish.

Mishongnovi
This was a pueblo of the Hopi in northeastern Arizona. The name means "at the place of the other which stands up"; the name referred to two large sandstone pillars on the middle mesa of Tusayan. This village was abandoned in 1680. During the mission period of 1629 to 1680, the site had the name of San Buenaventura.

Mishtapawa
A former village of the Chumashan located near the Santa Inez mission in Santa Barbara in California.

Mishtawayawininiwak
The name given to the Chippewa who lived in Canada, as distinguished from those who lived in Michigan and Wisconsin. This is the Chippewa name used by the Chippewa.

Miskwasi
Chippewa for the muskrat. See Musquash.

Mismatuk
A former village of the Chumashan, located in what is

now known as the Arroyo Burro in the mountains near Santa Barbara, California.

Misshawa

A division of the Potawatomi tribes.

Missiassik

This Algonquian tribe belonging to the Abnaki group lived in northern Vermont. Their name means "The wanderers." Their main village was located in Franklin County along Lake Champlain. It was abandoned in 1730 because of an epidemic, possibly smallpox.

Mission Indians

The Mission Indians of California were so called because they came under some 21 Spanish Missions which were established between 1769 and 1823. The first mission was established at San Diego. The Indians were taught and forced to work at agriculture. The land and the herds of sheep were theoretically owned by the Indians themselves, but were held in trust by the Franciscan fathers.

Missions

From the earliest discovery of America, missions were established. The Spanish and the French were the most avid in this field, establishing Roman Catholic missions. The expedition of Coronado in 1542 had such men as Father Padilla, Descalona. Father Olmos worked with the Indians of Texas. In 1642 the first Protestant mission was established in Massachusetts by Mayhew and Eliot. From then on almost every denomination carried on this work.

Missouri

The word Missouri is from the Algonquian dialect and means the "Great muddy," a name given to the river. The Missouri Indians were made up of the Iowa, Oto and Missouri Indians. In the middle 1800's the tribes migrated to Nebraska. They were later broken up and many were "removed" to Oklahoma.

Mittaubscut

A former village of the Narraganset located along the Pawtuxet River in Rhode Island. This village was active around 1676 in Kent County.

Miwok

This is one of the largest Indian "Nations" in California. The name means "man." They lived mainly in central California.

Miwuk

See Miwok and Fuller.

Mixed-bloods

A name given to those Indians who mixed with the whites and raised families and so were no longer pure-blood Indians, sometimes called "half-breeds."

Moache

A division of the Ute who formerly roamed over the southern part of Colorado and northern New Mexico. These Indians were sometimes called the "Taos Utes" because they used to gather in large numbers around the Taos pueblo in New Mexico. In March 2, 1868, they made a treaty with the government which defined the boundaries of their reservation.

Moah

This is the "wolf" gens of the Potawatomi.

Moapariats

This was a band of Paiutes who formerly lived near the Moapa Valley in Nevada. They were known as the "mosquito creek people."

Mobile

This Muskhogean tribe is supposed to have originated near Choctaw Bluff in Clark County, Alabama. The Mobile

Indians were very friendly to the French. In 1708 they were attacked by the Catawba, Cherokee and Alibamu. The name means "doubtful." The trade language known as the Chickasaw trade language and also as the Mobile trade language was used from Florida to Louisiana and north to Ohio. The Mobile Indians were mainly people of agriculture. After 1761, the tribe lost its distinction as a tribe and was lost to history.

Mobile trade language
See Mobile.

Mocama
These Indians of the Timucua lived near the present site of St. Augustine in Florida. The name means "on the coast."

Moccasin
There are generally two types of moccasins worn by most of the Indian tribes of the United States. The western or plains tribes wore a moccasin with a hard sole and a soft upper. The eastern or woodland Indians wore a moccasin with a soft sole and the upper part soft also. The woodland Indian had the typical "puckered toe" type of stitching. Certain tribes of the southeastern part of Texas did not wear moccasins but generally went barefoot, as did the tribes of the Northwest Coast Indians. It was not the usual thing for the women to wear the moccasin.

The shapes and designs and materials used in the making of the moccasin varied from tribe to tribe. This was influenced by the type of country lived in and the animals that were available for use. Dyes from plants such as roots, berries and leaves were used for designs as well as porcupine quills and later on, beads, shells and buttons. The design sometimes had a symbolism and the colors used also had a special meaning. Some moccasins were used for special ceremonies. Deer skin was the most generally used skin.

Moccason

The former way of spelling moccasin (q.v.). Derived from the eastern Algonquian dialects.

Mochgonnekonck

A former village of the Long Island, New York, Indians located near the present location of Manhasset, Long Island, New York.

Mochilagua

This pueblo of the Opata was visited by Coronado in 1540. The pueblo was located in northwestern New Mexico in the vicinity of Arizpe along the Sonora River.

Mocho

This Apache chief was prominent in Texas history in the 18th century. His name means "the cropped one," referring to an ear that he lost in a fight. The Spanish rulers at the time did not like "El Mocho" and did their best to kill him; after several plots failed they had to make peace with him. In 1784, he was finally put to death by the government.

Moctobi

This small band lived near the Gulf Coast around what is now Biloxi, Mississippi. They were mentioned by Iberville in 1699. These people belonged to the Siouan linguistic stock. The band disappeared shortly after the settlement and it is assumed that the tribe was broken up by smallpox and warfare; those who did survive were absorbed by the Choctaw and Caddo.

Mocuck

A term used to describe the birchbark container in which maple sugar was stored. This container would hold about forty pounds of sugar. The word is derived from the Chippewa and Algonquian dialects "ma'ka'k." The word has been spelled in various ways throughout the northeastern United States and Canada.

Modoc

These Indians lived in the area of northern California and Oregon. The Modoc language is much like that of the Klamath. The Modocs lived in the areas around Modoc Lake, Tule Lake and in the Valley of the Lost River. In 1864 the Modoc and the Klamath ceded their land to the United States and were moved to a reservation. In 1870 a chief named Kintpuash (q.v.) led a band which brought on the Modoc war (1872 to 1873).

An important element of the diet of the Modocs was water lily buds.

Moenkapi

This small settlement about 40 miles northwest of Oraibi in Arizona near the present town of Tuba City was used by the Hopi during the growing season. This village was seen by Oñate in 1604.

Mogg

A chief of the Abnaki in Maine. This chief had been converted to Christianity. In 1722 a Colonel Westbrook attacked and burned the Indian village. In 1724 the English killed many of the Indians. Mogg is written about in Whittier's poem "Mogg Megone."

Mogollon

This name was given to those Apache Indians who lived in the mountains of Mogollón in New Mexico and Arizona. The mountains were named after the Spanish governor of New Mexico in 1712, Juan Ignacio Flores Mogollón.

Mohanet

This was a settlement of the Iroquois, located along the eastern side of the Susquehanna River in Pennsylvania.

Mohave

This was a large tribe of the Yumans who lived along the Colorado River. They made no canoes but instead they used rafts made of reeds tied in bundles. These people did

much tattooing. Most of their food was raised. The name
Mohave means "three mountains," a name used to describe
the type of rock formation in the area in which they lived.

Mohawk
John Mohawk, see Odiserundy.

Mohawk
The name Mohawk means "they eat live things," sometimes also known as "man eaters." This was the most east-
erly of the Iroquoian confederacy. The Dutch and the Mohawk Indians carried on a large amount of trade. They
traded firearms which made them very powerful against
their neighbors the Delawares and the Munsee. The main
villages of the Mohawk were around Lake Mohawk in New
York state.

Mohegan
This Algonquian tribe lived near what is now New London, Connecticut. After the death of King Philip in 1676,
the Mohegan became the only strong tribe left in the New
England area.

Mohegan
Mohegan, Connecticut, see Sauquonckackock.

Mohock
This term was used by the early colonists to denote a
tough person or what would be our present "mugger" or
gangster. The early term was derived from the tough Mohawk (q.v.) Indians and was used in England as mohock
in the 18th century to describe street gangs.

Mohominge
A village of the Powhatan, located near the falls of the
James River in Richmond, Virginia. The village was active
around 1612.

Mohongo

This was the wife of Kihegashugah, a chief of the Osage. She was taken from New Orleans in 1827 and sent to France, where she and two other Indians were treated royally. The party died on the return voyage from the effects of small-pox.

Moich

The Virginia Indian word for filthy.

Moingwena

This small band of the Illinois was located near what is now Peoria, Illinois. It was visited by Joliet in 1673. Shortly after 1700, the tribe banded together with the Peoria and their name was not used after that.

Mojualuna

A former village of the Taos located north of the present Taos, New Mexico.

Mokaich

This was the Mountain Lion clan of the Keresan pueblos of San Felipe, Sia and Cochiti of New Mexico. They lived in the Mt. San Mateo area. They became extinct in the early days of the settlement.

Monanaw

The Virginia Indian term for the bird known as the turkey.

Monattecow

The Virginia Indian word for the fawn.

Mongolian

This is one of the major divisions of the human race.

Monida

Monida, Montana, see Winnemucca.

Monk's Mound

A large Ohio mound, so called because of a group of Trappist monks who lived in the area. See Cahokia mound.

Monnonfacqueo

The Powhatan word for bear, see also amonsoquath.

Monongahela

A river in Pennsylvania and also the name of the early American whiskey which was produced in the areas along the Monongahela River. The name is Algonquian.

Mono-Paviotso

This was one of the three divisions of the Shoshonean tribes of the great plateau area of California, Oregon and Nevada. This included the Mono of California, the Snake of Oregon and the Paiute of Nevada.

Monswidishianun

This was the division or phratry of the Menominee known as the Moose Phratry.

Montauk

A group of Indians that lived on the extreme eastern end of Long Island in New York. These people were closely related to the Indians of Massachusetts. The chief village of the Montauk was located at Ft. Pond near what is now Montauk Point. In 1875 the last full-blooded chief died (David Pharaoh).

Monterey

The Monterey Indians of Monterey County in California belonged to the Costanoan tribe in 1856.

Montezuma

This man, known as Carlos Montezuma, was a full-blooded Apache. He was born about 1866 near the Mazatzal Mountains in the southeastern part of Arizona. In 1871 he was taken prisoner by the Pima and taken to the Superstition Mountains in Arizona. He was sold by the Pima to a Mr. C. Gentile, a native of Italy who was prospecting in Arizona. Montezuma's Indian name was Wasajah, meaning "beckoning." He was taken to Chicago by Mr. Gentile and given the name of Carlos Montezuma. He was sent to school and later on he attended the University of Illinois at Urbana and also attended the Chicago Medical School. From 1890 to 1896 he served as a doctor at the Shoshone reservation in North Dakota. He left the Indian service to return to Chicago to teach at the College of Physicians and Surgeons (1907).

Montezuma Castle

This is a pre-historic cliff dwelling located along Beaver Creek and near the Verde River in Central Arizona. So called because it was supposed to have been occupied by the Aztecs of Mexico.

Montezuma Castle National Monument

This is a large several-story pueblo located near Camp Verde, Arizona, near U.S. Highway 89. Many interesting finds have been made here. There is also a small museum.

Moose

There are various ways of spelling moose by the Indians, such as "moos" of the Algonquian, "mos" by the Delawares, "monswa" by the Cree. They all, however, signify "he who strips off," which refers to the method of eating by the moose.

Moosehead Indians

This is the common name given to those Indians of the Penobscot who live around Moosehead Lake in Maine.

Moquats

This was a band of Paiutes which formerly lived near the Kingston mountains in California.

Moquelumnan Family
A linguistic stock, composed of the Miwok and other tribes of central California.

Moraine
A term used by geologists to describe the accumulation of rock and other material which is deposited by a glacier at its end.

Moratoc
This tribe lived along the Roanoke River in Virginia in 1586 and would not mix with the English in the area.

Moriches
Moriches, Long Island, New York, see Patchoag.

Mormon tea
See the Navajo, dl' oh' azihih.

Moroke
The Virginia Indian term for the tree known as the cedar.

Morphology
This is the science of structure and forms, such a form would be the skeleton of man.

Mortar
The mortar was used in various forms by nearly all of the Indians. They were made of wood, stone, bone or hides. A flat or hollow rock was used as a container and another rock was used to grind the grain in between. In some areas such as California, hollow or shallow places found on large boulders or on a hillside were used as a place to grind acorns. Wooden mortars were used by the Iroquois of New York and over into the Great Lakes regions. Rawhide basins were used by the Plains Indians and stone was used in the southwestern areas.

Mosaics
Several grave areas of California, Arizona and New Mex-

ico have fine specimens of mosaic work. Mainly bits of shell and bones are fastened onto handles and ceremonial objects with the pitch from trees and asphaltum.

Moshoquen
A village of the Abnaki located along the coast of Maine, active about 1616.

Mosilian
This village of the Delawares was located along the Delaware River in 1648. This is the present location of Trenton, New Jersey.

Mosquito Indians
During the Seminole War of 1835 to 1842, the Mosquito Indians played a large part. They derive their name from the Mosquito Lagoon which is located on the east coast of Florida and north of Cape Canaveral.

Moss
Moss was used by the Indians to make a form of cradle for their small babies. The baby was placed on a bed of moss which was then wrapped with deerskin. In the winter rabbit hair was added for warmth. The early settlers and those of the Hudson Bay Company who had small babies liked the idea so well that they too took up the idea for their own children.

Mota's Village
A village of the Potawatomi, located near Atwood in Indiana. The village was named for its chief.

Mother
See kick.

Mounds
Mounds are unusual formations made by pre-historic Indians. The effigy mounds are mainly found in the state of Wisconsin, although there have been others found in Ohio

(the serpent mound) and the bird mounds found in Georgia. Some mounds are made entirely of stone, others of fine dirt and still others have stones mixed in. The mounds were built long before the white settlement. The mounds themselves ranged from about three to six feet high and from 100 to 600 feet long. Very little is known of the actual life of the mound building people.

Mountain
See hill, pomotawh, romutton.

Mountain mahogany
This small tree is found in Navajo country. The bark from the roots of this tree is used to make a reddish brown dye.

Mount Vernon
Mount Vernon, Virginia, see Tauxenent.

Mouth
See mettone.

Movwiats
This was a band of the Paiutes who formerly lived in the southeastern part of Nevada in 1873.

Mowkowk
See mocuck.

Moxus
A chief of the Abnaki. He was the first signer of a treaty with the English in Maine (1699). In 1689 it was Moxus who captured Pemaquid from the English.

Moytoy
A chief of the Cherokee in Tennessee. It was he who led his people to the English and pledged themselves to be loyal subjects to King George. Moytoy, however, later on became bitter enemies of the English.

Mozeemlek

These were supposed to be a group of Indians who lived in the areas of the western Dakotas and Wyoming. It was said that they wore beards, had copper axes and that they dressed like whites. It was also said that they lived along a river which emptied into a large salt lake.

Msickquatash

The Narraganset word for corn as used in succotash (q.v.).

Muffanek

The Virginia Indian term for the squirrel.

Mufknis

The Virginia Indian term for the eyes.

Mufsetagwaioh

The Powhatan Indian word for a circle.

Mugg

A chief of the Arosaguntacook who fought with his people against the English in 1675. The English had gathered at a place which is now Scarboro, Maine. He treated his prisoners kindly, but later on when he came in peace he was taken prisoner and taken to Boston. He was later released but for this bad treatment he again attacked Black Point and was killed on May 16, 1677.

Mugwump

A political term used to denote someone who is an independent, who leaves his party as a protest and may even join the opposing side. The term was used in early New England and is derived from the Massachusetts dialect of the Algonquian, in which it meant a "man of great abilities," in other words he feels that he is better than the rest.

Mugwumpery

See Mugwump.

Muk

This was the "beaver clan" of the Potawatomi.

Mulatos

These were the people of west Texas who were baptized at the San José mission in 1784.

Mulatto town

This was a former town of the Seminoles located in Alachua county in northern Florida. Sometimes known as Mulatto Girls' Town.

Muller

A muller used by the Indians was usually a flat stone upon which grain was placed and then another flat stone placed on top. This was then rubbed back and forth to grind the grain. See mortar.

Mummychog

In the Narraganset dialect of the Algonquian, this was the name used to describe the killifish found along the northeast coast of the United States. The name means "he who travels together." Also used at one time for the smelt. Sometimes called Mummy.

Mundua

The word for whippoorwill, the name means "one that keeps calling or sounding."

Munsee

This was one of the three divisions of the Delaware. They formerly lived along the Delaware River and in New York, New Jersey and Pennsylvania. Their main village was at Minisink in Sussex County in New Jersey. Also spelled Munsi.

Murphy

Murphy, North Carolina, see Smith,

Muruam

This was a Texas tribe, most of its members were baptized at the beginning of the 18th century at the missions located at San Antonio in Texas. It is supposed that these Indians were Tonkawan and it is possible that some were members of the Ticmamare tribes.

Murzibusi

This was the bean clan of the Yoki or rain phratry of the Hopi Indians of Arizona.

Musalakun

This name was used to denote all of those Pomo Indians that lived along the Russian River south to a village called Geyserville in California.

Muscongus

A village of the Abnaki located in Lincoln county in Maine.

Mushalatubbee

A chief of the Choctaw who died of smallpox in Arkansas on September 30, 1838. He was a friend of Lafayette. He led his warriors against the Creeks with Jackson in the War of 1812.

Music

Music was an important part of Indian life, as every ceremony and important individual act was accompanied by music. This was generally vocal, often with accompaniment in a different rhythm. Instruments used were drums, various types of rattles, bone, wood or pottery flutes and whistles, and notched sticks which were rubbed with another stick. A few tribes used a musical bow. It was considered very important to sing songs accurately, and clans had special officers to insure the exact rendition and transmission of songs.

Muskeg

Meaning a "grassy bog," marsh or swamp. A term used by the Chippewa "muskig," and in the Kickapoo language "maskyag." Used by the Indians of the Great Lakes and along the Canadian border.

Muskhogean

This was a linguistic family, comprising the Choctaw, Creeks, Chickasaw, and Seminole. The term is Algonquian and is derived from Muskeg (q.v.). At the time of the settlement, it was estimated that there were over 50,000 Muskhogean. The general custom was to bind the heads of children to achieve a flat head. The name "flatheads" was given to many of these Indians, the Choctaw in particular.

Muskig

Chippewa for swamp or bog. See Muskeg.

Muskrat

See ofafquws.

Muskwessu

Abnaki for muskrat. See musquash.

Muspa

A village of the Calusa located along the southwest coast of Florida in 1570. The village is marked on some old English maps as Punta de Muspa. In the late 18th century these people were driven to the Florida Keys by the Seminoles.

Musquash

In the various dialects this refers to the muskrat and the reddish color of its fur, the name means "it is red."

Mussauco

An Indian village near Hartford, Connecticut, captured by the Uncas in 1654.

Muswasipi

Chippewa for the "Moose River."

Mutsun

A village of the Costanoan located near the San Juan Bautista mission in San Benito County in California. The name was also used for a linguistic family of those Indians who lived north of the Golden Gate and southward to below Monterey.

Muttamussinsack

A former village of the Powhatan located along the north side of the Rappahannock River in Caroline County in Virginia.

Muyi

This was the "mole clan" of the Hopi of Arizona.

Mystic

Mystic, Connecticut, meaning "great tidal river," because of the high tides in the area. The name was given to several villages in New England, one in Middlesex County in Massachusetts in 1649 and the other at Pequot village on the western side of the Mystic River near the present site of Mystic, Connecticut. The Pequot village was burned by the English in 1637.

N

Naa gar nep

See Nagonub, a chief of the Chippewas.

Naantam

The Virginia Indian term used to describe the wolf.

Naapope

A warrior of the Fox and Sauk. See Nahpope.

Nabedache

The ancient name of the "salt people" of the southern Caddoan confederacy. This village was located in San Pedro County in Texas.

Nabeyxa

A possible Caddoan tribe mentioned by Douay in 1691, located in the northeastern part of Texas.

Nabobish

Meaning "poor soup." This was a village of the Chippewa and was named after its chief. The village was located near the mouth of the Saginaw River in Michigan.

Nacachau

One of the nine tribes in Texas which was mentioned by the early explorer Francisco de Jesús María in 1691. A mission was established for this tribe which become known as the San Francisco de los Neches.

Nacaniche

This Caddoan tribe first was known by the French in 1690. They lived mainly along the Trinity River in Texas. They came under the rule of the Nacogdoches in the first part of the 19th century.

Nacbuc

A village of the Chumashan located in Ventura County in California. The Nacbuc village was active around 1542.

Nacheninga

A chief of the Iowa. The name means "no heart of fear," a name given to this chief because of his brave upstanding qualities. His son of the same name was painted by Catlin while he visited Washington, D. C., on official business and now is in the collections of the National Museum in Washington.

Nacisi

A small Caddoan tribe which lived along the Red River in Louisiana. They were first mentioned by Joutel in 1687. These people drifted to the area of the Nacogdoche (q.v.) in Texas.

Nacogdoche

One of the nine main tribes of Texas. Their main village was located in the same general area of the present city of Nacogdoches in Texas.

Nacotchtank

A tribe of the Conoy who lived along the Anacostia River, a branch of the Potomac River in Washington. Their main village was located near the present site of Anacostia.

Nadowa

A term used by many Indians to describe the Siouan, Iroquois, Iowa, Dakota, Teton and others. It was used for the rattlesnake. The name means mainly "he who seeks and eats flesh." The name applied often to the Iroquois.

Nagonabe

This was the name of a former Chippewa village located in the southern part of Michigan.

Nagonub

This was a Chippewa Indian who was born about 1815.

He came to the attention of General Lewis Cass. Nagonub was a favorite with the white ladies. He signed a treaty as chief of the Fond du Lac Chippewa at La Pointe, Wisconsin, in October 4, 1842. His portrait was painted by J. O. Lewis. This painting was destroyed in a fire at Washington, D. C., in 1865.

Naguatex

A Caddoan village visited by De Soto in 1542. Located in what is now Clark County in Arkansas.

Naguchee

A village of the Cherokee Indians, located at the head of the Chattahoochee River in Habersham County, Georgia.

Nahapassumkeck

A village of the Massachusetts Indians located in the northern part of Plymouth County in 1616.

Nahche

"The mischievous one," a name given to the second son of Cochise. He was a leading figure in raids on the early settlements in Arizona and New Mexico. Nahche was captured by General Miles and was confined to prison at Fort Sill in Oklahoma; he resided there and was about 49 years old in 1907.

Nahelta

A subdivision of the Chasta tribes of Oregon.

Nahpope

A warrior in the Black Hawk war, who fought against the Americans at Wisconsin Heights along the Wisconsin River near what is now Sauk City in Wisconsin. His portrait was painted by Catlin. He was released from prison at Jefferson Barracks and nothing more was heard of him.

Nahu

This was the Badger phratry of the Hopi of Arizona.

Nahuey

A village of the Chumashan located near the Purísima mission near what is now Santa Barbara, California.

Naig

A Costanoan village located near the Dolores Mission, San Francisco, California.

Nain

A mission built by the Moravian missionaries in 1757 near what is now Bethlehem, Pennsylvania. Used mainly by the converted Delawares. In 1763 the mission was abandoned and the Indians were removed to Philadelphia.

Nakai

Meaning "white stranger," this referred to the Spanish explorers who came through New Mexico. This term was also used to describe some Navajos who were descended from a white woman who had been captured by the Utes in New Mexico.

Nakankoyo

A village of the Maidu located on the north fork of the Feather River in California. The name has been used to describe all of the people of the Feather River Valley.

Nakasinena

This division of the Arapaho lived in the area around Colorado Springs, Colorado, and north to the Bighorn Mountains. They were known by the early settlers as the Northern Arapahos. Their name means "the sagebrush people." They claim to be the mother tribe of the Arapahos.

Nakaydi

This was a group of White Mountain Apaches made up mainly of Mexicans which were captured by the Apaches and their descendants. The name refers to these people's method of walking with their toes turned out.

Naked

See nepowwer

Nakhopani

This was a clan of the Navajo which originated at the Zuñi pueblo in New Mexico near a lake called Naqopà. The name means a "horizontal streak which is on the ground."

Nakhpakhpa

This was a group of the Brulé Teton Sioux. The name means to "take down your leggings."

Nakota

A name given to themselves by the Dakota (q.v.).

Nakuimana

This was a small tribe of southern Cheyenne, known as the "bear people."

Naltunnetunne

This tribe of Athapascan people lived along the coast of Oregon near Chetco. Their name means "people among the mushrooms."

Namakagon

This was a former village of the Chippewa, located in western Wisconsin at the northern part of St. Croix Lake.

Namanu

This was a lower phratry of the beaver gens of the Menominee of Wisconsin.

Namassingakent

In 1608 this was a village of the Powhatan Confederacy, located along the southern bank of the Potomac River in Fairfax County in Virginia.

Namatha

This was a section or gens of the turtle clan of the Shawnee.

Namaycush

This is one of several names given to the trout found in the Great Lakes, also the Mackinaw trout.

Nambe

This is a group of people who lived about 15 miles north of Santa Fe, New Mexico, at the Tewa pueblo. They lived along the Nambe River. This pueblo was the main section of a Franciscan mission in the early 17th century. There is still a pueblo village at this location.

Nameaug

This was a Pequot settlement near New London, Connecticut, active around 1647. The name means "the fishing place."

Namegos

Chippewan for the lake trout. See Namaycush.

Namekus

The lake trout of the Cree dialect. See Namaycush.

Namequa

A Sauk Indian who was the only daughter of Black Hawk. She was considered to have been very beautiful.

Names

Indian names are rather difficult for the average person to understand, some give us some idea of the person named and others seem to have no connection at all. Indian names were often changed during the lifetime of the Indian. They were governed sometimes by circumstances such as birth, puberty, warfare or retirement from the very active life of the tribe. Some names were derived from dreams that the individual had or some event that happened at the birth of the child, i.e., Crazy Horse, so named because of a wild horse that ran through camp while he was being born and so some special significance was placed on this event. Some names were inherited. Some names were taken from individuals without their consent or taken for revenge. Modern day Indians have taken many Christian names, however, there are still many Indians who have the old Indian names. Usually when translating the name of an Indian it "loses something in the translation!" The Indian may have had a special meaning for his name, for example, Takaibodal, a Kiowa name, when translated means "smelly or stinking saddle blanket." One gets an impression that he never washed his blanket, however, to the Indian it meant that he was on the warpath so much that he didn't have time to take off his saddle blanket and so was a great warrior.

Added to this, the early settlers themselves were not well educated and could not read or write well so the names that they did put down were sometimes written as they "sounded" to them.

Nammais
This is the Virginia Indian word for fish.

Namontack
A Powhatan exchange student who was exchanged by Captain Newport in 1608 for an English boy named Thomas Savage. Each was to learn the ways, habits and language of the other. Namontack was sent to England and on the return voyage to Virginia, he was killed by a fellow Indian in 1610.

Nampa woman
This is a small problematical figure which was brought to light during a well-drilling operation at Nampa, Idaho, in 1889. The figure is of baked clay about an inch and a half high and was pumped to the surface from a depth of 300 feet.

Namskaket
An Indian village located in Barnstable County in Massachusetts. It was sold to the settlers in 1644.

Nana

A lower chief of the Chiricahua Apaches. He was a strong leader and made many bold raids into New Mexico. In August of 1881 he was driven across the Rio Grande into Mexico. Nana is also the Birch Clan of the Tewa of New Mexico.

Nanabozho

A great spirit who formed the earth and the beings that inhabit the earth. It was said that he lived in the far north in the "ice country." This Algonquian belief of the formation of the earth was rather widespread. It was believed that such things as flint and fire were provided by Nanabozho.

Nanahuani

A former village of the Chumashan located on Santa Cruz island in California.

Nanamakewuk

This was the thunder gens of the Sauk and Fox Indians of Wisconsin and Michigan.

Nananawi

This was a phratry of the Hopi of New Mexico and was the sand or earth clan. Also a species of lizard found in the desert.

Nanatlugunyi

This was a settlement of the Cherokee known as the spruce tree place. Located at the present site of Jonesboro in Washington County in Tennessee.

Nanatsoho

A village of the Caddo Confederacy located along the Red River in Louisiana. Visited by Joutel in 1687.

Nanawonggabe

This was the main chief of the Chippewa who lived around Lake Superior. He was the father of the so-called "Chippewa Princess" who was the only female Chippewa allowed to become a warrior and to wear warrior's clothes and to participate in ceremonies dealing with warfare.

Nanepashemet

A chief of the Nipmuc Indians who lived in Middlesex County in Massachusetts, near Medford. He was killed in 1619 and his widow assumed his position and was known as the Squaw chief or sachem.

Nang

This was the stone clan of the Tewa of the San Juan area of New Mexico.

Nanibas

A tribe of the Choctaws who lived along the Alabama River and Mobile Bay. They were known as the fish eaters. After the middle of the 18th century they were absorbed by the Mobile Indians.

Nanihaba

A former Choctaw town, located at the present site of the town of Neshoba in Mississippi.

Nanikypusson

A Shawnee chief who was sent to sign a treaty of peace from Ohio. Sir William Johnson was the signer on behalf of the British government. The treaty was signed at Johnson Hall in New York.

Nansemond

A tribe of the Powhatan who lived along the James River in Virginia.

Nanticoke

This is an Algonquian tribe which lived mainly along

the Nanticoke River in Maryland. Their village was active around 1608. They were connected with the Delawares and the Conoy. In 1748, after many difficulties with the early settlers, they moved north up along the Susquehanna River and joined the Iroquois in New York State.

Nanuntenoo

A chief of the Narraganset. He was the first signer of the treaty of October, 1675. He fought against the English and was a strong supporter of King Philip. He was captured by the English in 1676 and was taken to Stonington, Connecticut, where he was killed by the English and his head cut off and sent to the city fathers of Hartford.

Napa

In 1877 this was listed as a tribe of the Patwin. The name is now given to a county and a city in California.

Napeshneeduta

A Sioux and the first Dakota full-blooded Indian to be baptized and accepted into the Christian church. He was baptized on February 21, 1840, and was given the name of Joseph Napeshnee. After several marriages he moved to an Indian village below Fort Snelling and became ill with fever. Because he had changed his faith his own people refused to feed or help him. He recovered and in 1862, like other Christianized Indians, he turned against his own people and fought against them on the side of the whites. He died in July, 1870.

Napetaca

A village of the Yustaga. It was the scene of one of the worst battles the Indians had against De Soto in Florida in 1539.

Napissa

A band or division of the Chickasaw; the name disappeared in the early 18th century.

Naraak

The Powhatan Indian word for the cedar tree.

Narraganset

One of the leading Algonquian tribes that lived in Rhode Island and along the Providence River. Because they lived on islands and away from the rest of the tribes, they did not suffer such losses from smallpox as did the other tribes and so after the plague they became very powerful. During King Philip's war, they fought a large battle in the celebrated swamp near Kingston, Rhode Island. On December 19, 1675, they lost over a thousand men. This and disease finally broke the once powerful Narraganset.

Nascapee

This is the most northeasterly of the Algonquian tribes who live along the St. Lawrence river and up into Labrador.

Nasheakusk

This was the eldest son of Black Hawk, whose name means "loud thunder." A portrait was painted by Samuel M. Brookes while Nasheakusk was a prisoner at Fort Monroe in Virginia. The portrait later became the property of the State Historical Society of Wisconsin at Madison.

Nashobah

A village of the Christian Indians located near Littleton, Massachusetts. During King Philip's War (1675) the people of this village were moved to Concord, Massachusetts. At that time they numbered 50.

Nashua

A tribe of Massachusetts Indians who fought in King Philip's War. They formerly lived around Worcester, Massachusetts. After the Indian war they were captured and most of the tribe were sold as slaves.

Nasiampaa

A tribe of the Mdewakanton Sioux who lived along the Mississippi River near St. Paul, Minnesota.

Nasoni
This tribe of the Caddo of Texas formerly lived along the Nacogdoche River. In 1719 a Spanish mission was set up in their midst. They are last mentioned in the Texas census of 1790.

Nassauaketon
This was one of the four divisions of the Ottawa who lived in northern Wisconsin and Michigan at the end of the 17th century. Their name means "forked river people," a name given them because they came from an area where several rivers joined together.

Natchez
A tribe that lived where the present site of Natchez, Mississippi, is located. They were first visited by the French in 1682. These people raised their food and practised head flattening. The language of the Natchez is made up of Muskhogean dialects.

Nation
A term used to denote the "five civilized tribes," Oklahoma, Choctaw, Chickasaw, Creek, and the Cherokee. The term formerly included many others such as the Catawba. The term was used to include those tribes of the Gulf States of the United States.

National Indian Association
A society that was organized in 1879 by interested whites. Organized to prevent "encroachments of the white settlers on the Indian." They also have published a paper called "The Indian's Friend."

Nattahattawants
A Christianized Indian chief who lived near what is now Concord, Massachusetts. He sold a large parcel of land to the whites for which he received in return . . . six lengths of beads, a waistcoat, and a pair of pants! He had a son named John Tahattawan who led the "praying Indians" who lived at Nashobah, Massachusetts.

Natuwanpika

A traditional stopping off place for the bear clan of the Hopi. It is located near the present town of Oraibi, Arizona.

Naugatuck

Naugatuck, Connecticut, see Paugusset.

Nauhaught

A Christian Indian of Massachusetts also known as Elisha. He was a deacon of an Indian church at Yarmouth, Massachusetts. He is remembered by Whittier's poem "Nauhaught the Deacon."

Naumkeag

An ancient Indian settlement, abandoned before the settlement by the whites. It was located at Salem, Massachusetts. Formerly used by the Pennacook Indians.

Nauset

A tribe of Algonquians that formerly lived on Cape Code in Massachusetts.

Nauvasa

One of the northernmost towns of the Catawbas of South Carolina. Located along the Santee River. The Catawbas now live on a reservation near Rock Hill, South Carolina.

Navaho

See Navajo.

Navahu

A former Tewa village or pueblo located west of the Santa Clara pueblo in New Mexico. The name means "a large cultivated area."

Navajo

This was a strong Athapascan tribe that lived in Arizona and New Mexico. The Navajos were visited by Oñate in 1598. The Navajo were very warlike and usually won their battles against the whites. They were beaten by

Colonel "Kit" Carson, who attacked them in 1863 and killed most of their sheep and so more or less starved them into submission. In 1867 there were 7,300 Navajos held in prisons. In 1906 there were over 28,000 Navajos. In a treaty with the United States at Canyon de Chelly in Arizona on September 9, 1849, the Navajo made peace and acknowledged the rule of the United States.

Navajo National Monument

A national monument of 13th Century pueblos located west of Kayenta, Arizona, in the Tsegi Canyon. It is about 130 miles from Flagstaff, Arizona. The two great pueblos located here are called Keetseel and Betatakin.

Navajo tea

A plant used by the Navajo for the making of an orange dye.

Navasink

This is a branch of the Delawares who lived in the highlands of New Jersey. Hendrick Hudson saw them on his way up the Hudson River in New York. He says that they were "clothed in feathers and wore copper ornaments."

Navawi

This is the name given to a group of Tewa ruins located in the Santa Clara Canyon southwest of San Ildefonso in New Mexico. The name means "the place of the trap."

Nawacaten

In 1608 this was a village of the Powhatans located along the banks of the Rappahannock River in Richmond County, Virginia.

Nayakolole

A village of the Willopah located in Pacific County in Washington.

Neamathla

Neamathla was a chief of the Seminoles who signed a

treaty at Camp Moultrie on September 18, 1823, with the United States. This treaty gave the Americans five million acres of land. However, most of the Seminoles did not agree with this arrangement and a war started led by Osceola. Neamathla left the Seminoles and joined the Creeks after this difficulty. By birth he was a Creek.

Neapope
A warrior of the Black Hawk War. See Nahpope.

Nechan
The Virginia Indian word for a child.

Neche
A tribe of Indians that lived along the Neches River in Texas near the present town of Nacogdoches, Texas. Farming was the main method of securing a food supply, though some hunting was done for bison.

Neckaun
The Powhatan Indian word for a child.

Neconga
A former village of the Miami, located in Miami County in Indiana.

Needle
The needle as we know it was a rare thing with the Indian. Some needles were made from bone and wood, also the spines from cactus and from the locust tree were used. The iron needle was brought over by the settlers; horsehair, human hair and certain plant fibers were used for thread.

Negahnquet
The first full-blooded Indian in the United States to become a fully ordained Catholic Priest was Albert Negahnquet. He was a Potawatomi Indian who entered the Catholic Mission school which was conducted by the Benedictine Monks at Sacred Heart Mission in Oklahoma. Later he

studied at Rome and in 1903 he was ordained as a Priest. He then returned to the United States to do religious work among the Indians.

Negas
A village of the Abnaki, located near what is now Penobscot, Maine.

Negeifp
This is the Virginia Indian term for I am full.

Negro slaves
Negro slaves were brought over in 1501 to work in place of the Indian slaves because they seemed stronger and easier to control. Negro and Indian mixed rather freely and many Indian tribes of today have little resemblance to the Indian.

Negrotown
A Seminole village which was used by escaped negro slaves. It was burned to the ground by the Americans in 1836.

Negwagon
This was a well-known chief of the Ottawa who lived in the Michilimackinac region of Michigan. He lost a son in the War of 1812. He then adopted a son known as Austin E. Wing. One time while he was alone in camp some English soldiers came by and saw that he was flying the American flag. They ordered him to take it down, which he did. He then wrapped the flag around his arm and took out his tomahawk and said "Englishmen, Negwagon is a friend of the Americans. He has but one heart and one flag; if you take one you must take the other." He was then left in peace. After the war he and his family would visit Detroit by canoe . . . each with an American flag flying from the stern. There formerly was a county in Michigan named after him but this has since been changed.

Nemat
The Powhatan Indian word for brother.

Neokautah
This was a Winnebago chief whose village was located at the present site of Neenah, Wisconsin. He was also a signer of a treaty which was executed at Prairie du Chien, Wisconsin, on August 19, 1825.

Neolithic
This is the age generally accepted as the period when man first domesticated animals and made pottery and raised crops.

Nepowwer
The Virginia Indian term for naked.

Neputts
The Virginia Indian term for a tooth.

Neron
A chief of the Onondaga tribe of the Iroquois. He was captured by the French in 1663 after it was said that he had burned over 80 prisoners and had killed over 60 of the enemy with his own hands. The French gave him the name Neron because of his cruelty.

Nererahhe
A peace chief of the Shawnee. He was present at the meeting of the Six Nations with Sir William Johnson at Johnson Hall, New York in April, 1774.

Nesâquake
An Indian settlement around 1643, located near what is now Smithtown, Long Island, New York.

Nescopeck
An Indian village located in Luzerne County, Pennsylvania. Formerly occupied by the Delawares, Iroquois and the Shawnee, it was abandoned in 1779.

Neshaw

The Algonquian name for the eels found off the coast of Massachusetts.

Nespelim

A tribe of the Salish living on Nespelim Creek, a tributary of the Columbia.

Neswage

In 1841 this chief of the Delawares was attacked by the Sioux at a place in Dallas County, Idaho; all but one was killed. In retaliation, over 500 Sauk and Fox attacked the Sioux war party and killed them all. The battle took place with the Sioux within what is now Des Moines, Iowa.

Nethkeon

A Virginia Indian term meaning nose.

Netop

This was a word used by the English as a form of greeting when they met the Indians. It means literally "friend" or "comrade" or "be my woman."

Neutrals

This was a division of the Iroquois, so called because they were neutral in the known wars between the Iroquois and the Hurons. They lived around Seneca Lake in New York.

Nevada City

Nevada City, California, see Ustoma.

Newark mounds

These are a series of Indian mounds and enclosures which have been recorded in Licking County, Newark, Ohio.

Newburn

Newburn, North Carolina, see Tuscarora.

Newcomer

A village of the Delawares, named after its chief, Newcomer. Located in 1766 at the present site of New Comerstown in Ohio. According to some authorities it was the chief's wife who was named Newcomer.

New Comerstown
See Newcomer.

New Haven
New Haven, Connecticut, see Quinnipiac.

New London
New London, Connecticut, see Stonington. Also see Pequot.

New Orleans
New Orleans, Louisiana, see Washa.

New Philadelphia
New Philadelphia, Ohio, see Schoenbrunn.

Newport
Newport, Oregon, see Tkhakiyu.

New Salem
New Salem, Illinois, see shickshack.

Newspapers
The first newspaper printed in any North American Indian language was the "Cherokee Phoenix" February 21, 1828. It was printed in English and Cherokee. The first issue of a semi monthly newspaper in the Shawnee language was the "Shawnee Sun," printed in March 1, 1835.

Newtown
A former Seneca village, located near Elmira in New York. The village was burned by General Sullivan in 1779.

Nez Percés
The Nez Percés were given this name because of the practice of piercing their noses so that they could insert ornaments. They were seen by Lewis and Clark in what is

now Idaho and west to Oregon. They belonged to the Shahaptian tribes. The Nez Percés were almost always on friendly terms with the whites, with one main exception, which was the Nez Percés War of 1877.

Niagara
A place name of Iroquoian origin, first used by the Jesuits for a village in Youngstown now in Niagara County, New York.

Niantic
This Algonquian tribe became extinct shortly after the Pequot War of 1637. They formerly lived in Connecticut and Rhode Island.

Nikikouek
The name is derived from the Chippewa meaning the "otter people." These were people who lived along the northern shore of Lake Huron. They left their villages regularly to hunt and fish. In 1653 they fought a battle against the Iroquois.

Nimham
This chief of the Wappinger Indians who lived along the Hudson River tried to recover Indian land from the English. In 1762 it was said that he traveled to England to plead for his land claims. He received favorable replies to his plea but the Revolution stopped his claims. He fought on the side of the Americans and was killed at the battle of Kingsbridge on August 3, 1778.

Nimsewi
This was a small division of the Maidu who lived along what was known as Butte Creek in Butte County, California.

Ninivay
See Ninivois, a Potawatomi chief.

Ninivois

This Potawatomi was a chief of the Fox and fought with Pontiac in 1763 at the siege of Detroit. His name has also been spelled Ninivay.

Nipinichsen

A village of the Manhattan Indians located on the east bank of the Hudson River in New York, north of Spuyten Duyvil.

Nipissing

This was a tribe of Algonquians who were first visited by the French in 1613. They became converted by the missionaries and were staunch friends of the French in Canada.

Nisqualli

A small Salish tribe living at the southern end of Puget Sound, Washington.

Nissaouakouad

See Nissowaquet.

Nissowaquet

A chief of the Ottawa. He lived most of his life at Michilimackinac, Michigan. In 1721 he was made head chief. His sister, Domitilde, married Charles de Langlade of Wisconsin. His name is also spelled Nissaouakouad.

Nma

This is the sturgeon gens of the Potawatomi.

Noatwhelama

The Indian name of Chief Newcomer. See Newcomer.

Nocake

This is an Indian food which was adapted by the early settlers. Its name is Algonquian and it consists mainly of parched corn meal which is eaten with a little water.

Nochpeem

This was a band of the Wappinger Indians that lived at

the present site of Matteawan in Dutchess County in New York. Their principal village was called Canopus, after their chief.

Noewe
Mentioned by Bartram in his travels in 1792 as a Cherokee settlement located in western North Carolina.

Nogales
This is a ruined pueblo located in the southeastern part of New Mexico. The name is Spanish and means "walnuts."

Noka
This was the bear foot gens of the Chippewa of Wisconsin and Michigan. Noka was also a chief of the Chippewa, known too as Old Noka. He led his people against the Mdewakanton at Crow Wing, Minnesota, in 1768.

Nokehick
The Narraganset dialect for parched corn meal, see Nocake.

Nondas
A village of the Senecas near Nunda in Livingston County, New York. This village was named after its chief. In 1791, it was visited by Colonel Thomas Procter. The name means "high or steep hill."

Nonfsamats
The Powhatan Indian word for cold.

Nonotuc
An active Indian village in 1653, located near what is now Northampton, Massachusetts. They lived in peace with the English until King Philip's War in 1675.

Nooksak
A Salish tribe living on the Nooksak River in Washington. Closely related to the Suquamish.

Noquet

This was one of the early Algonquian tribes which the French encountered in the Green Bay, Wisconsin, area and near Lake Superior.

Norfolk

Norfolk, Virginia, see Richahake.

Norridgewock

This tribe of the Abnaki became very friendly with the French and thus became enemies of the English. In 1724 the English attacked the village of Norridgewock and so broke up the tribe that they joined with other tribes in the area. This village was located near what is now Norridgewock, Maine; the name means "the people who live near the still water, between the rapids."

Norse

In 985 A.D. and up through 1500, the Scandinavian explorers ventured to our shores and settled on the coast of Labrador and parts of Nova Scotia. About 1450, no reports were received from these early settlers and they were more or less forgotten. It is believed that the Indian learned to build houses of logs from these early settlers.

Northfield

Northfield, Massachusetts, see Squawkeag.

Norwalk

A tribe, led by their chief Mahackemo, possibly of the Paugusset, who sold their land to the whites in 1640. The present site of Norwalk, Connecticut.

Norwalk

Norwalk, Connecticut, see Wecquaesgeek.

Norwich

Norwich, Connecticut, see Uncas.

Nose
See mefkewe, also nethkeon.

Notched plates
Stone plates have been found in Alabama, Ohio, Mississippi and other Gulf states. It has been suggested that these plates which were found in the mounds of the areas mentioned were used for the grinding of paint pigments. Their actual use has not been definitely determined in all cases, however. Some of the plates have intricate designs of birds, snakes and other forms of life.

Nottoway
This Iroquoian tribe lived in the southeastern part of Virginia, calling themselves Cheroenhaka. The Nottoway River is named after them.

Noufvmon
Powhatan word for below.

Nowadaga
A village of the Mohawk located in Herkimer County. It was the main village in 1750.

Nowe
One of the Cherokee towns mentioned by Bartram in his travels of 1792.

Nows
The Virginia Indian word for father.

Nowwanus
The Virginia Indian term for lost.

Nubobish
Chippewa for "poor soup." See Nabobish.

Nucassee
This village of the Cherokee was located along the Little

Tennessee River near what is now the town of Franklin in Macon County, North Carolina.

Numinundgum
A term used by the Virginia Indians which means to cut the hair from a man's head.

Nummanemennaus
The Virginia Indian word for the smallpox.

Nunkom
The Massachusetts term for a "youth or young boy."

Nuppawe
The Virginia Indian term for sleep.

Nutnur
This village was located in California and was occupied by the Kalindaruk, a Costanoan family.

Nutonto
A village of the Chumashan, located near the Santa Barbara Mission in California.

Nutqiu
This was an organization of warriors of the Cheyenne, including at least six societies.

Nut-stone
A type of stone found in Ohio and other places. Also called cupstones (q.v.).

Nyack
The present Nyack, New York, was the site of an Indian village up until 1652, when it was sold to the whites. This was the former home of the Delawares. The name means "point."

Nyuchirhaan
A village of the Tuscarora, formerly located near what is now Lewiston in Niagara County in New York.

O

Oakfuskee

One of the largest Creek villages located along the Tallapoosa River in Cleburne County, Alabama.

Oapars

A settlement of the Papagos of Arizona, located along the Gila River. It was visited by Father Garcés in 1775.

Oatka

This village of the Senecas was located at the site of the present village of Scottsville in Monroe County, New York.

Obozi

This is one of the thirty-six tribes mentioned by Juan Sabeata to have been living in Texas in 1683.

Obsidian

This is a black volcanic glass used by the Indians for the making of bladed spear points and arrowpoints. Obsidian is not usually found east of the Rocky Mountains in the United States. Specimens and artifacts found in other parts of the United States, such as the mounds of Ohio, have specimens made of obsidian, which must have been secured by trade.

Ocala

Ocala, Florida, see Tocaste.

Occaneechi

This small Siouan group was first met by the whites in 1670 when they were living along the Roanoke River in Virginia. They also lived in North Carolina. One of their villages was located at the present site of Clarksville in Mecklenburg County, Virginia.

Occom

Samson Occom was a Christianized Mohegan Indian who lived in and around New London, Connecticut. He was sometimes called the "pious Mohegan." He wrote several hymns, one of them "Now the shades of night are gone"; this was made a part of the Episcopal service but was later dropped from the hymn books. In 1759 he preached in Suffolk County, Long Island, New York.

Occow

A type of yellow pike found in the northern Great Lakes, derived from the Cree dialects.

Ocheese

This former Indian village of the Seminoles was located at the present site of Ocheese in Jackson County, Florida. The name means "the people."

Ochete

In 1539, this village was visited by De Soto. It was located in the northwestern part of Florida, not far from the Gulf.

Ochionagueras

A chief of the Onondaga who was Christianized in August of 1654 and given the name of Jean Baptiste. He was a successful warrior who fought with the Iroquois against the Erie.

Ochqueu

Delaware for squaw (q.v.).

Ocmulgee

The name given to the main town of the Creeks which was located along the north fork of the Canadian River in Oklahoma. The name was also given to a lower Creek town in Dougherty County in Georgia.

Oconaluftee

This town of the Cherokee was formerly located along

the Oconaluftee River in North Carolina. The present location of Birdtown, North Carolina. At one time there was a large mound in this area. The name means "beside" or "next to."

Oconee
A settlement of the Cherokee, located along Seneca Creek near what is now Walhalla in Oconee County, South Carolina.

Oconostota
This was a former chief of the Cherokee. At first he became friends with the English, however, soon after the English did not treat his people very well and he changed sides and fought with the French. At a battle of Fort Prince George in South Carolina, Chief Oconostota and his warriors fought against over 1500 soldiers. He died in 1783.

Odiserundy
A Mohawk chieftain who fought in the Revolution in 1777. Sometimes called "John Mohawk" and also "Deseronto," meaning the "lightning has struck."

Ofafquws
The Virginia Indian term meaning muskrat.

Ofawas
The Powhatan Indian word for brass.

Ofayoh
The Virginia Indian term meaning yesterday.

Ogeechee
A small tribe of the Yuchi who lived along the Ogeechee River in Georgia. They were wiped out as a tribe by the Creeks in the early 1700's.

Oglala
This was one of the main divisions of the Teton Sioux. They lived in what is now South Dakota. It was their Indi-

ans who had such well known leaders as Crazy Horse and Sitting Bull. The Oglala Sioux were the terrors of the west. On July 5, 1925, in South Dakota, they made a peace treaty with the United States.

Ohawas
The Virginia Indian word for the bird known as the crow.

Oiscoss
See Oshkosh.

Ojibwa
This tribe is usually called Chippewa (q.v.).

Okafalaya
One of the three divisions into which the Choctaw of the lower Mississippi were divided. Their name means the "long or tall people."

Okalusa
A Choctaw settlement located in Kemper County, Mississippi, active around 1732.

Okhorime
The Virginia Indian word for crooked.

Okisko
This chief of the Weapemeoc was one of the chiefs who gave information to Sir Walter Raleigh about the surrounding country. He pledged himself and his people to the English ruler, but was accused of treachery and with plotting secretly to massacre the settlers.

Okommakamesit
A village of Christianized or "praying Indians" located at the site of what is now Marlborough, Massachusetts. The village was active around 1674.

Okow
See Occow.

Okuwa

This Tewa clan was the "cloud clan" of several villages of the Tewa, such as Santa Clara, San Ildefonso and Nambe, all in New Mexico.

Olamon

A Penobscot village near Greenbush, Maine. The name means "paint."

Old Estatoee

The name for two former Cherokee towns. See Estatoee.

Old Knife

A famous chief of the Pawnee. He was a signer of several treaties. A painting done by John Neagle in 1821 was later presented to the Pennsylvania Historical Society.

Old Mad Town

A village of the Upper Creeks along the Catawba River near what is now Birmingham, Alabama.

Old Town

Old Town, Florida, see Suwanee.

Old woman

See tumpfeis.

Olotaraca

A chief who fought against the Spanish with the French. He distinguished himself in a battle at a Spanish fort near the mouth of the St. John River in Florida.

Omaha

One of the main tribes of the Siouan family. They moved west from Ohio, following the rivers. Their name means "against the current or wind." In a treaty at Washington, D. C., they gave all of their lands west of the Missouri to the government (March 16, 1854). Their houses were made mainly of earth and sod. Skin tents were used when they

traveled. In 1802, smallpox almost wiped out the Omahas
and reduced their numbers to less than 300.

Omaskos

This gens of the Menominee was the "elk."

Omenaosse

A tribe visited by Joutel in 1687 who lived along the
Maligne River in Texas; they were possibly Karankawa
people.

Ommunise

A band of the Chippewa who formerly lived around
Carp Lake in Michigan. Their name means "he who gathers
wood for a fire."

Omowuh

This was the Hopi rain cloud clan.

Ona

One of the three villages of the Chilula Indians who
lived along Redwood Creek in California.

Onagatano

A place in the mountains where it was said that the
Apalachee were able to find gold in the 16th century. Much
of the gold of the Florida Indians was secured from the
Spanish wrecks off the coast of Florida.

Onaghee

A settlement of the Seneca which had been abandoned
before the settlement. Located at Hopewell in Ontario
County, New York.

Onasakenrat

A chief of the Mohawk who is noted for his translations
of the Bible and other religious works into his native language. He died suddenly on June 15, 1877.

Onawmanient

This was a tribe of the Powhatan who lived along the

southern bank of the Potomac River in what is now West-moreland County in Virginia.

Onbi
A village of the Costanoan. In 1815 this village was located about nine miles from the Santa Cruz Mission in California.

Ondatra
In the Huron dialect of the Iroquoian language this is the muskrat.

Oneida
One of the tribes of the Iroquois, located around Oneida Lake, New York. The name refers to a large standing rock which was near one of their main villages.

Oneka
This Connecticut Chief of the Mohegan was born in 1640 and died in 1710. He fought with his warriors and the English in the King Philip War. He had a son named Mahomet.

Onekagoncka
This was a former town of the Mohawks who lived at the present site of Fort Hunter in Montgomery County, New York. In 1634 the village was visited by Arent Van Curler, who said that the houses were full of corn. At the time of his visit, he said that many of the tribe had smallpox.

Oneniote
This village of the Cayuga, located at the present site of Oneida, New York, was the scene of a great battle with the Hurons, who almost destroyed the village. They sent to the neighboring Mohawk towns for men and women to come and marry all of the single individuals in the town. This was a common thing for the Iroquois nations to do so that they would not be wiped out completely.

Oneota
A tribe of the Sioux in Nebraska, known until 1700.

One-seeded juniper
A plant used by the Navajo. See gad.

Onondaga
This was an important tribe of the Iroquois nation. The name means "on the top of." They lived in what is now Onondaga County in New York State.

Onondaga
An Iroquois reservation under the jurisdiction of the State of New York.

Ontikehomawck
A former village of the Stockbridge Indians of Rensselaer County in New York.

Ontonagon
The name means "my dish," so called because an Indian woman dropped a dish into the water and it sank to the bottom and she exclaimed "my dish, my dish!" This river in upper Michigan is still called Ontonagon.

Ontwaganha
Iroquoian for a foreigner, in other words one who speaks another language that is not understood.

Onuatuc
A village of the Algonquian, located along the Patuxent River in Calvert County, Maryland.

Oohinanpa
A band of Western Sioux.

Oony
A Choctaw town, located at the present site of Pinkney Mill in Newton County, Mississippi.

Ootun
This is the Powhatan word used to describe cheese or a milk product that has curdled.

Opa

The fourth village of the Chilula villages located along Redwood Creek in California.

Opechancanough

A chief of the Powhatan Indians of Virginia. It was he who captured Captain John Smith. After Smith's release, he went to the camp of Opechancanough on the pretense of buying food, however, he grabbed the chief and at gunpoint took him away. The Indians came with loads of food to ransom their chief. This did not agree with the chief who plotted secretly to attack Jamestown. One Indian who was a Christianized Indian told the settlers of the plot but too late to stop the attack. On March 22, 1622, Opechancanough attacked the settlement. On April 18, 1644, he was carried into battle on a litter and was captured and later killed by one of the men who guarded him.

Opok

A settlement of the Maidu located near the forks of the Cosumnes River in Eldorado County in California.

Opomens

The Virginia Indian term for the tree known as the chestnut.

Opommins

The Powhatan Indian word for chestnut.

Oponays

A settlement of the Seminoles, located in Hillsboro County, in the western part of Florida.

Opossum

See aposoum.

Oraibi

This was the largest village of the Hopi, located in the northeastern part of Arizona. The name means "the rock place."

Oratamin

A chief of the Hackensack in the early 17th century. After the Dutch attacked and killed most of the Indians at Pavonia, New Jersey, February of 1643, the Indians arose to avenge this outrage. A treaty was made which was promptly broken. Chief Oratamin died around 1667.

Oraton

See Oratamin.

Oregon

See Orejones.

Orejones

A name given by the Spanish to the Indians of the Northwest Coast, meaning the people with the "big ears," so called because of the large ornaments that they wore in their ears which stretched them. Also said to be the name from which Oregon was derived; this was done to distinguish the California Indians from the Indians of Oregon.

Orenda

This was a word used by the Iroquois for an unseen force, such as magical power or mystery.

Oronacah

This term is used by the Virginia Indians and is used to describe any ground that has been prepared and planted with corn.

Osage

This western division of the Sioux lived in Kansas, Missouri and Illinois. This was one of the most important divisions of the Sioux. They were first met by the whites in 1673 by Marquette.

Osanalgi

This clan of the Creeks was known as the "otter people."

Osass
This was a sub-phratry of the muskrat gens of the Menominee of Wisconsin and Michigan.

Oscalui
This was a village of the Conestoga located along the Susquehanna River in Bradford County, Pennsylvania.

Osceola
A chief of the Seminoles who was born about 1803. He fought the American army for a number of years and was only captured by the American General Jesup when he came under a flag of truce to talk. Osceola was then captured and jailed at Fort Moultrie, where he died in January, 1838.

Oshkosh
This main chief of the Menominee was born in 1795. He belonged to the Owasse gens. He fought with the English and helped to capture Fort Mackinaw, Michigan, from the American army in July, 1812. A painting of Chief Oshkosh done by Samuel M. Brookes was presented to the State Historical Society of Wisconsin. The name means "hoof or toe."

Oshonawan
An ancient village of the Zuñi, located near Ojo Caliente, New Mexico. The name means "the musty place."

Oskenotoh
This was the clan of the Hurons known as the "deer clan."

Oskoshe
See Oshkosh.

Osonee
A former village of the Creeks located in Shelby County, Alabama.

Osotchi

This was the name for the Lower Creek town located along the Chattahoochee River in Russell County, Alabama.

Osquake

This was the name of a former village of the Mohawks, located along Osquake Creek in Montgomery County, New York.

Ossahinta

A chief of the Onondaga from 1830 until 1846, when he died. He belonged to the turtle clan. His name means "frost," and he was sometimes known as "Captain Frost."

Osse

This is a Menominee subphratry, meaning the "old squaw duck."

Osunkhirhine

This Abnaki Indian known as Pierre Paul Osunkhirhine did much work in the translations of the Bible and other religious works into the Penobscot dialects. Books written by him were signed by the name of Wzokhiilan as this was the best translation he could make of his name.

Oswego tea

This was a tea made by the Indians of medicinal value, the plant is called Monarda didyma. It was also used by the white settlers.

Otatshia

This was a gens of the Menominee known as the "cranes."

Otaue

The Virginia Indian word used to describe a woman's breast.

Otherday

John Otherday was a Christianized Indian of the Wahpeton Sioux. He was born in 1801. He married a white woman and tried to live as much like the whites as he could. He lived on a reservation until his death from tuberculosis in 1871. He is buried in Roberts County, South Dakota.

Otkon
See the Iroquois, Orenda.

Oto
This was the name of one of the three Siouan tribes who lived in the Wisconsin area. The name means "the lechers."

Otopali
A village visited by the explorer Fontaneda in 1575, said to be occupied by the Chicora. Located at the present site of Charleston, South Carolina.

Otowi
An ancient Tewa pueblo, located on a mesa in the northeast part of Sandoval County, New Mexico.

Otsaandosti
See Sandusky.

Otsiquette
Peter Otsiquette was a chief and was one of the signers of a treaty in 1788 for the Oneidas, he was also present at a signing for the Onondagas, both New York tribes.

Ottachugh
In 1608 this was a village of the Powhatan, located along the Rappahannock River in Lancaster County, Virginia.

Ottawa
In 1615 Champlain met the Ottawa, these woodland tribes were traders and their name means "to barter or trade with others." They lived mainly around the Great Lakes of the United States and up into Canada.

303

Otter
   See cuttak, pohkewh.

Ouananiche
   This is a species of salmon and in the Algonquian dialects means "unclean."

Ouheywichkingh
   A village of the Algonquian, located on the western end of Long Island, New York.

Ouhshawkowh
   The Virginia Indian word for the codfish.

Ouray
   Chief Ouray was born in Colorado and was a chief of the Uncompahgre Utes. He was a well educated Ute and spoke both Spanish and English. He was always friendly to the whites. For his efforts on behalf of the government he received a special salary for as long as he remained a chief of the Utes. He died on August 24, 1880.

Ourcar
   The Virginia Indian word for grave.

Ouxe
   The Virginia Indian term for the animal known as the fox.

Owasse
   This was a phratry or gens of the Menominee of Wisconsin known as the "bear."

Owassissas
   In 1822 this was a Seminole town located along the St. Marks River in the northwestern part of Florida.

Owego
   A Cayuga town located in Tioga County in New York. In 1779 the village was burned by General Poor of Sullivan's army.

Owl's claw
See the Navajo word, g'asdah bee gah.

Owl's town
Located in Coshocton County, Ohio, this was a former village of the Delawares.

Oxidizing
This term is used to describe what happens to pottery, metals, etc., which have been exposed to air or heat and so have changed their outward appearance. Examples are copper, which changes from a reddish color to a green in the process of oxidizing, and iron from a grey to a reddish brown.

Oxidoddy
The name given to plant used by medicine men and the early patent medicine men for Culver's black root.

Oyaron
A spirit being of the Iroquois who watches over and controls the destiny of everyone.

Oyateshicha
This was a group of Mdewakanton Sioux who lived along Rice Creek in Minnesota. Their name means "bad people."

Oyike
This is one of the divisions that each Tewa village was divided into. The name means "the winter frost people."

Oyster
See cauwaih.

Oyster Bay
Oyster Bay, Long Island, New York, see Secatoag.

Ozark
This tribe of Quapaw who lived in the mountain areas of Missouri and Arkansas were named by the French Aux

Arcs and the name was corrupted by the Americans to Ozarks.

Ozenic

A Powhatan village in 1608, located along the Chickahominy River in New Kent County, Virginia.

Ozinies

A village of the Nanticoke which was visited by John Smith in 1608. Located up the Chester River about fifteen miles in Maryland.

P

Pa

This term was used by the Tewa of San Ildefonso of New Mexico to denote the "Fire Clan." Also used by the Deer Clan of certain pueblos of Pecos, New Mexico.

Paakfetowee

The Powhatan Indian term for bringing something into a boat, such as supplies.

Pabaksa

This was a division of the Yankton Sioux who formerly lived in Minnesota and west to Devils Lake in North Dakota. The name means "cuthead."

Pachade

A village of Christianized Indians that lived around Middleboro, Massachusetts, in 1703.

Pack strap

See tump line.

Pacohamoa

This was one of the gens of the Sauk of Wisconsin, known as the "trout."

Pacus

The Powhatan Indian word for a chest.

Paddle and anvil

This is a technique in which pottery is finished by pounding with a paddle to make it smooth. An object is held inside the piece of pottery to help keep its shape during this process.

Pafeme vppook
The Virginia Indian expression, give me some tobacco.

Pagaits
This was a tribe of the Paiutes who formerly lived near Colville in southeastern Nevada. The name means "the fish eaters."

Paguan
A tribe of Texas Indians, active about 1690.

Paguate
A pueblo of the Lagunas of Valencia County in New Mexico. This is one of the oldest pueblos of the Lagunas.

Paguits
Also known as the "fish people," this was a group of Paiutes who lived around Fish Lake in the southwestern part of Utah.

Pahatsi
This was one of the three main divisions of the Osage. The name means "those who camp on the mountains."

Pahcunnaioh
The Virginia Indian term for dark.

Pahquetooai
Supposed to be the village of the ancestors of the Tigua village of Isleta, New Mexico.

Pahvant
This was a division of the Utes who lived over a large area of the west central part of Utah.

Painting
Painting was done on the body, on horses and on all sorts of objects. Paints were made from a variety of materials, minerals, plants, even blood, charcoal and colored sands.

Paiute

It has been the belief that the Paiutes were of Shoshonean derivation and lived in Utah, Arizona and Idaho. The name means "true water."

Pajalat

This was one of the tribes mentioned by Espinosa in 1746. These people lived around the Conception Mission near San Antonio, Texas.

Pakab

This clan of the Hopi was known as the Arrow or reed clan.

Pakachoog

A village of the Nipmuc occupied by the Christian or Praying Indians. Located near Millbury and also Worcester, Massachusetts.

Pakadasank

A village of the Munsee people, located in Orange County, New York.

Pakataghkon

This was a former village of the Delawares, meaning "split wood." Located not far from Margaretsville in Delaware County, New York.

Paki

A village of the Maidu located north of Chico in Butte County, California.

Palatka

Palatka, Florida, see Pilatka.

Palatki

This is a pre-historic cliff dwelling located south of Flagstaff, Arizona. It is believed that this was one of the places that was visited by the Hopi Cloud Clan. This is the Hopi name for "red house."

Paleolithic

An age of man during which he was devoted mainly to hunting rather than agriculture. Articles made of stone were usually made by percussion rather than pressure flaking.

Palewa

This is the "turkey" gens of the Shawnee.

Paloos

The Paloos were visited by Lewis and Clark in 1805. This Shahaptian tribe lived in Idaho.

Paltatre

A former village of the Chumashan, located near Point Concepcion, California. The village was active around 1542.

Paluna

The war god clan of the Hopi of Arizona.

Pamacocack

A settlement of the Powhatan, located along the Potomac River about thirty miles from Alexandria, Virginia. This name was also used for a village on the Maryland side of the river, near what is now Pomonkey, Maryland. Both villages were visited by Captain John Smith around 1608.

Pamaque

In 1760 this tribe lived along the Texas coast near the Nueces River.

Pamlico

This was a small tribe of Algonquians who formerly lived in Beaufort County, North Carolina. In 1696 they were hit with the smallpox plague. Later on they fought against the English and the Tuscarora in the war of 1711, after this fight those that lived were made slaves and so the tribe disappeared.

Pamunkey

This tribe fought the English in King William County, Virginia; however, they aided the English against invading tribes.

Panamint

A Shoshonean tribe formerly living in the Panamint Valley, California. Also known as Koso. Now almost extinct.

Pani

This name was used by the Indians and the early settlers for any Indian who had become a slave, especially the Pawnee (q.v.). Most of the tribes of the middlewest and the Great Lakes region used the Pawnees as a source for slaves.

Panisee

A cure or remedy, also signifying a medicine-man or shaman, used by the Algonquian of the Northeastern part of the United States.

Panka

This was a division of the Kansa tribes, sometimes spelled Ponca.

Pannee

See Pani, Pawnee.

Paouites

A tribe that is supposed to have lived in Texas around 1690. They were mentioned during the testimony regarding the death of La Salle.

Papago

This Piman tribe lived south of Tuscon, Arizona, and over into Mexico. They are known as the "bean people." They are the people of the arid and desert lands of the southwest. A large number of them live in the Grand Canyon, where they may be visited.

Papagonk

A tribe that formerly lived in Ulster County in New York around 1776, they were a tribe of the Lenape.

Papoose

A small child or infant. Also spelled Pappoose, pappouse, papeississu.

Parched corn Indians

A name given to those Indians who have become "civilized" and yet still do many of the old things of their people. A collective term to denote those Indians who farm for a livelihood.

Parfleche

This is a tough bag or box made from rawhide with the hair removed. It is usually painted or decorated and used to carry a variety of items. Made mainly by the Plains Indians and those in the Rocky Mountain areas.

Parker

This was a Seneca of New York. He was a mixed-blood of the Wolf Clan. Eli Samuel Parker studied in public schools and became a civil engineer. At the start of the Civil War, he joined with General Ulysses S. Grant and fought with Grant at Vicksburg. In 1863 he became Assistant Adjutant General and later became secretary to General Grant. It was Eli Parker who wrote the terms of surrender in his own handwriting which Lee and Grant signed to end the Civil War.

Parker became the Commissioner of Indian Affairs in 1869. He died in Fairfield, Connecticut, August 21, 1895.

Pashipaho

A chief of the Sauk, he was a signer of a treaty with the Americans to cede the Sauk lands in Illinois and Wisconsin to the whites. This eventually led to the Black Hawk War.

312

Pashka

A settlement of the Modoc who formerly lived along Tule Lake in the southwestern part of Oregon.

Paskwawininiwug

This was one of the divisions of the Plains Cree, whose name means "the prairie people."

Paspahegh

In 1608 this was one of the main groups of Indians with whom the settlers at Jamestown had contact. They lived along the James River in Virginia.

Pasquasheck

A village of the Nochpeem, located along the east side of the Hudson River in Dutchess County, New York.

Pasquotank

In 1700, this was a tribe who lived along the north side of Albemarle Sound, North Carolina. The tribe was Algonquian.

Passaconaway

A former chief who lived near the Pennacook on the Merrimac River.

Passadumkeag

This was a former village of the Penobscot. The village was destroyed by the English in 1723; it was located near the present town of Passadumkeag, Penobscot County, Maine.

Passamaquoddy

Passamaquoddy, Maine, see Quoddy.

Passamaquoddy

This small group of Abñaki lived along the boundaries of Maine and New Brunswick. Their name means "much fish" (pollock).

Passayonk

A former village of the Delawares who lived along the Schuylkill River in Pennsylvania. The village was active around 1648.

Pasukdhin

One of the ancient settlements of the Osage, located along the Verdigris River in Oklahoma. The settlement was active around 1850.

Pataheuhah

A village of the Mdewakanton Sioux which was formerly located along the Minnesota River in Minnesota.

Patchoag

Also known as the Poosepatuck, these were the tribes that lived on the southeastern end of Long Island, New York, near what is now Patchogue, Long Island, in Suffolk County. They also had villages at Westhampton, Mastic, and the Moriches, all on Long Island. The name means "where they divide in two."

Patchogue

Patchogue, Long Island, New York, "where they divide in two." See Patchoag. Also see Secatoag.

Patica

A tribe of Florida Indians named by Bartram in his travels, who lived in the northeastern part of Florida. This name was given to two villages, one of which was located near Fort Caroline and the other near the mouth of the St. John River. This village was near the present site of Jacksonville, Florida.

Patina

This is the crust or oxidized film formed on objects that have been buried or exposed, such as the green coating found on copper or the minerals which are formed on objects found in caves.

314

Patiquin

In 1542 this was a village of the Chumashan people who lived on the Island of Santa Rosa, California.

Patki

This was the cloud clan of the Patki phratry of the Hopi of Arizona.

Patoqua

One of the former villages of the Jemez. Also a site of a Spanish mission (San Joseph de los Jemez), this mission was abandoned in 1622 because of the fear of the Navajos.

Patung

This was the squash clan of the Hopi of Arizona.

Patuxent

This Algonquian tribe formerly lived in what is now Calvert County, Maryland. In 1639 they became fast friends with the settlers.

Patuxet

A village of the Massachusetts, located at the present site of Plymouth. In 1617 most of the population was wiped out by smallpox.

Patwin

This was the name given to those tribes of the Copehan family who lived in what are now Colusa and Solano Counties in California. The name means "man."

Paugusset

A small tribe of Algonquians who lived along the Naugatuck and Housatonic Rivers in Connecticut. In 1660 they sold most of their lands to the settlers. They also had villages at Milford and Naugatuck.

Paviotso

A group of Shoshonean tribes of western Nevada. See

Mono-Paviotso. Some authorities identify the Paviotso with the Paiute.

Pawating
This is a former village site of the Chippewa, located on the south bank of the St. Mary's River in Michigan. They were also called Saulteurs by the early French Explorers.

Pawipits
This was a band of the Paiutes of the southeastern part of Nevada.

Pawnee
Known also as the "horn people" because of the method of fixing their hair. This group is part of the Caddoan family. They were also called "men of men," a name given to them because they were used as slaves by many of the other Indian tribes in the area. The Pawnee never made war on the United States.

Paxinos
He was a Minisink and a Shawnee chief, who fought with the Mohawk against the French in 1680. He was friendly with the Moravian missionaries and his wife became a convert.

Paxtonville
Paxtonville, Pennsylvania, see Peixtan.

Payne's Town
Located in Alachua County, Florida, this was a town used as a refuge by escaped slaves. It was named after its chief, Payne.

Peag
A name used by the Massachusetts for wampum, or the white and purple beads made from shells. The settlers used the word wampum or peag because the Indian word was too long and hard to say (wampampeag).

Pearls

The Gulf Coast Indians used pearls for decoration and for burial ceremonies. De Soto dug up many Indian graves to get the pearls that were buried with the dead. Pearls appear in the mounds of Ohio and other inland areas.

Pecan

The nuts from the pecan tree were used by many Indians for food and much sought after in Illinois, Iowa, Louisiana and Texas. Also known as the "Illinois nut."

Peccarecamek

A settlement in southern Virginia which had stone houses which were built by the Indians. It is said they learned to do this from those settlers who escaped the massacre of Sir Walter Raleigh's colony at Roanoke.

Peccataas

The Powhatan Indian word for beans.

Peckwes

A village of the Munsee or possibly the Delawares who were on the move around 1694, located about ten miles from Hackensack, New Jersey.

Pecos

This was one of the largest pueblos in New Mexico, located along the Pecos River about 30 miles southeast of Santa Fé, New Mexico. The Jemez who lived here were first met by the Spanish explorer Coronado in 1540. He estimated that the pueblo had about 2,500 people after battles with the Spanish, smallpox and raids by the Comanche; the pueblo population was reduced in 1790 to less than 17.

Pecos Monument

In 1838 these pueblos and their mission were abandoned. The ruins are located near U.S. Highway 85 about 25 miles southeast of Santa Fé, New Mexico, near Pecos, New Mexico.

Pedee

Sometimes spelled Peedee, this small tribe of Siouan people lived near what is now Cheraw, South Carolina. By 1775 most of the Pedee lived with the whites and the Catawbas (q.v.).

Peekskill

Peekskill, New York, see Sackhoes.

Peepchiltk

A village of the Pima Indians who formerly lived in southern Arizona. Their name meant "concave" and referred to the type of nose that they had.

Peixtan

A village of the Shawnee, located along the lower Susquehanna in Dauphin County, near the present site of the city of Paxtonville, Pennsylvania.

Peketawas

The Virginia Indian term for beans.

Pemmican

A food product usually made of deer meat dried in the sun or over a slow fire. The dried meat was pounded, and one part of melted fat mixed in. Dried berries were sometimes added. The mixture was then packed into skin bags and would keep for four or five years.

Penah

This is a former village of the Fox, located at Cassville in Grant County, Wisconsin. The name means "turkey."

Penateka

A former division of the Comanches who lived in eastern Texas. Their name means "honey eaters."

Penikikonau

This is a phratry of the Eagle clan of the Menominee, known as the "fish hawks."

318

Pennacook

Located in New Hampshire and Massachusetts and the southern part of Maine, this Algonquian confederacy was between the English and the French. They occupied both banks of the Merrimac River. Their main village was located at the present site of Concord, New Hampshire.

Penobscot

One of the larger Abnaki people who live in Maine yet, they are still living on land which was theirs in the early days of the settlement.

Pensacola

These Indians lived in the area which is now Pensacola, Florida. As a tribe, this Choctaw band was exterminated before the Spanish arrived in 1696. Their name means "the hair people."

Penutian

A language group of central California.

Peoria

This was a former tribe of the Illinois Indians who lived along the Mississippi and Wisconsin Rivers. The name means "he comes, carrying a pack on his back." The name is a personal one, after a chief of the Illinois.

Peoria

Peoria, Illinois, see Pimitoui.

Pequea

This former village of the Shawnee was located along the Pequea Creek where it joined the Susquehanna River in Lancaster County, Pennsylvania. Around 1730, the village was abandoned.

Pequimmit

This was a former village of the Christian Indians who lived near what is now Stoughton, Massachusetts, in 1658.

Pequot

This Connecticut tribe of the Algonquians was considered to be one of the most dangerous of the tribes of New England. Their villages were located near what are now Groton, New London and Stonington. In 1637 they were at war with other tribes and the settlers and by 1638 they lost the battles and those who surrendered were forbidden to call themselves the Pequots. Their name means "the destroyers."

Perage

An ancient Tewa pueblo, located along the west bank of the Rio Grande about a mile west from San Ildefonso, New Mexico.

Percussion flaking

This was the method of shaping stone articles by the process of hammering with another stone or heavy bone.

Periphery

A term used to describe those areas in between various cultures (q.v.), or those at the edge of an area which is being studied.

Perry

Perry, Maine, see Sebaik.

Persimmon

The fruit of this tree was used by the Indians in many ways, dried, cooked and mixed with other food plants. First seen by John Smith, who said "It draws a man's mouth awry with much torment!" A beverage called persimmon beer was made in the south.

Peruka

This clan of the frog or toad belonged to those people of the San Felipe pueblo of New Mexico.

Pesawa

This was the horse gens of the Shawnee.

Pescadero

A pueblo located along the Gila River in Arizona, belonging to the Pima in 1775. Also a Zuñi summer village located about 15 miles from Zuñi, New Mexico. The name is Spanish and means "fisherman."

Peshewah

A former chief of the Miami Indians of Indiana, he was born in an Indian village located near what is now Fort Wayne, Indiana, about 1761. Also known as John B. Richardville. He became very wealthy and a town in Indiana was named for him . . . Russiaville, which is a corruption of his name from the Indian and French. He died August 13, 1841.

Pessacus

In 1623 this was a chief of the Narraganset. He died in a battle with the Mohawk.

Pestle

One of the devices used in the grinding of grains into flour. Some are plain and some are carved. Used in conjunction with a mortar or bowl, usually shaped like a bowling pin or rolling pin with no handles.

Pestle

See pocohaac.

Petalesharo

This former chief of the Pawnee was the son of Old Knife, and was born about 1797. He was a signer of a treaty in Nebraska on September 24, 1857.

Petaocawin

The Powhatan word for bed, see also cawwaivuh.

Peyote

This name means "caterpillar" in Spanish. Also called by the whites "mescal," which is a different plant, however. Peyote "buttons" are dried and eaten during special ceremonies, causing dreams and other hallucinations. The button appears on this cactus after it has bloomed. It is found mostly in the arid sections of the Gulf States and northwest to the Rocky Mountains.

Phase

This is a term of archaeology which covers a section of a culture which has been affected by outside influences.

Philadelphia

Philadelphia, Mississippi, see Schekaha.

Philadelphia

Philadelphia, Pennsylvania, see Shackamaxon.

Philip

See King Philip.

Piasa

The name of the thunderbird, also meaning a large bird to the Chippewa. This name was given to a pictograph (q.v.) seen on the rocks near Alton, Illinois. Seen by Marquette in 1673 as he traveled down the Mississippi. Part of this rock was quarried away in 1867.

Piba

This was the tobacco clan of the Hopi of Arizona.

Pichikwe

The clan of the Pueblo at Zuñi, New Mexico, which was known to the Indians as the "parrot people."

Pick

The Indian pick was usually made of stone and was used to cut stone and wood, used as chisels, adzes and celts.

Pickawillanee

This was a former village of the Miami, located near what is now Piqua, Ohio. The village was destroyed in 1750 by the English and the Indians.

Pickewh

This is the Virginia Indian term used to describe the gum that is gotten from the Virginia maple.

Picolata

A former Seminole village, located on the St. Johns River, just west of St. Augustine, Florida.

Pictograph

This is a form of picture writing. Pictographs have been made on cave walls, sides of cliffs, shells, wood, hides and human beings. The drawings depict real or supernatural beings or objects. Usually pictographs are simple with only the essential features being included. Some pictographs are colored, others are cut into the material upon which it is drawn. Pictographs are not necessarily found only in the United States but are found all over the world in much the same circumstances.

Picuris

A Tigua pueblo about forty miles north of Santa Fe, New Mexico. It is still occupied.

Piegan

This is one of the tribes of the Blackfoot confederacy in Montana and Canada. Their name means "poorly dressed hides."

Pierced tablets

Rather flat plates, usually several inches long with a hole or two drilled through the edge, possibly used as ornaments, similar to banner stones.

Pieskaret

This Algonquian chief lived along the St. Lawrence River. He was a very brave warrior and fought against the Iroquois a number of times. He became a Catholic in 1641 and was then known as Simon Pieskaret. He was killed by the Iroquois in 1647.

Pikuni

Another name for Piegan (q.v.), a division of the Blackfoot.

Pilatka

A former Seminole village located along the west side of the St. John's River near Crescent Lake and the town of Palatka. The name means "into the water."

Pillagers

This was a group of Chippewas who were what could be termed an advanced guard of the Chippewa who entered the Sioux country to become established there. They formerly lived in Minnesota. Their name for themselves was the "robber people."

Pima

This name was used for those people who lived around the Gila and Salt Rivers in the southern part of Arizona. The Pima were placed on reservations with the Papago, Maricopa and other desert dwelling tribes. The Pima did not take scalps as they considered their enemies as something evil and so did not want to touch them when they were dead.

Pimitoui

In 1722 the Illinois abandoned this village and moved toward the Mississippi. They lived also near what is now Peoria, Illinois.

Pinal Coyotero

This was a band of the Apache who used to gather in

the Pinal Mountains. They moved all over southern Arizona and down into the Pueblo country of the southwest.

Pinaleños

This division of a very warlike group of the Apaches lived in the Pinaleños Mountains in the southeastern part of Arizona. In 1883 they were forced by General George Cook to surrender to the Americans and were then placed on reservations. The name meant the "Pinery people."

Pinedrop

The entire plant of the pinedrop is used by the Navajo Indians for the making of a dull brown dye.

Pine Plains

Pine Plains, New York, see Shecomeco.

Pinkney Mill

Former Indian village, see Oony.

Pink sterns

See chebacco.

Pintiats

This was a band of the Paiutes who formerly lived in the Moapa Valley in the southeastern part of Nevada, around 1873.

Pinutgu

A term used by the Cheyenne for those members of their own people who did not bear arms during the Indian outbreak of 1874.

Pious Mohegan

See Samson Occom.

Pipe

The Indian pipe had various forms; some were long and resembled the present day "cigar holder," others had the conventional shape of a pipe, with a bowl for the tobacco and a stem. Some pipes were used only for ceremonial purposes, such as the calumet. During the Colonial Period many pipes were made in Europe for use as a trade item, many of these had initials and were made of metal.

Pipsissewa
A plant used by the Indians as a medicine, especially for the removal of gall stones. A beer named Pipsissewa beer was made from this plant, made with the addition of ginger root, sugar and a type of yeast to cause fermentation.

Piqua
This name was used for several towns of the Shawnee who lived in Ohio near what is now Springfield, Ohio.

Piqua
Piqua, Ohio, see Pickawillanee.

Piros
In the early 17th century this was one of the main tribes of Pueblo Indians who lived in New Mexico. They lived in an area east of the Rio Grande.

Piscataqua
This small band of the Pennacook confederacy lived along the Piscataqua River, near what is now Dover, New Hampshire.

Piscataway
This was a village of the Conoy Indians who became Christianized around 1634. In 1642 this mission was moved because of the fear of the Conestoga Indians.

Piskakauakis
This small tribe of the Cree lived along the northwest part of our country and traded with the members of the Hudson's Bay Company in 1856.

Pissacoac
Part of the Powhatan confederacy who formerly lived

near what is now Leedstown, Virginia. They also lived along the Rappahannock River.

Pitahauerat

Spoken of by the French as Tapage Pawnee, this was a group of the Pawnee Confederacy who lived in Kansas and Nebraska. In 1857 they were placed on reservations in Oklahoma.

Pitchlynn

This chief of the Choctaw, known as Peter Perkins Pitchlynn, was a mixed-blood who was born January 30, 1806. He went to school to learn to read. When he returned, his people were about to sign a treaty which he read. He said that the treaty was frauding his people and he would not shake hands with General Jackson. He was met by Charles Dickens in 1842, who subsequently wrote about him. During the Civil War he fought for the North while his sons fought for the South. He became a member of the Lutheran Church in Washington, D. C., and also became a Mason. In 1865 he became an Indian agent at Washington, where he represented his people. He died January 17, 1881. He is buried in the Congressional Cemetery.

Pitkachi

One of the larger tribes of the Mariposa who lived in central California in the foothills of the Sierra Nevada Mountains.

Pizhiki

A chief of the Chippewa of Wisconsin. Born on Madeline Island approximately in 1759. He was the signer of many treaties. He was also known as "Buffalo," a name which the whites used for him. He lived at what is now Buffalo, New York, at one time; from there he returned to La Pointe, Wisconsin. He died September 7, 1855.

Planoconvex
Archaeological term used to describe an article that is convex on one side and flat on the other.

Plates
Plates found in mounds of the Gulf States, see Notched Plates.

Playa
This is a shallow spot or dry lake bed in which water collects during the rainy season.

Playwickey
A village of the Delawares, located in Bucks County, Pennsylvania, which was active around 1737.

Plummets
Objects made by the Indian for use as net sinkers, somewhat egg shaped, sometimes grooved and drilled. Used by some tribes for ceremonial purposes and carried as charms. They were made of stone, copper, wood and other materials of special significance.

Pluvial
This is the action of water or rain, also applied to dry regions which formerly had rainier climate.

Plymouth
Plymouth, Massachusetts. See Patuxet.

Pocahontas
Matoaka, Pocahontas, Lady Rebecca and Mrs. John Rolfe are all names for the Powhatan Indian woman who is supposed to have saved Captain John Smith from death. After 1609, Captain Smith departed for England. In the meantime Pocahontas was taken aboard an English ship and taken to Jamestown in 1612, where she was ransomed by her father, the chief. It was here that she met John Rolfe and in April, 1613, they were married. Pocahontas had be-

come a Christian and received the name of Lady Rebecca. In 1616 they traveled to England. A year later in March, 1617, Pocahontas caught smallpox and died aboard ship. Her one son, Thomas Rolfe, returned to Virginia where he became wealthy. He had one daughter.

Pocohaac
The Virginia Indian term for the pestle.

Pocosack
The Virginia Indian term for a gun or firearm.

Podunk
A word from the Algonquian meaning "neck or point of land," or "away." The term was used for a pond in Connecticut and an Indian village on Long Island, New York.

Pogamoggan
Another name for a club, from the Chippewa and the Cree word for hammer (pakamagan).

Poghaden
See porgy.

Pogonip
A type of fog seen by the Shoshonean tribes in the mountain country of Nevada.

Pohkewh
The Virginia Indian word for the animal known as the beaver, see cuttak.

Pohkopophunk
A village of the Delawares, located in 1740 in eastern Pennsylvania in Carbon County.

Poison
Many tribes used poisons for hunting, warfare and in special ceremonies. Poisons were used to stupefy fish, such as the Cherokee use of walnut bark pounded to a powder

and thrown in small pools. The California Indians used the soapbush for a fish poison. The Zuñi poisoned certain springs in their area with the juice from varieties of yucca plants in order to stop the Spanish invaders. Many tribes dipped their arrowpoints in decayed substances and thus infection was caused in the wounds inflicted.

Pojoaque

A small Tewa pueblo located about twenty miles northwest of Santa Fe, New Mexico. It was abandoned around 1696. However, there is a modern pueblo of this name.

Pokagon

One of the last full-blooded chiefs of the Potawatomi, he was born in 1830 at an Indian village in Berrien County, Michigan. He attended college at Oberlin in Ohio. He became a Catholic. He was active in the Chicago Worlds Fair in 1893. He was an author and poet. It was he who finally secured a claim of $150,000 from the government for the Potawatomi. A monument was erected to his memory in Jackson Park, Chicago.

Pokanoket

A village of the Wampanoag, located on the Bristol Peninsula in Rhode Island. It was also the home of King Philip. It was abandoned in 1675 at the outbreak of King Philip's War.

Pokegama

A former village of the Chippewa, located on Pokegama Lake in Pine County, Minnesota.

Pokekooungo

This was the turtle clan of the Delaware tribes.

Pokeloken

An Indian term used by the whites for a swamp or marsh, used mainly by those who were lumbermen.

Poke weed
A plant used for the making of a red dye used by the Indians, also known as Indian poke.

Pokunt
Shoshonean for an unseen force, see Orenda.

Polychrome Pottery
A term used to describe that pottery which has three or more colors on its surface.

Pomeioc
This was a former village of the Algonquians located in Hyde County, North Carolina. This is one of the villages that was painted in color by the artist John White in 1585.

Pomo
The people of north central California and those of the extreme southern part of California. Pomo means "the people."

Pomokey
Pomokey, Maryland, see Pamacocack.

Pomotawh
The Virginia Indian term for a hill or mountain.

Pomouic
A former Algonquian tribe that lived along the Pamlico River on the coast of North Carolina. The village was active around 1585.

Pomperaug
A sacred place where those who passed would place a rock on a pile that was left there, located near what is now Woodbury, Connecticut.

Pompton
This was a former settlement of the Munsee who lived

along the Pompton River in New Jersey. They were first mentioned by the whites in 1695 in a land deed.

Ponca
One of the five tribes of the Sioux who lived along the Missouri River and in the Black Hills of the Dakotas.

Poningo
In 1640, this was a village of the Siwanoy, located at the site of what is now Rye, New York.

Ponpon
A Yuchi village located in the southwestern part of South Carolina.

Pontiac
This chief of the Ottawa was born about 1720 in Ohio. In 1760 he met with Major Robert Rogers at a place now known as Cleveland, Ohio; here he agreed to the surrender of Detroit to the British. He did this in order to save another attack on the rest of his tribe. He did not, however, like the British and because of the raw treatment that he received from them, he organized all of the tribes northwest of the Ohio River. He proceeded to attack all of the British posts on the Great Lakes. Eight of the ten forts were taken, all but Detroit and Fort Pitt fell to Pontiac's men. On August 17, 1765, he finally made peace with the English at Detroit. In 1769, he was killed by another Indian.

Pontotoc
A former settlement of the Chickasaw, the present site of Pontotoc, Mississippi.

Poodatook
A Mohegan village located near what is now Newtown in Fairfield County, Connecticut. It was active around 1660.

Poosepatuck
This is one of the 13 tribes of Long Island, New York.

They lived on the south shore of Long Island out near the Montauk Indians. They were placed on a reservation in 1666.

Pope
This Tewa chief set out to get rid of all the Spanish influence in the southwest; around 1675 there were some 2,500 Spanish settlers and missionaries in the area. On August 10, 1680, he attacked Santa Fe, New Mexico, and killed over 400. The Spaniards gathered and returned the attack, but were forced to retreat down the Rio Grande to El Paso, Texas. After much success he finally had to fight the old enemies such as the Apache and the Utes, as well as the Pecos. He died in 1692.

Poquosin
An Algonquian and Cree dialect word for land which is flooded at certain times of the year. Used for such areas as the Dismal Swamp. Applied mainly to those areas in Virginia and North Carolina and Maryland.

Porgy
A fish found along the North Atlantic coast, also known as the bream, a rather bony fish, known also as the pin fish, pogy, pogie and poghaden.

Portage
This was a division of the Winnebago who lived at what is now Portage, Wisconsin, around 1811. This is a spot where the Wisconsin and the Fox Rivers come together.

Porter
This is one of the last chiefs of the Creeks of Oklahoma. He was a Christianized Indian and his full name was Pleasant Porter. He fought on the side of the South during the Civil War. He died September 3, 1907.

Port Royal
Port Royal, South Carolina, see Wayon.

Potano

This was a tribe who formerly lived in northern Florida and were visited by De Soto in 1539. They later became Christian Indians. They were exterminated by their enemies to the north around 1705.

Potawatomi

This is a tribe that speaks the Chippewan dialect and who lived in Wisconsin and along Lake Huron. Also known as the "Fire Nation." The Potawatomi fought for the French until about 1773; during the Revolution, they fought against the United States and then in the War of 1812, they fought the English. During the removal, they were placed in Iowa and Kansas.

Poteskeet

A tribe of Algonquians who formerly lived along the shores of Albemarle Island, North Carolina around 1700.

Potlatch

The potlatch was a type of ceremony which was mainly, as the Indian name implies, "giving away." At certain times of the year, an individual would give away everything he had, houses, hides, canoes, slaves, etc. He would then expect the other individual to "go him one better." This was kept up until one was destitute. The property which wasn't destroyed was divided amongst the rest of the village.

Potomac

The name means "something which is brought." This former Indian village was a spot to which certain tribes of the Virginia area came and "brought tribute" to the local chief.

Potomac

An important tribe of the Powhatan who lived on the Potomac River in Virginia.

Pot sherds
See sherds.

Pottery Hill
This name was given to a pueblo ruin located on the north side of the Salt River near Linden in Navajo County, Arizona.

Powevwh
The Virginia Indian term used to describe a woman with child.

Powhatan
This was a strong confederacy of the Algonquian tribes of Virginia. They also included some of the tribes in Maryland. In 1570, the Spanish started a mission in their midst. The Powhatans were friendly with the settlers at Jamestown in 1607, and continued until around 1621, when, after much cheating of the Indians by the settlers and the death of the chief, hostilities broke out. After this a war continued for 14 years. The settlers continued a "war of extermination"; they were ordered to carry out three expeditions a year, to prevent the Indian from planting or building. They even went so far as to offer peace to the Indians who came under a truce, only to be massacred by the settlers. In 1636 a peace was finally made between the Indians and those of Jamestown.

Powhigwava
The Virginia Indian term used to describe the juice or milk that is made from crushed walnuts.

Powow
This term has been used in many ways and has several meanings to Indians in various parts of the country. It usually means a gathering to talk, especially for political reasons. The term is also used to mean the practice of witchcraft or medicine.

Prairie du Chien
Prairie du Chien, Wisconsin, see Red Thunder.

Prairie la Crosse
A village of the Winnebago in the southeastern part of Wisconsin to which Chief Black Hawk went in 1832.

Prairie Potawatomi
This largely broken up division of the Potawatomi lived south of Lake Michigan and throughout Wisconsin and Michigan, Illinois and Indiana, now mainly living in Kansas and southern Wisconsin.

Praying Indians
This term was used to describe those Indians who became Christians of one faith or another. The term was applied mainly to those Indians of New England and Massachusetts in particular. As the settlers and the missionaries spread, so did this term.

Pressure flaking
The method whereby objects are shaped from stone by the use of pressure against the surface, this differs from percussion flaking (q.v.).

Prickly pear cactus
See hwoshntxyeeli binesd'a'.

Projectile point
This is the point of an arrow point, spear or harpoon.

Property
As a general rule, property that a person wore was his own. Such things as a canoe, a crop or field belonged to the tribe or family; names usually belonged to the clan (q.v.). Sacred articles belonged to an appointed guardian. In the case of areas of land where wild foods could be gathered, such as wild rice in the Chippewa areas, it was necessary to occupy the area before it could be classed as property of the tribe.

Prophet

The Prophet, see Wabokieshiek.

Prophetstown

Prophetstown, Illinois, see Wabokieshiek.

Ptansinta

Meaning "otter tail," this is a former village of the Santee Sioux who lived around Lake Traverse in Minnesota.

Puaray

A former village of the Tigua who formerly lived along the Rio Grande in New Mexico, near the town of Bernalillo. It was visited by Coronado in 1540 and was the site of a battle which lasted almost two months when the Tigua people fought the Spanish invaders. In the early 1700's the pueblo was abandoned and was never used again.

Puccoon

A plant used by the Indian for dyeing hides and other articles, often the plant known as "blood root."

Puchkohu

This clan of the Hopi of Arizona is known as the "rabbit stick clan." The rabbit stick was similar to a boomerang and was thrown at rabbits when hunting.

Puckna

This former village of the Upper Creeks was located in the southwestern part of Clay County in Alabama.

Pueblo

The Spanish word for village, applied to the Indians that live in parts of Arizona and New Mexico. Their houses are made of adobe and are situated in groups on the mesas. [The term Pueblo Indian is used collectively and not for one particular tribe. It includes such people as the Zuñi, Hopi and Tewa.] These Indians are descendants of the prehistoric Indians that lived in this area over fifteen hundred years ago.

Pueblo Alto
This pre-historic pueblo is located on top of a mesa near Chaco Canyon in northwestern New Mexico. This ruin was very hard to reach through a rock crevice in back of Pueblo Bonito.

Pueblo Bonito
This is one of the largest and most important pre-historic ruins found in the Chaco Canyon area of New Mexico. Articles found in this ruin are now at the American Museum of Natural History in New York.

Pueblo Grande Park
This is a partially excavated ruin located in Phoenix, Arizona, on East Washington Street.

Pufsagwun
The Powhatan Indian word for clay.

Pujunan Family
A language family consisting of only one tribe, the Maidu of northern California.

Pukwaawun
A former village of the Chippewa who lived in western Wisconsin.

Pumham
A chief of the Narragansets who lived around what is now Rhode Island. During King Philip's War, his village was burned by the English in 1675.

Pummy
An Algonquian term used in New England which meant "fish oil," especially of the porgy (q.v.).

Pung
A type of sled or toboggan made from split pieces of wood which were fastened together.

Pungwe

The Powhatan Indian word for ashes.

Punkapog

A village of "praying Indians" (q.v.) who lived near Stoughton, Massachusetts. After King Philip's War, this was one of the few towns of praying Indians left (1792).

Punkie

Also spelled ponk by the Lenape, meaning "living ashes," a term used for the sandfly which is small like an ash and yet burns when it lands on you. This gives some indication of the bite of this fly.

Punta de la Loma

Punta de la Loma, California, see Swino.

Punxsutawny

A village of the Delawares, located in Jefferson County, Pennsylvania, in 1755. It was also known as "Gnat town," and was abandoned in 1758.

Puttaiquapifson

The Powhatan Indian word for a hat or head covering.

Puttawus

A term used by the Virginia Indians for a cape or mantle made of feathers.

Puyallup

A Salish tribe on the Puyallup River in western Washington.

Puye

This pueblo and cliff houses are located on the Santa Clara Reservation about 15 miles from Espanola, New Mexico.

Pyquaug

A former village of the Mattabesec, meaning "open area" or "clear land." The present site of Wethersfield, Connecticut.

Pyrite

These crystals of iron pyrite were used to strike against rocks for the starting of a fire.

Q

Quabaug

This village of the Nipmuc formerly located near what is now Brookfield, Massachusetts; the village was abandoned after 1675. The name means "red pond."

Quantisset

This was a former village and fort of the Nipmuc, located on Thompson Hill in 1727. Now the site of Thompson in Windham County, Connecticut.

Quapaw

Those who go "downstream," this was the southwestern branch of the Sioux who followed the Mississippi and the Arkansas Rivers. They were visited by the Spanish in 1541.

Quaras

A village of the Karankawa, located not far from Matagorda Bay in Texas. It was visited by La Salle in 1688.

Quasky

This is the Algonquian name for the trout (Salmo oquassa).

Queen Anne

This was a woman chief of the Pamunkey tribe. The English called on her for men to aid in a battle known as Bacon's Rebellion of 1675. It was in this battle that her husband Totopotomoi was killed, along with many warriors. For this she and her people were promised a reward. After some twenty years of waiting, she appeared with her son to plead for herself and her tribe. After another promise and a silver crown which was inscribed "Queen of Pamunkey" she left. Shortly after 1715 she died. The "crown" was presented to the Society for the Preservation of Virginia Antiquities at Richmond, Virginia.

Querecho

This is the pueblo name for the Apache who hunted the bison on the plains of Texas and New Mexico. They were first met by Coronado's men in 1541. They were also known by the names of Jicarillas, Faraones and the Mescaleros, and included all the Apaches who lived mainly on the meat of the bison.

Quesinille

A former village of the Luiseño who lived in San Diego County, California.

Quiburi

Several houses or a village of the Sobaipuri and a mission which was established by Father Kino about 1697. Located near the present town of Benson in southern Arizona.

Quigaute

This was a town in Florida which was seen by De Soto in 1541 on his way from Quapaw (q.v.).

Quigyuma

This Yuman tribe lived on the Colorado River below the Gila River around 1604.

Quileute

A tribe of the Chimakuan linguistic family, living at and around Lapush, on the coast of Washington.

Quillwork

The quills of the porcupine and of birds were used to make a form of embroidery. Porcupine quill work was done throughout the United States in all areas except California and those areas on the southern plains where the porcupine did not live. Quills were dyed with the juice from berries, etc. They were flattened between the teeth when they were needed for use. They were also softened with hot water and then flattened with rocks. They were laced into moccasins, shirts, pipe covers and any number of articles. Quillwork was gradually replaced by the trade beads of the settlers.

Quinahaqui

A large Indian village located between the Wateree and the Catawba Rivers in South Carolina. It was recorded by Juan Pardo in 1567.

Quinaielt

A Salishan tribe living along the Quinaielt River in Washington.

Quinebaug

A tribe of the Nipmucs who were conquered by the Pequots. They formerly lived in an area near Jewett City, Connecticut.

Quinet

This tribe lived near the Bay of Matagorda in Texas. In 1687 La Salle made a peace agreement with these people.

Quinnat

A type of salmon which was caught off the northwest coast of Canada and Alaska. Also known as the Chinook and tyee salmon.

Quinney

This Mohegan, known as John Quinney, aided in the translation of various things such as prayers into the Mohegan language. One of his sons, Joseph, became the deacon of a church at Stockbridge, New York (1817).

Quinney, John W.

A former chief of the Stockbridge Indians who was born in 1797. He was chief of the tribe in Wisconsin from 1852 until his death in 1855. He studied in Westchester, New York. In 1822 he went to Green Bay, Wisconsin, where a treaty was signed which gave lands in the Green Bay area to the Stockbridge Indians who were being moved from New York to the Green Bay area. The Menominee were caused to move from the area to make room. In turn the government made an effort to repurchase this land, which they did, so the Stockbridge were made to move again to an area around Lake Winnebago, Wisconsin. A painting of John W. Quinney was presented to the State Historical Society at Madison, Wisconsin. The Quinney family was prominent in the history of the Stockbridge tribe.

Quinnipiac
A village of the Quinnipiac was located near the present city of New Haven, Connecticut.

Quisiyove
In 1570 this was a village of the Calusa, located on the southwest coast of Florida.

Quitoles
This was one of the tribes mentioned by Cabeza de Vaca during his stay of seven years in Texas (1527), they were possibly the Karankawan.

Quittaub
In 1698 this was a village of praying Indians located just southwest of Plymouth, Massachusetts.

Quiver
The quiver was used to hold arrows. Its size was determined by the size of the bow and arrows. Deerskin was used in Canada and east of the Rockies. The Pacific coast areas used quivers made of cedar. The skins of the otter and coyote and mountain lion were also used.

Quivira
Quivira Historical Society, see Tatarrax.

Quoddy

This was a name for the type of herring which was caught off the coast of Maine near Passamaquoddy, Maine. The name means "a large number of pollack or herring." Fishing boats were also known as quoddy boats.

Quoratean Family

The linguistic family of the Karok tribe of northwestern California.

R

Rabbitbush

See the Navajo, g'iiltsoih.

Race

The Indian had various names for the white man who came into his country, such as the Chippewa word, waya-bishkiwad, meaning "white skin." The Delaware, woapsit, meaning "he is white." Iroquoian names variously are assar-icol or "big knife," or asseroni, "he who makes axes." Kiowa, bedalpago, meaning "hairy mouths," referring to their mus-taches and another, ta-'ka-i, meaning "his ears stick out." Big knife, long knife, etc., were used to designate the Ameri-cans as distinguished from the French, English and the settlers before the Revolution. The English were known as "wautacone" or the "coat men, or one who wears clothes." The Scotch were known by the Mohawk as kentahere, which applied to the type of hat that they wore, which reminded them of cow and buffalo droppings. The French were known as "wameqtikosiu" or "builders of wooden ships." The Ger-man and Dutch were known generally as "yah yah algeh," for "those who talk ya ya." The negroes were known as "ma'kadäwiyas," meaning black flesh or black face. The Chi-nese were known for their long "pig tail" and so were called "gooktlam."

Rain-in-the-Face

This was a chief of the Sioux who was born along the Cheyenne River in North Dakota. He was a full-blooded Hunkpapa Sioux. He received his name from a fight that he had when he was a boy. While in the fight his face became cut and his blood and his war paint became streaked and this caused others to say that he looked "rained upon." He was re-named, or his name was confirmed, after he had fought all day in the rain and his warpaint became smeared by the rain. He fought in many battles and one of the most notable was with Sitting Bull at the battle of the Little Big Horn. It has been said, but not yet proven, that he himself killed General Custer. It was said that Chief Rain-in-The-Face had seven wives.

Rappahannock

The Lenape name for the river that alternates which means that it was affected by the tides. Located in Virginia. Also a tribe of the Powhatan named for this river.

Raputtak

The head of an arrow in the ancient Virginia Indian language.

Raritan

This was a division of the New Jersey Delawares who lived in the area of the Raritan River of New Jersey. The name means an area where the "stream overflows," meaning that at times water floods the area from streams and rivers. In 1832, they sold their land to the whites and moved to Green Bay, Wisconsin.

Rathroche

This was one of the sub-gens of the beaver gens of the Iowa tribe.

Rattles

The Indian had many forms of rattles made from beaks of birds, hooves of animals, bones, pods, shells, tortoise shells and scrotum of various animals. Rattles are used in ceremonies and in witchcraft.

Rawhide

The skin of animals was dehaired, fleshed, stretched and

dried. It was then ready for use. It was used for drum heads, cut in strips and used to fasten handles, as it shrinks when it becomes dry. The parfleche (q.v.) was made from rawhide.

Rawottonemd
A term used by the Virginia Indians which denotes God (q.v.).

Reaum Village
This village, named after a Chippewa chief, was located along the Flint River in Michigan, between Saginaw and Genesee Counties. This village was given to the United States in a treaty signed on January 14, 1837.

Rechquaakie
Meaning sandy land, this was a former village of the Long Island Indians at Far Rockaway, Long Island, New York.

Rechtauck
The people of the Wacquaesgeek who lived in this village in 1643 were massacred by the Dutch who attacked this village on Manhattan Island, New York.

Red Bank
This was a former Cherokee village located near what is now Canton in Cherokee County, Georgia.

Red Bird
This was the name of a Winnebago chief who was a friend of the settlers of Prairie du Chien, Wisconsin. In 1827 two Winnebagos were falsely accused of killing a family who were making maple sugar. They were arrested and turned over to the Chippewa for punishment, and were promptly beaten to death. When Red Bird heard of this he led an uprising of his people. After a few days, troops came and Red Bird surrendered and was put in prison, where he died on February 16, 1828, while he was awaiting sentence.

Red Cedar Lake
A village of the Chippewa located in Barron County, Wisconsin.

Red Cloud
Red Cloud was one of the main chiefs of the Oglala Teton Sioux. He was born in 1822 along the Platte River in Nebraska. From 1865 to 1868 he fought against great odds to hold lands he felt were needed to keep a food supply for his people. He prevented a road from being built through Montana. He would not even be present to sign a treaty until all of the troops had been removed. Thus he was able to win a complete victory. On November 6, 1868, he finally did sign a treaty at Fort Laramie in Wyoming. He died at Pine Ridge, South Dakota, on December 10, 1909.

Red Fish
A chief of the Oglala Sioux around 1840. He fought against the Crows in 1841. He was last seen at Fort Pierre in South Dakota.

Red Head
This Onondaga drew a map of the St. Lawrence River for the Englishman, Sir William Johnson, in August, 1759. He died at Oswego, New York, in August of 1764.

Red Horn
This chief of the Piegan fought a losing battle with the troops on January 23, 1870, when Colonel E. M. Baker surprised his village on the Marias River in Montana and killed many of the inhabitants, including women and children and also Chief Red Horn. This was at a time when most of the Indians in the village had smallpox.

Red Jacket
This Seneca Indian was born about 1756 at Canoga, New York. He died at what is now Buffalo, New York, on January 20, 1830. He fought with the British during the Revo-

lution and he received his name from the bright red jacket that he wore, a present from the British who kept him supplied with a new one. In 1821 New York State laws were passed which forbade any residence of white men on Indian lands. Red Jacket spoke out against the missionaries who came to live with the Indian, and in 1824 he finally won out and a mission on the reservation was removed. The reason Red Jacket gave for disliking the missionaries was, "Because they do us no good. If they are not useful to the white people why do they send them to the Indians, why do not they keep them home? . . . these men know that we do not understand their religion, we cannot read their book, they tell different stories about what it contains . . . the black coats tell us to raise corn and yet they do not themselves."

Redlands
Redlands, California, see Tolocabit.

Red Men
The Improved Order of Red Men was originally organized by those who admired Indian character and who adopted as their "patron" Chief Tammany (q.v.). It is now an organization that does charitable and benevolent acts. The first idea was started in Philadelphia around 1772 when a society met called "The Sons Of Tammany." They met at the home of Mr. James Byrn.

Red mud
Used by many Indian tribes in the United States, especially in the Southwest. The muddy water is collected after a rain and is used as a dyestuff. The color comes from the red mesas and the red clays in an area.

Red Thunder
This chief of the Yanktonai Sioux was at the Great Council meeting at Prairie du Chien, Wisconsin, in April, 1806. He fought with the English in the War of 1812. He

fought at Fort Meigs and Sandusky, Ohio. He was killed by the Chippewa in 1823.

Red Town
A rallying point for the Seminoles located on Tampa Bay, Florida.

Redwing
The name belongs to several chiefs of the Mdewakanton Sioux who formerly lived along Pepin Lake in Minnesota, the present location of Redwing, Minnesota. The name disappeared after 1865.

Renape
A term used by many Indian nations to mean the true man, or all races of man.

Renville
Gabriel Renville, the last chief of the Sisseton Sioux, was born near Big Stone Lake in South Dakota in April, 1824, and died at the Sisseton reservation on August 26, 1902. During the Sioux wars of 1862 he was a friend of the whites.

Reservations
Indian reservations were established in order to place some control on the Indians in the early days and also as a place to put the Indians that had been moved away from their native areas when the settlers moved in, in large numbers. Certain rights were given the Indian who lived on the reservations. These reservations were usually not the most choice of lands and the Indian feelings were not always considered during their "removal." Much has been done to improve the lot of the Indian on the reservations but at the same time a movement is also under way to "terminate" these people, which will absorb the Indian and his land. As a race he will soon disappear. See Indian Reservations.

Retouch
A term used when a point is broken and it is reworked;

sometimes the article is made into another thing altogether.

Rhinebeck
Rhinebeck, New York, see Sepascoot.

Rhombus
See bullroarer.

Rice
See wild rice.

Rice Lake
In 1700 this was the area where a village of the Chippewa was settled, located in Barron County, Wisconsin.

Richahake
In 1612, this was a village of the Powhatan, located near Norfolk, Virginia.

Richardville
John B. Richardville, a former chief of the Miami, see Peshewah.

Richmond
Richmond, Virginia, see Totopotomoi.

Rique
This village of the Erie was a former stockaded town. It was attacked in 1658 by the Iroquois. It was located at the present site of Erie, Pennsylvania.

River Indians
A term used by the early settlers to denote those Indians in general who lived along the Connecticut River.

Roanoke
This is an Island off the coast of Virginia which is about twelve miles long. Also spelled Roanoak, meaning a curve or bend, which is the shape of the island. The name was also applied to an Indian village at the end of the island.

Roanoke

Roanoke, Virginia, see Peccarecamek.

Robber People

See pillagers.

Robbiboe

A type of soup or broth made by the Chippewa and other Algonquian tribes, made from pemmican and flour.

Robin

See the Powhatan word, cheawanta.

Robinson

Alexander Robinson was a chief of the Potawatomi. He was born at Mackinaw, Michigan, in 1789. He did much to make peace between the settlers and the Indians. He served as an interpreter for General Lewis Cass during the treaty negotiations at Prairie du Chien, Wisconsin, on July 29, 1829.

Rockaway

Meaning the sandy land, this was a tribe of Long Island Indians who formerly lived near what is now Far Rockaway, Inwood and Cedarhurst, Long Island, New York.

Rock Hill

Rock Hill, South Carolina, see Sugeree, Catawba.

Roe

See the Powhatan word woock.

Roman Nose

This was a war chief of the Himoiyoqis, better known as the Cheyenne, called "Roman Nose" because of the shape of his nose. The Indian name was Woqini or "hooked nose." Roman Nose State Park in Oklahoma was named after chief Roman Nose. He was killed in a battle with the soldiers at Beecher's Island, Colorado, in September, 1868.

Romutton

The Virginia Indian term for a small hill or mountain.

Ross

This man, John Ross, was born in Rossville, Georgia, on October 3, 1790. His father was Scotch and his mother a Cherokee. He went to school at Kingston, Tennessee. In 1817 he worked on the Cherokee Council, which was set up to settle what lands the Cherokee would or would not have. He was later removed himself to a reservation. He died on August 1, 1866.

Roundhead

A town in Ohio named for a chief of the Wyandot Hurons who fought for the English in the War of 1812. He died in battle in 1813.

Rsotuk

A former village of the Pima, located just northwest of Casa Blanca in southern Arizona.

Rubberplant

The rubberplant (Hymenoxys metcalfei) is used by the Navajo Indians for the making of a bright yellow dye. The plant name in Navajo means the eared owl's foot.

Running Water

In 1782 this was an active Cherokee town, located along the Tennessee River, below the present city of Chattanooga, Tennessee. The village was destroyed in 1794.

Runonvea

This was another of the Iroquoian towns which was burned by General Sullivan on August 31, 1779. It was located near "Big Flats," in Chemung County, New York.

Runtee

An ornament of value, made of a shell cut round to make a sort of disc, which was drilled and strung around the neck. The runtee was made from a part of the conch. Some Atlantic coast tribes prized these so highly that one runtee was worth one beaver skin. Others valued them as six small or three large ones being worth one beaver. They were also made by the settlers so the value went down because of the discs that were made commercially.

Russia

The Russian traders came to America and along the northwest coast of Canada and Alaska beginning around 1741. The American Eskimo and the Siberian natives as well as other hostile Eskimos helped to discourage the early Russian traders. Those that did manage to get through met with hostile Spanish and English traders and the well armed Haida and Tlingit tribes of the Northwest Coast. The Hudson's Bay Company drew most of the fur trade in the early days. The Russians bought a small piece of land at Bodega Bay and later on one on the Russian River, both in California. They did this so that they would have a place to raise food supplies for their traders. At one time they did visit as far south as Santa Barbara in the late 1880's.

Russian River Pomo

This was a term used to describe those Pomo Indians who lived along the Russian River in California.

Russian thistle

The Navajo Indians use the entire plant of this thistle for the making of a dull green dye.

Russiaville

Russiaville, Indiana, see Peshewah.

Rye

Rye, New York, see Poningo.

S

Sabeata

A Christianized Indian of the Jumano. As chief of his tribe, he asked the Governor of Texas for protection against the Apaches and for a mission to be established for his people. He led Domingo de Mendoza's explorers into the interior of Texas in 1683 to 1684. At this time there was ill will between Sabeata and the Spanish, and he left to join his people. He was seen again in 1691 while leading a bison hunt with his people.

Sacagawea

This was a Shoshonean woman who accompanied Lewis and Clark on their trip west. She had been captured by the Hidatsa of North Dakota at age fourteen. She acted as interpreter. In return for her work, she would be able to return to her people in the Rocky Mountains. When the expedition met the Shoshone, they provided Lewis and Clark with horses which they used to cross the mountains. Sacagawea gave birth to a son during the trip west. She died near Fort Washakie in Wyoming on April 9, 1884. Her grave was marked with a brass tablet erected by Mr. Timothy F. Burke of Cheyenne, Wyoming. A bronze statue was erected in her honor in Portland, Oregon, in 1905. Another statue was erected at Bismarck, North Dakota.

Sacaton

This was formerly a trading station of the Pima, located along the Gila River in Arizona. Located at the present reservation of the Pima Agency at Sacaton, Arizona.

Sachem

This was a term used mainly by the Indians of Massachusetts. It denotes the supreme ruler or chief, followed by lesser rulers known as the sagamores (q.v.).

Sackhoes

In 1684 this was a village of the Kitchawank Indians. Named after their chief, the name means "black pot or kettle." Located at the present site of Peekskill, New York.

Saconnet

A small tribe of the Narraganset or Wampanoag who had a woman chief. During King Philip's War (1675) they took the side of the English. In 1700 they sold their lands to the whites. After an epidemic in 1763 and for a few years after, their tribe went down in size to less than a dozen individuals who were then living at Compton, Rhode Island.

Sacramento

Sacramento, California, see Sekumne.

Sacrifice

Most people think of primitive individuals who make a sacrifice as those who kill some special person and offer parts of the individual as a meal for those who want or need special powers.

The Indians north of Mexico did very little in the way of what could be called "human sacrifice." It was part of the Indian religion and way of life to appease the spirits; much of his "sacrifice" was done with a pipe because tobacco was used for such sacred purposes. Throwing certain objects into fire or leaving rocks at a certain spot were considered as a sacrifice. Such things as self inflicted wounds done during the Sun Dance or the cutting off of certain joints of the fingers were considered as a sacrifice. The early settlers and missionaries sometimes had a rather biased or distorted view of the "savages" and so things that they saw were not always what they thought they saw. What was roasting in a fire may have been a wild pig, but to the early whites it looked human!

Sagakomi

This is the name of a type of plant known as the bearberry bush which is used by the Indians in place of, or mixed with, tobacco. The leaves and sometimes the bark are used.

Sagamite

This is soup made from boiled corn. It was a favorite dish of the early settlers.

Sagamore

This is the Abnaki name for a ruler who is next under a sachem (q.v.).

Sagaunash

A chief of mixed blood, his father was Irish and his mother was a Potawatomi. He was born in 1780. He became a Catholic and fought for the English. In 1820 he moved to Chicago. On September 28, 1841, he died at Council Bluffs, Iowa.

Sagawamick

This was one of the main villages of the Mille Lac Band of the Chippewas who lived along the shores of Mille Lac Lake in Minnesota. The site has many mounds which were used by the recent Indians as burial places for their dead.

Saghwareesa

In 1752 this was a chief of the Tuscarora.

Saginaw

Meaning "mouth of the river," this was a former village of the Sauk who lived at the location of what is now Saginaw, Michigan. The village was abandoned and later occupied by the Chippewa, who lived there until 1837 when they were "removed."

Sagonaquade

Also known as Albert Cusick, which was his Christian

name. He was a former chief of the Tuscarora who was born on the reservation on December 25, 1846. He lost his rights as a chief when he became Christianized, however. He later moved to the Onondaga reservation in New York. His Indian name meant "he who angers them."

Sagoquas
In 1614 this was a village of the Massachusetts, located near what is now Cohasset in Norfolk County, Massachusetts.

Sagunte
This possible Costanoan village was located near what is now San Francisco, California, at the mission.

Saia
This was formerly a tribe of California Indians. In 1862 they were taken prisoners and placed on the wrong reservation until 1868, when the reservation was abandoned. They were then placed on a Hupa reservation, where for ten more years they led a hard life. By 1877 they became almost extinct as a people.

St. Augustine
St. Augustine, Florida, see Picolata.

Saint Francis
In 1844 this was a mission which was established on the Wolf River in Winnebago County, Wisconsin. In 1852 the Menominee were moved to another reservation, this time to Shawano County. It was here that a new mission was established, called St. Michael.

St. Regis
An Iroquois reservation under the jurisdiction of the State of New York, with the state holding the lands in trust.

Saituka
This was a name applied to those Indians of the state

of Oregon, especially the Shahaptian, known as the "camas eaters." The name was used by the Paiutes.

Sakaweston

This was an Indian captured on one of the small islands off the coast of New England by a Captain Harlow in 1611. He took the Indian to England, where he lived and eventually became a soldier and was sent to Bohemia to fight.

Sakeyu

An ancient Tewa pueblo, located on a mesa near the San Ildefonso pueblo and west of the Rio Grande in New Mexico.

Salabi

This was one of the spruce clans of the Hopi Kachina phratry.

Salem

In 1781 this was a Moravian Delaware village, located about a mile from Port Washington, Ohio. The mission was abandoned in the same year.

Salinan

A California linguistic family living in San Luis Obispo and Monterey Counties. Little is known about them.

Salisbury

Salisbury, Connecticut, see Weataug.

Salish

This was a large group of Indians who inhabited the areas of western Montana, also known as the Flatheads. They were mainly hunters. The Salishan family covered an area of Montana, Idaho and parts of Oregon and Canada.

Salishan Family

A language family covering Northern Washington, northern Idaho and western Montana. The Salish, Chimakuan and Wakashan are related, and have a few similarities with

Algonquian. These people built houses of planks and beams. They depended on fish for a great deal of their food, even those in the interior being able to secure large amounts of salmon.

Salt

Many tribes in the United States did not use salt. Tribes such as the Omaha traveled to areas such as are found around Lincoln, Nebraska, where they gathered rock salt which they ground to the desired size. See sawwone.

Saltketchers

This was a former village of the Yuchi of South Carolina, which was active around 1715.

Salt Lick

A former village of the Delawares, located at the present site of Warren, Ohio. An early salt works was operated at this site by the settlers in 1796.

Saluda

A small tribe which was a part of the Shawnee who lived along the Saluda River in South Carolina.

Samoset

In 1620, he was one of the chiefs who appeared amongst the Pilgrims and informed them that he was the sagamore (q.v.) of the Pemaquids of the Bristol, Maine, area. He also introduced the Pilgrims to Massasoit (q.v.). In July, 1625, he made the first deed between the English and the Indians which gave some 12,000 acres to the English. Shortly after 1653 Samoset died and was buried near Round Pond, Bristol, Maine. His name means "he who walks over much."

Samp

This is a kind of mush or cereal made with beaten corn which is cooked. This was an important article of food for the colonists and the Indians.

Sana

This was one of the central Texas tribes, possibly the Tonkawan which were met by the Spanish in 1691. They lived in an area now known as San Marcos, Texas.

San Antonio

This was a former settlement of the Tigua. Several Spanish missions were established in this area. One called the San Antonio de Valero church or mission is better known by the name of the Alamo. In 1773 the lands around the mission were divided, but not among the Indians. The building was then occupied by the del Alamo de Parras Company from which its name is now derived. On March 6, 1836, this mission was the center of a battle between the Texans and the soldiers of Mexico.

San Antonio, Texas, see Pajalat.

San Carlos Apache

This name was given to those Apaches who lived along the Gila River in Arizona. Also the present name of the San Carlos Indian Agency in Arizona.

Sandal

The sandal was worn mainly by the desert peoples, some in California and a few areas of the Gulf Coast.

Sandia

This was an ancient pueblo, located about 12 miles north of Albuquerque, New Mexico. It was visited by the Spaniards, Coronado in 1540 and Oñate in 1598. It was abandoned in 1680. However, there is a modern pueblo of the same name at approximately the same location.

San Diego

This was the first Spanish mission to be established in California; July 16, 1769, the mission was formally dedicated by Father Junípero Serra. It was then called San Diego de Alcalá (Saint James). Most of the Indians in the area belonged to the Yuman stock and those who came within the reach of the mission were known as Diegueños.

Sand-painting
Done by the Hopi and Navajo of the Southwest. See dry-painting.

Sandusky
This name was used for two villages of the Wyandot Hurons who lived at the present site of Sandusky, Ohio. The name means "cool water" in Huron (Otsaandosti). See Red Thunder.

Sandwich
Sandwich, Massachusetts, see Skauton.

San Felipe
A pueblo of Keresan Indians, located near Bernalillo, New Mexico. It has existed as a pueblo from the seventeenth century to the present.

San Francisco
San Francisco, California, see Sagunte.

San Ildefonso
A Tewa pueblo located about 18 miles from Santa Fe, New Mexico. In 1617 it became one of the main Spanish missions. Now a well known center for Indian potters.

Sanipao
A tribe of Christianized Indians, formerly belonging to the Coahuiltecan tribes. In 1755, a number of these people came to the Concepción mission near San Antonio, Texas (q.v.). They were the first tribe to appear on the marriage books . . . in one day, they were instructed, baptized and remarried.

San Juan
A Tewa pueblo about twenty-five miles north of Santa Fe. It is still occupied.

San Marcos
San Marcos, Texas, see Sana.

Sanpoil
A Salish tribe living on the Columbia River in Washington.

Sans Arcs
This was a division of the Hunkpapa and Teton Sioux who lived in the Dakotas. On October 20, 1865, at Fort Sully, South Dakota, they made peace with the United States.

Santa Ana
Several pueblos of this name were used in the United States and Mexico. One was a Keresan pueblo located in central New Mexico along the Rio Grande. The village was active in 1598 and was one of those pueblos visited by Oñate.

Santa Barbara
This was the tenth Franciscan mission to be founded in California, established in 1782. The Indians in the area were mostly Chumashan and some Yokuts.

Santa Clara
A Tewa pueblo north of Santa Fe, which has existed to the present day.

Santa Clara Indians
A term used to denote those Indians who lived in the area and influence of the Santa Clara Mission (mission number eight) which was founded in 1777 in California.

Santee
This was a tribe of the Sioux who lived along the Santee River in South Carolina. They were active around 1700. They fought against the English. After 1716 what was left of the tribe joined with the Catawba of South Carolina.

Santee Dakota
A division of the Dakota living in Minnesota.

Santo Domingo
A Keresan pueblo near Bernalillo, New Mexico, north of San Felipe pueblo.

Santsukhdhin
This was one of the larger divisions of the Osage who lived around Missouri. By 1810 they had moved along the Verdigris and Arkansas Rivers.

Saopuk
This was a large Pima village located along the Gila River in Arizona, the name means "many trees," meaning the cottonwoods.

Sapohanikan
This was the Delaware trade center of Hoboken, New Jersey. It was from here that the furs and other trade items were taken across to New York City.

Saponi
This was a former tribe of the Sioux who lived in North Carolina and Virginia. Soon after 1780 they disappeared from history, due to treaties, wars and smallpox.

Sarasota
Sarasota, Florida, was a former settlement of the Seminoles in 1841.

Saratoga
This was a village of the Mohawk; the name means the place "where ashes float," referring to the mineral waters which are found there. It was located on the west bank of the Hudson River in Saratoga County, New York. The name was also given to a trunk, called the "Saratoga Trunk," so called because so many people used this type of trunk when

365

they visited Saratoga. Saratoga chips were a type of potato chip which was made famous there.

Sarontac
A former Costanoan village located near the Dolores mission near San Francisco, California.

Sarrochau
This was a former village of the Winnebagos who lived in Fond du Lac County in Wisconsin.

Sarsi
These people live in the Rocky Mountain area and into Canada.

Sassaba
A chief of the Chippewas. He attended a treaty signing at Sault St. Marie, Michigan, in 1820. He disliked the Americans intensely and argued against selling any land to them. He died from drowning in 1822.

Sassacus
He was one of the last Pequot chiefs, born near Groton, Connecticut, about 1560. In 1630 the colonists decided to make war on the Pequots. He was killed by the Mohawks near New York in June, 1637.

Sasuagel
A former village of the Chumashan located on Santa Cruz Island, California.

Satanta
This chief of the Kiowa was born about 1830. He was known as the "Orator of the Plains." He was one of the signers of the Medicine Lodge Treaty of 1867 which forced his people to live on a reservation. He was taken prisoner by General Custer and after some time, he committed suicide while he was in prison. He died October 11, 1878.

Satquin

In 1614 this was a village of the Abnaki located along the coast of Maine near the mouth of the Kennebec River.

Satucket

A former village of the Nauset located near what is now Brewster, in Barnstable County, Massachusetts. The village was active around 1687.

Saturiba

This was a former village of the Timucuans who lived along the St. John's River in Florida around 1565. Before the end of the 16th century all of these Indians became Christians.

Saucita

This was a former village of the desert Indians known as the Papagos and was active around 1863, located in southern Arizona.

Sauk

This was a group of Algonquian tribes who lived in what is now Michigan. They were first met by the Frenchman Allouez in 1667. They also lived in Wisconsin and Illinois, and were woodland Indians.

Sauquonckackock

This was a former Pequot village, located on the western side of the Thames River near Mohegan, Connecticut. Active around 1638.

Savannah

Savannah, Georgia, see Tomochichi, also Yamacraw.

Sawanogi

This was a combined town of Shawnee and Creeks who lived along the southern side of the Tallapoosa River in Macon County, Alabama, around 1773.

367

Sawcunk

This was a former village and trading center of the Delaware, located along the Ohio River near the mouth of Beaver Creek, Pennsylvania. This village was abandoned in 1758 by the French traders. The present location of Beaver, Pennsylvania.

Sawwone

The Virginia Indian term for salt.

Saydegil

Saydegil, see Una Vida.

Scalps

Scalps were taken by comparatively few tribes of the United States in the early days. The practice was carried out mainly by the Iroquois and was not common with the New England or Atlantic Coast tribes. It was unknown to the Plains Indians and those of California. The spread of the practice of taking scalps was the direct result of the early governments of England, France, Spain and Holland. They offered bounties for the scalps of their enemies. This was one way that they could tell the results of a war party. The scalp was taken from the back crown of the head (the part where the hair seems to grow in a circle). This was cut from the head. This was sometimes done while the person was alive and then he was returned to his people as an insult to them. Scalps were braided and knotted, and sometimes dyed certain set colors. These could then be turned in for payment . . . certain colors for soldiers, settlers, women, etc., they would receive payment according to the amount of danger involved. As the settler spread, so did scalping.

Scandinavian

See Norse.

Scarface Charley

Scarface Charley was a warrior who fought with Kintpuash (q.v.). He was a witness at the trial of the Indian prisoners at the Modoc trials, 1874. He died in December, 1896.

Scaticook

This was a former village of the Mahicans located along the East bank of the Hudson River near the Hoosac River in Rensselaer County, New York.

Schekaha

This was a former village of the Choctaw, located about six miles northeast from Philadelphia in Neshoba County, Mississippi. The name means "town of sand."

Schenectady

This was a former village of the Mohawks which was active in the late 1600's. The name means "near the pines," referring to the large pine woods in the area. In 1690 it was attacked by the French and Indians.

Schira

This was the former clan of the crows of the Sia and San Felipe pueblos located in New Mexico.

Schodac

This ancient village of the Mahicans was formerly located on the east bank of the Hudson River in Rensselaer County, near what is now Castleton, New York. It was active in 1664.

Schoenbrunn

This was a former town of the Munsee Indians located near New Philadelphia, Ohio. The Indians of this village were all Moravians and were moved to this village in 1773. During the Revolution these Indians were forced to move to Sandusky, Ohio, and in 1782, the village was burned.

Scottsville

The city of Scottsville, New York, see Oatka.

Scraper
A device used to scrape hides, bone, woods, etc. They are usually named by the way that they are used, such as side scraper, bottom scraper, etc.

Scrub Oak
The Navajo use the galls that are found on this oak for the making of a rather golden-colored dye.

Scuppaug
This was a name used in New England for the porgy (q.v.), a small fish caught off the Atlantic Coast.

Scuppernong
A type of white grape which was used by Captain John Smith to make a table wine. The grape was found growing in and around Columbia, North Carolina. This name was also given to a river in North Carolina.

Seattle
This was the name of a chief of the Dwamish who lived in the Puget Sound area of Washington. He was born about 1790. He became a Catholic. During the Indian outbreaks of 1855 to 1858, he remained friendly to the whites. In 1890, the people of Seattle, Washington, erected a monument over his grave.

Sebaik
This was a former village of the Passamaquoddy, located near what is now Perry in Washington County, Maine. The name means "at the water passage."

Secacawoni
In 1608 this was a village of the Powhatan who lived along the bank of the Potomac in Northumberland County in Virginia.

Secatoag
Meaning the "burned land," this was a former Long

370

Island tribe that lived on the south side of Long Island between Oyster Bay and Patchogue.

Secawgo

In 1807 this band visited the Indian meeting which was held at Greenville, Ohio. They belonged to the Potawatomi.

Seccasaw

In 1614 this was a village of the Massachusetts who lived along the coast in the northern part of Plymouth County, Massachusetts.

Secobec

In 1608 this was a village of the Powhatan which was located along the southern banks of the Rappahannock River in Caroline County, Virginia.

Secotan

This Algonquian tribe lived on the Albemarle Peninsula and in several counties in North Carolina. The tribes were active about 1584 and were met by Sir Walter Raleigh during his travels.

Sego

The root of the sego lily was used by the Indians for food, especially by the Indians of Utah and those in the surrounding areas.

Segocket

In 1614 this was a village of the Abnaki who lived near the mouth of the Penobscot River in Maine.

Segotago

This was a former village of the Abnaki who lived near the mouth of the Kennebec River, Maine, in 1614.

Segunesit

This was a village of the Nipmuc Indians who gathered with other hostile Indians of northeastern Connecticut during the uprising of 1675.

Seh

This was the eagle clan of the Jemez and Pecos pueblos of New Mexico.

Sekumne

This was a former Maidu settlement, located north of Sacramento, California.

Sekhushtuntunne

This tribe, known as the people of the big rocks, formerly lived along the Coquille River in Oregon.

Seminole

These Muskhogean people were a mixture of other tribes such as the Yuchi, Upper Creeks and Creeks. Their name means runaway or the peninsula people. About 1775 they began to be known by the name of Seminoles. In 1817 the first official Seminole war began. General Andrew Jackson invaded Florida with over 3,000 men and forced Spain to cede the land to the United States. By a treaty of 1823, the Seminole were supposed to remove themselves from Florida within three years. In 1835 Osceola (q.v.) prepared his people to fight against this and in a few months, the second Seminole war started. This war lasted for nearly eight years. Some of the Seminoles were removed to Oklahoma. Those that stayed in the Everglades never officially made peace with the government.

Seneca

These Mohegan people lived around what is now Seneca Lake and the Geneva River in northwestern New York. They were then a part of the great Iroquois Nation. Their name means "people of the rocks." Seneca of Sandusky, see Cayuga.

Seneca Oil

Seneca Oil, see Wenrohronon.

Sepascoot

A tribe of the Munsee or Wappinger who lived along the Hudson River at Rhinebeck, New York.

Seping

This Tewa clan of the San Juan Pueblo of New Mexico was known as the painted eagle clan.

Sequoia

Sometimes spelled Sequoya, this Cherokee was born in Taskigi, Tennessee, about 1760. Sequoia developed a Cherokee alphabet in 1821 which enabled his people to read and write. He felt that the whites had great power because they could read and write. The government named the redwoods of California after him, "Sequoia."

Sequoya League

In 1902, Mr. Charles F. Lummis and others founded an organization in Los Angeles, California, known as the "Sequoya League," named after the noted Cherokee. It was incorporated to "make better Indians." They have done much to help the Indian with food, clothing, legal assistance and to right many of the wrongs done the Indian since the settlement.

Serpent Mound

This great mound is located in Adams County, Ohio. The mound measures about 4 feet high, about 16 feet wide and some 1,300 feet long from head to tail. In 1900 the mound and the land around it became the property of the Ohio Historical Society. See mounds.

Serrano

A Shoshonean group, living in the San Bernardino Mountains and Valley of California. There were two groups, Kitanemuk and Alliklik.

Serrated

This means tooth-edged or saw-like.

Sesum

This Maidu village was located on the western side of the Feather River just below Mimal in Sutter County, California.

Setangya

A medicine man and chief of the Kiowa and also the war leader of his tribe. Also known by the name of Satank. He was born about 1810. He was one of the signers of the treaty at Medicine Lodge in 1867. His son was killed by the whites in Texas in 1870. He went to Texas to get his bones and while doing so he attacked several wagon trains. About a year later he was in Oklahoma and he talked about his deeds in Texas and he was promptly arrested. As he was about to be sent to Texas for trial, he drew a knife and a guard shot and killed him. He is buried in the military cemetery at Fort Sill, Oklahoma.

Setauket

This was a former Algonquian village located on the north shore of Long Island, New York, near what is now Wading River. Also the town of Setauket, New York.

Setokwa

This village of the ancient Jemez was located just south of the present pueblo in New Mexico.

Setsi

The name of a mound and an ancient Cherokee village, located near Valleytown in Cherokee County, North Carolina.

Sewackenaem

In 1658 this was one of the chiefs of the Esopus Indians who lived along the Hudson River across from Hyde Park, New York, and the present town of Esopus, New York.

Sewan

This was a general term used by the early settlers of New England and New York for the loose shell money of the Indians. One purple bead was worth two white ones. This name was used to describe those beads which were loose and not strung.

Sewee

In 1701 this small tribe was living along the Santee River in South Carolina. They were of Siouan origin and later joined with the Catawbas of South Carolina.

Sewickley

This Shawnee village was a trading center. It was located along the Allegheny River near what is now Springdale, Pennsylvania.

Shabbona

Shabbona, Illinois, see Shobonier.

Shabonee

This was a former chief of the Potawatomi and a nephew of Pontiac. He was born in Illinois around 1775. He did much to save the whites during the Indian wars. He died July 17, 1859.

Shabwasing

This was a tribe of the Chippewa who formerly lived in lower Michigan.

Shackamaxon

This Delaware village was located near what is now Philadelphia, Pennsylvania. This was the place where William Penn made his treaty with the Indians in 1682.

Shadjwane

For the Yuchi Indian, this was the rabbit clan.

Shaganappi

This was a long thong or rope of rawhide, cut from

hide. This was an invaluable article for the Indians and the settlers.

Shahaptian

This was the Salish name for the linguistic family known as the Nez Percés (q.v.), who formerly lived in what is now Washington, Oregon and Idaho.

Shakashakeu

This was the heron sub-phratry of the Menominee of Wisconsin.

Shakehand

In 1804 this was a chief of the Yankton Sioux who met with Lewis and Clark at a meeting near the present site of Yankton, South Dakota.

Shakopee

Meaning six, this was the name used by a series of chiefs of the Mdewakanton Sioux who lived in Minnesota.

Shakori

This was a small tribe of people who were associated with the Eno of North Carolina. They lived near the present city of Durham, North Carolina.

Shaman

Also known as a medicine man. This is an individual who is supposed to have special healing power and who gets his power directly from another world. He is the spiritual leader of a tribe.

Shamokin

The name means where the horns are plenty, meaning deer antlers. This was one of the largest Lenape settlements in Pennsylvania. It was located near the forks of the Susquehanna River, near what is now Sunbury in Northumberland County, Pennsylvania.

Shanel

A former village of the Pomo, located along the Russian River about a mile north of Centerville, California. See Russian River Pomo.

Shanhaw

This was formerly one of the six towns of the Choctaw, this one located in Mississippi.

Shannopin's Town

This was an early trading center, located at the present site of Pittsburgh, Pennsylvania. It was active around 1730. The village was occupied mainly by the Delawares.

Shapashken

This former Modoc village was located on the southern side of Klamath Lake in the northern part of California.

Shapata

This was formerly the Shawnee raccoon clan.

Shasta

Around 1840 this tribe of California Indians lived in the northern parts of California.

Shaugawaumikong

This ancient Chippewa village was located along the coast of Lake Superior in Ashland County, Wisconsin. Later moved and known to have been located at Bayfield and La Pointe, Wisconsin.

Shawangunk

A village of the Waranawonkong which was fortified and located near what is now Tuthill in Ulster County, New York. In 1663 it was burned by the Dutch.

Shawiangto

In August, 1779, General Clinton burned this village of

the Tuscarora. It was located near what is now Windsor in Broome County, New York.

Shawnee

At one time the Shawnee lived in South Carolina, Pennsylvania, Ohio and Tennessee. Their name means the south or from the south. The Shawnee belong linguistically to the Central Algonquian. They were the enemies of the Catawbas of the Carolinas. These people moved about a great deal and some went to Ohio in 1748 and on into Missouri. Chillicothe, Ohio, was one of their villages.

Shawnee Cabins

This was a trading post located along the Indian trail along the Ohio River, the present site of Bedford, Pennsylvania. This was a well-known starting point for those traders who went west.

Shaya

This was the former squirrel clan of the Yuchi tribes.

Shaytee's Village

Located in Illinois, see Grand Bois.

Shecomeco

In 1740 this was the site of a Moravian mission which was established at the Mahican village, located about two miles south of the present Pine Plains in Dutchess County, New York. The name means large or great village.

Shediac

This was a former village of the Micmac Indians, active about 1670. Located at the present site of Shediac, New Brunswick.

Sheffield

Sheffield, Massachusetts, see Skatehook.

Shell heap

A shell heap, as such, was a refuse pile or kitchen midden which was used by the Indians. Usually found along a bank of a stream, river or other large body of water wherein shellfish could be found, collected and eaten. Some of the mounds are large and cover several acres. These are gradually built up after years of use in one area.

Shenango
This name was used for several Indian trading centers in Ohio and Pennsylvania. One was located at Economy in Beaver County, Pennsylvania.

Sherd
A term used by the archaeologist which means a piece of pottery.

Sheshebe
This was formerly the duck gens of the Chippewa.

Sheshequin
The various spellings of this word in Cree, Chippewa, Lenape, and Menominee mean the rattle, usually made from a gourd.

Shiankya
This was the former clan of the Pueblo at Pecos, New Mexico, known as the mountain lion clan.

Shickshack
This was a former chief of the Winnebago who lived in Illinois. He and his people lived about 11 miles west of the present New Salem, Illinois. He became known through the book by Mrs. Mary Catherwood called "Spanish Peggy."

Shield
A shield was used mainly by the Indians of the plains and further south into Mexico. The shield was not used by the eastern and the woodland tribes. Many shields were only used for ceremonial purposes.

Shigom
This was a former village of the Pomo who lived along Clear Lake in Lake County, California.

Shikshichela
This name means the bad ones and was a group belonging to the Hunkpapa Sioux and the Sans Arcs.

Shingabawassin
This Chippewa chief was born about 1763 and lived most of his life along the St. Mary's River in Michigan. He tried to get special reservations set up for those Indians who were "half-breeds."

Shinnecock
This Algonquian tribe lives on the southeastern shore of Long Island, New York, from Shinnecock Bay to Montauk Point on Long Island. Their reservation comprises some 700 acres. The Presbyterians and Seventh Day Adventists have churches there. Because of intermarriages with the negroes, very little is left of the original characteristics of the Shinnecock Indians.

Shipaulovi
The name means the mosquitoes. A name given because the people of this abandoned pueblo had to leave their village site because of the hordes of mosquitoes. The pueblo was located on Middle Mesa of the Tusayan in northeastern Arizona.

Shiptetza
This was a former band of the Crow Indians. The name is used when talking about an arrow as it glances off the side of a bison when it happens to hit a rib.

Shitaimu
This was the former pueblo of the eagle clan of the Hopi, situated near Mishongnovi in Arizona.

Shiu

This was the former eagle clan of the pueblo at Isleta, New Mexico.

Shivwits

In 1873 this tribe lived on the plateau named after them in the northwestern part of Arizona. They were later removed to reservations in Nevada and Utah.

Shiyosubula

This band of the Brulé Teton Sioux was known as the sharp-tailed grouse.

Shobonier

This was a former village of the Potawatomi located in De Kalb County, Illinois, about 1830. The village was named after its chief. The present site of Shabbona, Illinois.

Shodakhai

This was the name of the Pomo people who formerly lived in what was then known as Coyote Valley along the east branch of the Russian River in Mendocino County, California.

Shoe

See chapant.

Shopakia

This is an ancient ruin of the Zuñi, located about five miles north of the present Zuñi, New Mexico.

Short Bull

This chief of the Brulé Sioux was born about 1845 in Nevada. He became a Christian Indian and took part in the Ghost Dance activities and thought of himself as the Messiah. He later became a Congregationalist.

Shoshoko

Sometimes this term is used for a division of the Shoshoni. It is also used to describe those of the tribe who did not have a horse and so were known as the "walkers."

Shoshoni

This group of people lived in what is now Wyoming, Nevada and parts of Idaho. They were visited by Lewis and Clark in 1805, when they were living along the Missouri River and in Montana. They were also known by the name of grass people because they lived on the plains, and used the bison for food and the horse to get around on. They were not an agricultural people.

Showtucket

A former Mohegan settlement located near what is now Lisbon in New London County, Connecticut. After the war in 1678 the village was occupied by a band of Indians known as the "Surrenderers," it was later left by these people too because of warfare among local tribes.

Shubuta

Shubuta, Mississippi, see Yowani.

Shumway

This was a former pueblo which is now a ruin located about 40 miles south of Holbrook, Arizona.

Shungikcheka

This band of the Yanktonai Sioux was known as the common dogs.

Shup

A former village of the Chumashan, located near what is now Santa Barbara, California.

Shushuchi

This was a former village of the Chumashan located near Point Conception, California. The present site of La Fuemada.

Shuta
This was the former crane clan of the Sia pueblo in New Mexico.

Shutaunomanok
This was a former village of the Pomo who lived around Clear Lake in California.

Sia
This small tribe of the Keresan lived along the Jemez River about fifteen miles from Bernalillo in New Mexico. They fought against the Spanish in 1696. There is also a modern pueblo by this name.

Sibley
General Sibley and the Sibley tent, see tipi.

Signals
The Indian had many simple signals which were used to show trouble, fresh game, friendship or enemy. Smoke signals, dust thrown in the air or fires which were lit in a conspicuous place, all of these were used by the various tribes. Such things as walking or riding in circles, zig zag riding were used.

Sign Language
A system of communication by using gestures by tribes speaking different languages. It was used chiefly by plains Indians, only traces of sign language being found in other areas. A well-developed system arose, the sign representing the article or idea it stood for. "Man" is indicated by holding out the hand with the back outward and one finger pointed up, to show one who walks erect.

Sihasapa
This is a division of the Teton Sioux, better known as the Blackfeet. So called because of the black moccasins that they wore. They lived in the Dakotas.

Sihu

This is the flower clan or the bush clan of the Hopi.

Sijame

This tribe of the Tonkawan lived around the San Antonio mission (q.v.). They were active around 1719. Many of the members of this tribe became Christianized.

Siksika

The Blackfoot tribe proper, sometimes called North Blackfeet.

Sikyatki

This prehistoric Hopi pueblo was known as the yellow house. It was located at the base of Walpi Mesa near Tusayan in the northeastern part of Arizona.

Siletz

This Salishan tribe lived along the southern coast of Oregon.

Silt

A term used for the accumulation of sand or clay. It is usually made up of many sizes but separated according to size.

Silver Bluff

This former village of the Yuchi was located along the Savannah River in Barnwell County, South Carolina.

Silverwork

At the time of the discovery, silver was not in general use by the Indians north of Mexico. The working of silver was learned from the Spanish explorers.

Sinaesta

In 1570 this was an active village of the Calusa who lived on the southwest coast of Florida.

Sinago
This is the Chippewa word for the grey squirrel.

Sinew
This is a part of an animal known as the tendon. It is taken from along the backbone of the deer, bison or other large animal. It is pounded and dried for use in sewing. Fish lines and ropes were made from braided or twisted sinew.

Sing
See kantikantic.

Single-flowered actinea
The stems, flowers and the leaves of this plant are used by the Navajo for the making of a yellow dye.

Sinkyone
This was a group of Athapascan who formerly lived in Humboldt County, California.

Siouan
Next to the Algonquian, this was the largest linguistic family of Indians north of Mexico. Their influence extended from the Mississippi west to the Rocky Mountains.

Sipapu
A term used to describe the hole from which a mythological figure arises from a kiva.

Sisseton
This Dakota tribe lived along the Mississippi and the Minnesota Rivers. The name meant "the water people" or "those who lived along the water."

Sister
See the Powhatan word, cuvfmc.

Sitting Bull
This was a chief and leader of the Hunkpapa Teton

Sioux who was born in South Dakota, 1834. As a boy he had the name of Jumping Badger. After a battle that he participated in he took the name of Sitting Bull in 1857. Because Sitting Bull made good medicine in the hills before the Battle of Little Big Horn, and had foretold that he would win the battle against Custer, he received higher honor for actually having done what he started out to do. On December 15, 1890, while some of his people were trying to rescue him from prison, Sitting Bull was killed by two members of the Indian Police named Tomahawk and Bullhead.

Siuslaw
A Yakonan tribe formerly living on the Siuslaw River in Oregon.

Siwash
This is not a tribe, but an uncomplimentary term for Indian used by white people in the Northwest. It is said to be a corruption of the French word "sauvage" (savage).

Skagit
A group of the Salish who lived on the Skagit River and on Whidbey Island, Washington.

Skahasegao
This was a former Seneca village, located at the present site of Lima, New York, in Livingston County.

Skaniadariio
This former chief of the Senecas was a half-brother of Cornplanter (q.v.), who was born near what is now Avon, New York, about 1735. Around 1796 he became very sick and stayed so for almost four years, until he had a vision and suddenly recovered and started a new Indian faith which he preached to the Iroquois. He died near Syracuse, New York, in 1815.

Skatehook
In 1736 the Westenhuck people moved from the village

which was located near what is now Sheffield to Stock-bridge, Massachusetts.

Skauton
In 1685 this was a village of the Nauset or Wampanoag Indians. Located near what is now Sandwich, Massachusetts.

Skeinah
This was a former Cherokee settlement, located in Fannin County, Georgia. The tribe was "removed" in 1839. This was also known as "Devil Town."

Skenandoa
This was a chief of the Oneida. He became a Christianized Indian and was a friend of the whites. He persuaded the Oneida to remain neutral during the Revolution. He died at Oneida Castle, March 11, 1816, in Tryon County, New York. He requested that he be buried at the side of his friend, the Reverend Samuel Kirkland, a missionary who was buried in a cemetery at Clinton, New York.

Skidi
A member of the Pawnee confederacy, closely related to the Arikara.

Skidirahru
This was a group of the Skidi Pawnee who killed a large number of bison while they camped along the Loup River in Nebraska. The carcasses which were left on the ice attracted many wolves.

The translation of Skidirahru is "wolves standing in pools."

Skokomish
A Salish tribe which was a division of the Twana. They lived on the Skokomish River in Washington, and their name means "river people."

Sleep
See nuppawe.

Sleeping Wolf

This second chief of the Kiowa was a delegate of his tribe at Washington in 1872. The name is a hereditary one and so there are at least five known chiefs with this name; the name means actually, "wolf lying down."

Sleepyeye

Sleepyeye, Minnesota, see Sleepy Eyes.

Sleepy Eyes

This name was given to a chief of the Sisseton Sioux who was born in Minnesota near what is now Mankato. Sleepy Eyes became a chief of his tribe around 1822. He was a signer of several treaties, one at Prairie du Chien, Wisconsin, in 1825. He died in South Dakota after 1851. His remains were removed to Sleepyeye, Minnesota, and he was buried under a monument erected by the people of that town.

Slip

A term used in the pottery crafts, meaning a thin coating of clay, usually colored, which is applied to a piece of pottery to add color to it.

Smallpox

See nummanemennaus.

Smith

Chief Nimrod Jarrett Smith was born near the Valley River at the present site of Murphy, North Carolina, around 1838. During the Civil War he enlisted on the side of the Confederates. After the war he worked continuously for his people. He arranged to establish Indian schools for his people. He died in August, 1893.

Smohalla

This Indian became a religious teacher and started a new way of tribal life for the Indians of Oregon, Washington and Idaho. He had quite a following. He believed that the Indian should drop the white man's religion and way of life and go back to the old ways. "Smohalla Indians" was the name his followers became known by, also called the "dreamers."

Smoking
At the time of the settlement, the Indians were well advanced in the practice of smoking the plant tobacco along with other plants mixed in. The early explorers said that they met persons who were carrying coals for fumigation. Smoking was done mainly at ceremonies and other special occasions. Tobacco and its use spread all over Europe and Asia. At one time it was considered a beneficial and healthful thing to smoke and children in English schools were ordered to smoke as a measure against the plague!

Smutty Bear
A Yankton Sioux leader who was the signer of a treaty at Portage des Sioux in 1815, and also in 1858, when the tribe had to give up their lands and the tribe was removed to a reservation in South Dakota in 1859. Smutty Bear died shortly after the removal.

Snake Dance
This is a ceremony that is held every two years by the Hopi of several pueblos in Arizona. This dance seems to be the best known of Indian ceremonies, especially by those who know little about the Indians. The snake dance is mainly a ceremony for rain making. It starts about eight days before the public sees it, as much of the ceremony is done secretly. The dance and pageantry culminate with the snakes, which are carried in the mouth and after songs and special rites are carried out the snakes are released at certain designated spots to go and return with the needed rain. This is followed by feasting and games by everyone in the tribe.

Snakes

This is a name which is applied to many groups of Indians, mainly those of the Shoshonean groups such as are found in Nevada, Oregon and California.

Sneeze

See zanckone.

Snohomish

A small group of Salish that lived on Puget Sound, Washington.

Sockobeck

In 1608 this was a village of the Powhatan located along the north side of the Rappahannock River in King County, Virginia.

Socorro

This is the site of an ancient pueblo of the Piro, located at the present site of Socorro, New Mexico. The name is Spanish and means "help," so called by the Spanish explorer Oñate, who visited there in 1598 and received help and friendly treatment from the Indians there.

Sofk

This is a type of food made from corn meal. The ground corn is placed in a pot of hot water and let cool, to this is added water which is dripped through wood ashes, forming a lye. When this is thick, ground nuts such as the hickory are added and also some bone marrow. This food is prepared mainly by the Creeks and other tribes of the Gulf States area.

Soldier

At the time of the settlement there were no Indians who were called soldiers in the strict sense of the word. They had wars and battles which they fought in but they did not do this for pay. There was a class of wariors in a tribe whose only reward was honor. There were usually six grades of soldiers that an Indian had to pass through from early youth on up to an adult.

Somo

A name which belonged to a former village of the Chumashan who lived in Ventura County, California.

Sonoma

This name is taken from one of the chiefs of the Indians who lived at the present site of Sonoma, California. In the early days this was the site where the last mission was established in California. The name meant ground or place or area.

Sonsa

This clan of the Jemez pueblo of New Mexico was known as the badger clan. The name was used also by those people of the Pecos pueblo in New Mexico.

Sopone

This was a Chumashan village located near what is now Santa Barbara, California.

Soquee

This was a settlement of the Cherokee who formerly lived in an area near the present site of Clarkesville in Georgia.

Souhegan

This Pennacook tribe lived along the Souhegan River in Hillsborough County in New Hampshire. This is the present site of Amherst, New Hampshire.

Souligny

This was a chief of the Menominee who was born about 1785. He was one of the chiefs who fought with the English and captured the fort at Mackinaw from the Americans.

He also fought against the Americans in the War of 1812 and the Black Hawk War. In 1864 he died at a place known as Great Falls, which is along the Wolf River in Wisconsin.

Spade stone

This is an artifact which was found in several areas where mounds are found; they resemble spade or shovel blades but because of the materials used this could not always be their actual use. They are what might be called "ceremonial, problematical."

Spall

This is the term used for a small chip or flake which is broken from a larger piece of rock or mineral.

Spanguliken

This term was used by the Delawares of New York when they spoke of someone as being vain. In other words a person who raises his eyebrows when he is speaking in a haughty manner.

Spanish Influence

The main influence of the Spanish explorers was felt by the Indians of Florida, the Gulf Coast area and the southwest into California. The Spanish quest for gold led them into long trips into Indian country which were followed by the missionary work. The Indians at first welcomed these new people, but gradually they found their own customs being abolished and the protection from their enemies that they expected from the Spanish turned into a necessity for a protection from the Spanish.

The Spanish did introduce the horse, sheep, goats, hogs and chickens. Methods of planting and the different crops such as oranges, grapes, etc. were introduced. The handicrafts such as silversmithing and other trades were improved upon.

Spemicalawba

This was a chief of the Shawnee. As a child he was taken prisoner by General Logan, who was fighting in Ohio at the time. He raised the boy and gave him the name of James Logan. He later became a captain and during the War of 1812 he fought on the side of the Americans. He died November 24, 1812, after several wounds that he received in a battle. Logansport, Indiana, is named for this Shawnee chief.

Spia

This was the clan of the Sia pueblo in New Mexico known as the hawk clan.

Spike Town

Also known as Spike Buck Town, this was a former village of the Cherokee who lived along the Hiwassee River near what is now Hayesville in Clay County, North Carolina.

Spirit Walker

This Wahpeton Sioux chief was born near Lacquiparle, Minnesota, around 1795. He became a Christian Indian and fought against the Sioux in 1862. After the battle of Little Crow he fled to the Dakotas.

Spokan

This name was used by several small bands of the Salish who lived along the Spokane River in the northeastern part of Washington.

Spoons

The Indian made spoons from a variety of articles, mainly from horns of sheep, gourds, shell, wood and pottery. As a general rule the spoon was rather large as compared to our present day spoon.

Spotted Arm

This Winnebago Chief was born about 1772 and lived

in and around Michigan and Wisconsin. His name is derived from the fact that he had a very bad arm wound and he used to paint it to look like a fresh wound. He was also known as Broken Arm. He was one of the signers of a treaty at Green Bay, Wisconsin, in 1832. His main village was located near what is now Exeter in Green County, Wisconsin.

Springdale
Springdale, Pennsylvania, see Sewickley.

Springfield
Springfield, Ohio, see piqua.

Spruce Tree House
This is one of the largest cliff houses in Colorado. It is located in the Mesa Verde National Park in Colorado. The building is some 220 feet long and has about 115 rooms with some of the sections of the building being three stories high. Much repairing has been done on these ruins in recent times.

Squantersquash
The early spelling for the squash.

Squanto
This was the name for the Wampanoag Indian of Patuxet who it is said was the only one to escape the plague of 1619 in New England. He died in 1622.

Squantum
The name means door or entrance, or as we know it an "open house" or a party. Generally used in New England to denote a feast or picnic where many people attend.

Squash
A plant in use at the time of the settlement, used by the Indians of the northeastern part of the country. The Indian name meant that it was green or could be eaten green. Also spelled squantersquash (q.v.).

394

Squaw

The word squaw is now used by tribes all over the United States to mean a woman; the word was from the Narraganset "eskwaw," the Delaware, "ochqueu," the Chippewa "ikwe."

Squawkeag

This was the tribe of the "red earth people" who lived along the Connecticut River near what is now Northfield in Franklin County, Massachusetts, in 1688.

Squeteague

This was a kind of fish which was caught off the coast of New England and used by those tribes. Parts of this fish were used by the Narraganset for the making of a glue, their name meaning they who make glue.

Squirrel

See muffanek.

Standing Bear

This was a former chief of the Ponca who lived in Nebraska. On January 15, 1877, Standing Bear and several other chiefs were taken to Kansas to select a site for a reservation that they were to be "removed" to. They did not like the site selected for them and they asked to be taken home. This was refused and so they walked almost 500 miles to their old village only to be refused a hearing. In May Standing Bear and his people were arrested and "removed." The new climate caused much sickness. The chief tried to take the bones of his son back to the old village site for burial and he was again arrested. A writ was drawn up for his release but the United States Government denied that a prisoner had the right to a writ, that he was not a person within the meaning of the law. However, in April of 1879, a Judge Dundy handed down the decision that "an Indian is a person within the meaning of the law of the United States." Chief Standing Bear died in September, 1880, after traveling around the country telling of the sorry dealings that his people received at the hands of the government.

Standing Stone

This was a landmark located near the present site of Huntingdon in Pennsylvania. This was a rock which was covered with pictographs (q.v.) and was about 15 feet high. After 1754 it was removed by the Indians and replaced by another one which was used by the early traders as a spot to stop. They put their marks on it also.

Steatite

A soft stone sometimes called soapstone. It was used by the Indians for the making of bowls and other containers.

Stikayi

This was a name used for three different villages of the Cherokee in Georgia and North Carolina. One was located near what is now Whittier and the other at the junction of the Nantahala with the Little Tennessee River, both in North Carolina, and the other one was located near what is now Clayton, Georgia.

Stilts

A game played by the children of the Hopi and Shoshone. Stilts were also used in Mexico.

Stockbridge

The present city of Stockbridge, Massachusetts, was the site of several Indian villages in 1736; it was abandoned in 1787. The name was also used for Indian village sites in New York and Wisconsin, both of the same name and tribes. See Skatehook.

Stogie

This name is derived from the Indian name of Conestoga, Pennsylvania, a town of the Iroquois where a short cigar was made which became known as a stogie. This is also the same city where many covered wagons were made known as the Conestoga Wagon (q.v.).

Stonington
This was a former village of the Pequots who lived near New London, Connecticut, about 1825. See Pequot.

Stono
In 1562, this tribe of the Edisto were active around the present site of Charleston, South Carolina. Their village was raided by the English in an effort to secure slaves in the early days of the settlement.

Storage
See caching.

Stoughton
Stoughton, Massachusetts, see Pequimmit, Punkapog.

Strata
This term is used to describe the layers of earth which are encountered when digging a site of Indian or other ruins, the oldest being the deepest.

Struck by the Ree
This was a head chief of the Yankton Sioux who was born at Yankton, South Dakota, on August 30, 1804. When he was born Lewis and Clark happened to be in the village and they asked to see the baby. They wrapped it in the flag and stated that it was hereby an American. This chief took great pride in what had happened to him as a child and he became a strong friend of the whites, even during the Indian wars of 1862 in Minnesota. He died on July 29, 1888.

Sturgeon
See cuppotoon.

Succotash
This was the corrupt name of the Narraganset word for

corn, "msickquatash," meaning grains are whole (corn). This was a mixture of green corn which was cut from the cob, beans, milk and some form of meat, usually bear meat.

Suckquahan
The Virginia Indian term for water, see suckquohana.

Suckquohana
The Virginia Indian term for water.

Sugeree
This small tribe of the Sioux lived near what is now Waxhaw, in Mecklenburg in North Carolina and another tribe near Rock Hill, in York County, South Carolina. Around 1715 they merged with the Catawba.

Suhub
This was a clan of the Hopi known as the cottonwood clan of Arizona.

Sukaauguning
This was the location name of a tribe of the Chippewa who lived around Pelican Lake in Oneida County, Wisconsin.

Sukiaug
This was the village of a small tribe of Algonquian who lived along the Connecticut River near Hartford. In 1730 they moved to Farmington, Connecticut.

Sulapin
This was a former village of the Chumashan, located in Ventura County, California.

Sun Dance
This is a ceremony typical of the Plains tribes. The ceremony is performed in the summer. The ceremony usually lasts for eight days. Some of the ceremony is secret, lasting from one to four days. Smoking, fasting and the completion of certain rites are done during these days. Every act is

performed in a set way. Penance and self torture are the main object of the ceremony. In some tribes, a bison skull was pulled around the lodge by means of a thong and a peg which was inserted through the skin of the chest. Other tribes, such as the Kiowa, did not want any bloodshed during the ceremony and there was no form of self-torture. The missionaries and the government frowned upon the ceremony to such an extent that the rites are now almost forgotten and the true meaning, which the government and the missionaries did not understand then, has been lost.

Suquamish
A Salish tribe living at the west side of Puget Sound, Washington. Seattle was a chief of this tribe, and the city was named after him.

Susquehanna
In 1608 this was a town of the Iroquoian people which was located along the lower reaches of the Susquehanna River. The name was spelled "Sasquesahannocks" by Captain John Smith. They were friends of the early settlers, who even helped them in battles against their enemies.

Sutaio
A small tribe related to the Cheyenne, which eventually combined with the Cheyenne.

Suwanee
This was a town of the Seminoles which was deserted around 1763 and then rebuilt. In 1818, after the Seminole War, it was again destroyed. There is a village located there now called Old Town, Florida.

Sweat lodge
The sweat lodge was almost a universal thing for all of the tribes north of Mexico. This was usually a small round house made of sod, sticks or hide. The individual entered and hot rocks and water were placed inside to cause steam.

The individual would remain for a specified time and would then plunge into snow or cold water. The sweat lodge was used for religious purposes, to purify oneself and also to cure disease. Special rituals were carred out in sweat lodges.

Swift Bird

This was the son of a trader who married a Teton Sioux. Swift Bird was born about 1842 along the Missouri trade route; he became a sub chief. He died in 1905.

Swino

This was the former village of the Chumashan Indians who lived in Ventura County at a place now called Punta de la Loma in California.

Swinomish

A small Salish tribe of northwest Washington, related to the Skagit.

Syracuse

Syracuse, New York, see Skaniadariio.

T

Ta
This was the deer clan of the second Kansa gens and the grass clan of several Tewa pueblos of New Mexico and Arizona.

Tabeguache
This division of the Utes lived in southwestern Colorado around Los Pinos. They were later removed to a reservation and were then called the Uncompahgre Utes.

Tabo
This was the rabbit clan of the Hopi of Arizona.

Tachi
This was one of the larger Mariposan tribes who lived in the south central part of California.

Tachikhwutme
This former Athapascan village was located along the coast of California, just north of the Klamath River.

Taconnet
This was a village of the Abnaki, located at the start of the 17th century near the present Waterville in Kennebec County, Maine.

Tacquacat
This is the Virginia Indian word for frost.

Tacquison
This was a former village of the Papago, located along the Arizona-Sonora border in 1871.

Tahchee

This was a chief of the Cherokee who lived in Arkansas. He became a scout for the army. His portrait was painted by George Catlin in 1834.

Taimah

This was a lower chief of the Fox tribe of the Thunder Clan. He lived for some years on Flint Creek a short distance from Burlington, Iowa. He was friendly toward the whites. He warned the Indian agent at Prairie du Chien of danger at one time. He was a signer of a treaty at Washington for the Foxes and the Sauk in 1824. He was known as the bear.

Ta-'ka-i

See race.

Takaibodal

Kiowa, see names.

Takelma

This linguistic family of people live along the Rogue River in Oregon. They are allied with the Shasta of northern California. Tobacco was the only plant that they cultivated.

Takhchapa

This group of the Miniconjou Sioux was known by the name of the deer heads.

Takimilding

A former village of the Hupa of California. This village could be called the religious center of the tribe. Sacred horses were located here and such ceremonies as the acorn feast and others were held here.

Taladega

This was a town of the Upper Creeks who lived along the Coosa River. This was located at the present site of Taladega, Alabama.

Talakhacha

In 1823 this was the location of a town of the Seminoles who lived along the west coast of Florida.

Talapoosa

In 1715 this was a name given to some 13 Creek towns that were along the Tallapoosa River in Alabama. They all belonged to the Upper Creeks.

Talasse

Talasse, Alabama, see Tukabatchi.

Talawipiki

This clan of the patki or cloud people was known as the lightning clan of the Hopi of Arizona.

Talking Rock

This village of the Cherokee was located along the Coosawatee River in northern Georgia. The name was given this village because of the echoes that can be heard in the area, especially near the falls.

Tall Bull

This Cheyenne name is hereditary among the Cheyenne who lived in Kansas and over into Colorado. One chief in particular fought against the Fifth cavalry at Summit Springs in Colorado and on July 11, 1869, he was killed by the troops of General E. A. Carr.

Tama

This term was in use in Texas by the Indian and the Spanish. It was used for someone who was a "pusher" or an overseer who saw to it that things were done when they should be.

Tama

Tama, Iowa, see Taimah.

Tamaha

In about 1775 this chief of the Mdewakanton Sioux was

born near Winona in Minnesota. Because he lost an eye while he was a boy, he was known as One Eye by the English. He fought with the Americans in the War of 1812. He was always known to wear what was known as the stove pipe hat. He died at Wabasha, Minnesota, in April, 1860.

Tamanos

This term was used by the Indians of the northwest of Oregon, Washington and up into Canada. It signified a person who had magic power, not the shaman or medicine man, but the act of magical power by any indivdual.

Tamaque

This chief of the Delawares was a great trouble to the settlers of Pennsylvania. He was friendly with the English until Braddock was defeated in 1755, after which he became a friend of the French. After 1764 he came under the influence of Moravian missionaries and became a Christian. He died about 1770.

Tamaroa

A division of the Illinois tribe.

Tamarox

This was formerly a village of the Costanoan who were connected with the San Juan Bautista mission in California.

Tammany

One of the most famous chiefs of the Delawares, his name means affable or friendly. He was so well liked by the whites that legends grew up about him; he was known as St. Tammany and also the Patron Saint of America. The Tammany Society of New York became a political factor for the Democratic Party.

Tammufcamcuwh

This is the Virginia Indian word for flowing water.

Tampa Bay

Tampa Bay, Florida, see Totstalahoeetska.

Tano

In ancient times this was the southern group of the Tewa of New Mexico, this was the name given to several villages of these people. In 1541 they were seen by Coronado. By 1630 most of the people of the Tano villages had become Christianized. After 1680 most of the people had left and joined the Hopi tribes, those left died of smallpox.

Tanques

This pueblo of the Tigua was located along the Rio Grande near Albuquerque, New Mexico. The word is Spanish for pools or water holes.

Taos

This name is derived from the Tewa name of Towih or Tuatá, known also as the red willow place. In 1540 the pueblo was visited by the Spanish explorer Hernando de Alvarado. In 1598 it was again visited by the Spanish, this time by Oñate and soon after it became a main Spanish mission site. Today Taos, New Mexico, is an active Indian center.

Taposa

This tribe lived along the Yazoo River in Mississippi around 1699, they eventually were combined with the Chickasaw.

Tappan

This was a tribe of the Delawares who formerly lived on the west side of the Hudson River in Rockland County, New York, and also in Bergen County, New Jersey.

Tarapins

Tarapins, see terrapin.

Tareque

This was a village of the Wichita who lived in eastern Kansas and was considered to be the main village of the Quivira.

Tarhe

This was a well-known chief of the Wyandots, also known as the Crane. He was born about 1742 near what is now Detroit, Michigan. He was a great warrior and fought the whites until 1795, when he signed a treaty. He kept his word after that. He fought for the Americans in the War of 1812 and became well-known to the early settlers in Ohio. He died at Cranetown, near Upper Sandusky in Ohio in 1818.

Tasawiks

This was a village of the Paloos which was located along the Snake River about 16 miles from its mouth in southeastern Washington.

Tascalusa

This former chief of the Alibamu tribe led his people against De Soto in a battle which was held in October, 1540. He led this fight against De Soto's soldiers who wore armor and who rode horses. The battle was one of the greatest Indians fights in our history. It took place at the Indian town of Mabila, located along the Alabama River in Alabama. There were almost 600 Spaniards who fought against a large number of Indians. After the battle there were over 2,500 Indians killed and some 175 of De Soto's men were killed or wounded. The battle started over De Soto's threats to persuade Tascalusa to supply men to carry the Spanish burdens.

Tasetsi

This was a former village of the Cherokee who lived along the Hiwassee River in Towns County, Georgia.

406

Tashkatze

This pueblo of the Keresan was located near Cochiti in north central New Mexico. The name means the place of broken pottery.

Tasikoyo

This village of the Maidu was located near what is now Taylorsville in Plumas County, California. The name means north valley.

Tasqui

In 1711 this was an active fortified town of the Tuscarora, located in North Carolina.

Tatamaho

This is the Virginia Indian term for the garfish.

Tatarrax

This chief of the Pawnee met Coronado along the Kansas River in Kansas, late in 1541. Chief Tatarrax is remembered by a monument which was erected by the Quivira Historical Society, located at Manhattan, Kansas.

Tatemy

This Christianized Indian, known as Moses Fonda Tatemy, was born near Cranberry, New Jersey. He became an interpreter for the English. As a Delaware chief, he spoke for his people. In 1757 Tatemy's son was killed. This strained relations between the Indians and the whites; however, it was promised that the young man who killed his son would be punished. The son was buried near Bethlehem, Pennsylvania, with services given by the Moravian Church. Sometime after 1761 Chief Tatemy died.

Tatlatunne

This was the former village of the Tolowa who lived along the coast of California, at the present site of Crescent City, California.

407

Tatumasket

This was a former village of the Nipmucs who lived in the southern part of Worcester County in Massachusetts around 1675.

Tautog

This is the word used by the New England tribes of the Algonquian for the fish called the blackfish.

Tauxenent

This was a former village of the Powhatan Indians who lived along the Potomac River in Fairfax County, Virginia, the present location of Mount Vernon. The village was active around 1608.

Tavibo

This was the name of a chief of the Paiutes who was a medicine man. When the whites were pushing his people out of their lands, he said that he had a vision whereby all people, including the Indians and the whites, would be swallowed by a giant earthquake and only the Indian would return to a land of plenty. He had a large following of hopeful Indians from Nevada, Idaho and Oregon. He died about 1870.

Tawasa

This tribe was known to have been located along the Tallapoosa River in Alabama. They belonged to the Muskhogean tribes that were met by De Soto. By 1705 they left the area because of attacks by other tribes.

Tawsee

This was a former settlement of the Cherokee which was located along the Tugaloo River in Habersham County, Georgia.

Taylorsville

Taylorsville, California, see Tasikoyo.

Tazaaigadika

This was a tribe of the Shoshonean people who lived along the Snake River in Idaho. Their name means the salmon eaters.

Tchataksofka

This was a former town of the Creeks of the area near Eufaula, Oklahoma. The name means the cliff or precipice.

Teatontaloga

In 1666 this village of the Mohawks was destroyed by the French. It was rebuilt a short distance from the former site and became the Jesuit mission of St. Mary. In 1693 it was again destroyed by the French. They were located along the Mohawk River in Montgomery County in New York.

Tecumseh

About 1768, this chief of the Shawnee was born in the village of Piqua on the Mad River, a few miles from the present city of Springfield, Ohio. Tecumseh did not like the whites taking land from the Indian and he tried to organize all of the Indians from Ohio to Florida for a strong resistance against the whites. A premature battle ruined the plan. In the War of 1812, he sided with the English and on October 5, 1813, he died in battle.

Teeth

See mepit.

Teguayo

This was a name used in several instances for cities that were seen or visited by the Spanish explorers, they were located at various spots on Spanish maps and were in the Tewa country of New Mexico.

Tekanitli

In 1839 this settlement of the Cherokee in upper Georgia

409

came to an end. It was also known by the name of Tick-anetly.

Telmocresses

This former town of the Lower Creeks was located along the Chattahoochee River in Jackson County, Florida.

Temecula

In 1875 this village of the Luiseño was moved from Riverside County, California, to Pachanga Canyon and so they were then known as the Pichanga Indians.

Temesathi

This was a village of the Chumashan who lived in the area around San Luis Obispo County, California.

Temoksee

This small tribe of Shoshonean lived along the Reese River in north central Nevada.

Temper

A term used in the ceramic arts and crafts to denote how much cracking or other changes are made in pottery objects when they are fired.

Tenawa

This downstream division of the Comanche became extinct shortly after a battle with the tribes to the south of them in 1845.

Tendoy

This was a chief of mixed people who lived in the Lemhi Valley in Idaho. He spoke up for his tribe and the terrible conditions that they were in. Because of his pleas the tribe was helped by the government and in return, he and his people kept the peace. He died on the Lemhi reservation in 1907.

Tenino

A small tribe of Shahaptian who formerly lived along

the Des Chutes River in Oregon. In 1855 they were placed on a reservation.

Tennessee
This was the name used for several villages of the Cherokee. One was located in eastern Tennessee and the other located in a place near Webster, North Carolina. The meaning of the name has been lost.

Tenskwatawa
This man became a prophet of the Shawnee. He is supposed to have had a vision which said that the Indian should return to his old ways or no hope would be his in the hereafter. He had a large following for some time. In 1832 he was interviewed by George Catlin, who also painted his picture. He died in 1837 and was placed in an unmarked grave.

Tenyo
This clan of the Tewa people was known as the pine people.

Tepemaca
In 1757 this was a tribe that lived near what is now Laredo, Texas. Also known as the burnt skins.

Teracosick
This village of the Powhatan was located along the western side of the Nansemond River, Virginia, in 1608.

Terebins
Terebins, see terrapin.

Terrace
Geologically, this is the steplike formation which is seen when a stream or river cuts through a section of land and so exposes the various layers of earth, some harder than others. This results in the gradual wearing away of the softer materials, thus forming terraces or steps.

Terrapin
This word is spelled in many ways: the Delaware, tulpa; Abnaki, turebe; terebins and tarapins in the Massachusetts dialects.

Tessuntee
This was a former village of the Cherokee, located near what is now Franklin in Macon County, North Carolina.

Tesuque
This was the name for one of the most southern of the Tewa Pueblos, located about eight miles north of Santa Fe, New Mexico. It became a center for the Spanish missionaries. In 1680 it was abandoned by the Indians in the pueblo revolt. There is a modern pueblo of this name at approximately the same site.

Tetanauoica
This was the name of an Indian who was buried at the San Francisco Solano mission in Texas.

Teton
This was the western division of the Dakotas and the Sioux. The name means the people of the prairie. They now live mainly in North and South Dakota on reservations.

Tewa
This group of people were known as the moccasin people and they belong to the Tanoan language family. They live mainly in the pueblos of New Mexico, such as San Ildefonso, Santa Clara, San Juan and Nambe. They were visited by Oñate in 1598.

Texas
A name used by the Spanish to designate the combined tribes of what is now the state of Texas. The tribes were made up mainly of the Hasinai. It was variously spelled, but the general meaning was allies, or friends, it was used as a form of greeting by the Indian. As used on the Mississippi

412

River boats it designated the upper deck around the pilot house (1877).

Tfepaih
To be dead in the Virginia Indian language.

Thamien
A name used to designate those Indians who belonged to the Costanoan family and who lived around the Santa Clara Mission in California.

Thayendanegea
This was a well-known chief of the Mohawk Indians. He was born in 1742. His family lived near what is now Canajoharie, New York. Through re-marriage of his mother, he secured a new name, Brant, and he then became known as Joseph Brant. After marriage, he joined the Episcopal Church. He took part in the Pontiac War of 1763, where he fought for the English. He died on November 24, 1807, and was buried near a little church in Brantford, Ontario. In 1879 a doctor and some medical students opened the grave and stole the body.

Thigh
See apome.

Thompson
Thompson, Connecticut, see Quantisset.

Three Fires
A term used during the Revolution to designate the three tribes of the Ottawa, Potawatomi and the Chippewa.

Thunder Bay
This was a village of the Chippewa who formerly lived in the area which is now Alpena County, Michigan.

Thunderbird
The thunderbird is the Indian answer to just what thunder and lightning are caused by. The general conception is

that there is a great bird in the sky and when he flaps his wings you will hear the thunder; as he is so large, naturally you will hear thunder in distant spots. If you are hit by lightning and live, you are considered to have certain mystical powers. The thunderstorm itself is supposed to be a contest between the thunderbird and a giant serpent.

Thur
This is the sun clan of the people of the Tigua pueblo at Isleta, New Mexico.

Tigua
This term is used to designate a group of three pueblo tribes of New Mexico—Taos, Picuris and Sandia.

Tihehip
Powhatan word for a bird.

Tikwalitsi
This was a former town of the Cherokee which was located along Tuckasegee River near what is now Bryson City, Swain County, in North Carolina.

Tilapani
This name was on a map made by De L'Isle in 1700, located near Atchafalaya Bayou in Louisiana.

Tilkuni
This tribe was located around the area of Warm Springs in Wasco County, Oregon.

Till
This is the deposit left by a glacier which is not in layers or stratas, it is usually composed of many types of rocks and clays.

Tillamook
An important Chinook tribe formerly living on Tillamook Bay, northwest Oregon.

Timigtac

This former village of the Costanoan was located near the Dolores mission in San Francisco, California.

Timpaiavats

This division of the Utes lived near the mountains in Utah around 1865. In 1873, they were placed on a reservation and were then known as the Uintah and Ouray agency.

Timpoochee

This man, known as Chief Barnard Timpoochee, fought with the Americans against the Creeks in the War of 1814, at the battle of Camp Defiance, Alabama. He was also a signer of the Creek treaty on August 9, 1814, at Fort Jackson, Alabama.

Timucua

This name was given to the principal tribe of the Timucuan family of tribes of Florida who lived along the east coast from Cape Cañaveral to the St. Johns River and northwest to about the Ocilla River.

Tinne

A term used sometimes to designate the northern divisions of the Athapascan family of tribes.

Tintaotonwe

This was a former village of the Mdewakanton Sioux, located along the lower Minnesota River in Minnesota. Known as the village on the prairie.

Tioga

This former Iroquois village was located near the present Athens, Pennsylvania. This was a center area for those tribes that went north and south. In 1778 it was burned by Colonel Hartley.

Tiou

This was a group of people who lived along the lower Mississippi and Yazoo Rivers in Louisiana in the early 1700's, through warfare they became extinct at a very early date.

Tipi

The Siouan word for dwelling or house. A term used to describe the type of dwelling of the Plains Indians, it was a cone-shaped house made from the skins of animals, especially the bison. The tipi differs from the wigwam, hogan and wickiup. The army Sibley tent which was developed by General Sibley was a direct result of the influence of the Plains Indian tipi. The Indian tipi was made from ten or more bison skins and some twenty or more long cedar poles, depending on the size of the family. These were tied together at the top and the hides, which were sewn together, were fastened around the framework. An open top was left to let out the smoke and a flap covering was left. Sleeping was done on mats around the wall.

Tippecanoe

This was a village site on the Wabash River near the mouth of the Tippecanoe River in Indiana. It was occupied by the Potawatomi and the Miami. The name means at the place of the buffalo fish. The slogan "Tippecanoe and Tyler Too" came from a battle that William Henry Harrison had with the Indians of Tecumseh and the Prophet (Tecumseh's brother). General Harrison marched on the village and on November 7, 1811, defeated the Indians at the Battle of Tippecanoe. This was used as a rally cry in the presidential election against Tyler.

Tiwa

See Tewa.

Tiyochesli

This name was given to a band of Oglala Sioux and means dung in the lodge.

Tkhakiyu

A former village of the Yaquina, located along the Yaquina River near what is now Newport, Oregon.

Tlelding

This was the name of a former village of the Athapascan who lived along the Trinity River in California. They spoke the language of the Hupa and were later removed to the Hupa Reservation at Eureka, California.

Tobacco

Tobacco is an American Indian plant, the use of which has spread all over the world; cigars and cigarettes were made by the Indians and were being used at the time of the discovery . . . as Columbus said, he had found men with "half burned wood in their hands." See Kinnikinnick. Also see apooke.

Tobacco bag

See chamange.

Tobacco boats

See chebacco.

Tobacco pipe

See apokan, also see vppocano.

Toboggan

A type of sled or pung (q.v.), made from flat pieces of wood bent and lashed together. Used mainly by the tribes of the northeastern part of the United States, the toboggan and the name were used by the whites.

Tocaste

This was an ancient Indian village which was visited by De Soto in 1539, located at the present site of Ocala, Florida.

Tohopeka

This was a fortified village of the Creeks, located at the

bend of the Tallapoosa River in Alabama. It was here that General Jackson fought the Creeks on March 27, 1814, killing over 500 Creeks.

Toisa

This was a former village of the Potawatomi who lived along the Tippecanoe River near what is now Bloomingsburg in Fulton County, Indiana.

Tokaunee Village

A village of Winnebago and Menominee who lived near what is now Mauston in Juneau County, Wisconsin. The village was active about 1837.

Tolemato

In 1595 this village of the Yamasee was located on the coast of Georgia. In 1597 the Indians revolted against the missionaries and drove them away for several years.

Toloawathla

In 1823 this was the site of a Seminole village, located along the western side of the Chattahoochee River in Florida.

Tolocabit

A former village site of the Cahuilla or Serranos, the present site of Redlands, California.

Tolowa

This was a former Athapascan tribe who lived in the northwestern part of California near Oregon. In 1862 they were placed on a reservation which was then abandoned in 1868, leaving the Tolowa to shift for themselves.

Toltu

This was the Sun Clan of the Hopi of Arizona.

Tolungowon

In 1836 this was a village of the Oneida Indians who lived near what is now Green Bay, Wisconsin.

Tomahawk

The name tomahawk is used rather freely by individuals to mean a war-club, an ax, a club, a type of pipe shaped in the form of an ax, a hammer. The word is Algonquian and no doubt came into common use through the Virginia Indian language. It has been spelled in various ways, almost as many ways as the uses to which it is attributed. The word tomahawk can be applied to a group of tools and weapons which had a handle and could be used as a tool or a weapon. The tomahawk, with some exceptions could be considered much as our ax . . . it was used to chop wood, to drive stakes in the ground and many other uses . . . even as a weapon if the occasion arose!

Tomau

This chief of the Menominee was born about 1752 and he died July 8, 1818, and is buried at Green Bay, Wisconsin. He acted as a scout and guide for Zebulon Pike and was a friend of the whites, or at least he stood for peace. However, he did side with the English and help in the attack on Fort Mackinaw.

Tomochichi

A former Creek chief who was active in the early history of Georgia. In 1733 he appeared in Georgia at the colony founded by Oglethorpe and helped to bring about a treaty with the Lower Creeks and the Colonists. He died on October 5, 1739, and a monument was erected to him at Savannah, Georgia, by the Colonial Dames of America.

Tomsobe

This was a former village of the Calusa located on the southwest coast of Florida. The village was active about 1570.

Tonawanda

An Iroquois reservation under the State of New York, with the state holding the lands in trust.

419

Tongue

See maratsno.

Tonikan

A linguistic family composed of the Tunica tribe of the lower Mississippi River.

Tonkawa

This was a linguistic family of people who lived in the central part of Texas. Their name meant "those who stay together," they were a combination of several tribes.

Tonto Monument

This National Monument is located near Roosevelt, Arizona, on Arizona State Highway 88. Here you can see a small museum and two very well preserved ruins of 14th century pueblos.

Tontos

This was a Spanish word for "fool," a name the Spanish applied to the tribes who were made up of Yuma, Mohave and Yavapai, also applied to some Apache bands. This name was used by early writers to designate those who lived near the White Mountains and in Arizona.

Tooth

See neputts.

Totheet

In 1614 this was a village of the Massachusetts, located in Plymouth County, Massachusetts.

Totoma

This village of the Maidu was formerly located on the east side of the Feather River in Butte County, California.

Totopotomoi

He was one of the main chiefs of the Pamunkey Indians of the colony of Virginia in 1650. In 1656 he and his warriors joined with the Virginians in a battle against other

Indians, the battle was such a failure that Colonel Edward Hill was stripped of his rank and property and made to pay personally for the cost of the battle. It was in this battle that Totopotomoi was killed. The battle took place at the present site of Richmond, Virginia.

Totstalahoeetska
This was a former town of the Seminoles but after the Creek war of 1813, it was made up mainly of Upper Creeks who fled to this village. Located near Tampa Bay, Florida.

Touenho
In 1688 this was a village of the Onondaga, located at the present site of the town of Brewerton, New York.

Touladi
This word derived from the Micmac and Abnaki dialects is the name for the lake trout found in the Great Lakes.

Towakwa
This name has been used in early accounts of the exploration of New Mexico by the Spanish but the location of the pueblo of this Jemez people is unknown.

Towha
This is an extinct clan of the coyote of the pueblo at Taos, New Mexico.

Trait
A term used to describe some specific element of a culture (q.v.).

Travois
Because the Indian had no wheeled wagons, he used the travois. This was a method used mainly by the Plains Indians who moved about with his tipi (q.v.). These devices were drawn by dogs as early as 1540, when they were seen by Coronado. As the Indian secured the horse he made good use of this animal. The travois consisted of poles, such

as the tipi poles, a bundle of each was tied on either side of the horse or dog and then bundles or the tipi hide were fastened in the middle similar to a sulky without wheels. The ends were dragged on the ground. Sometimes a small hut made of branches was made to carry small children.

Treaties

With the formation of the government of the United States, it became necessary to deal with the Indians in a legal way and such official actions as treaties were made. The government claimed complete sovereignty over the Indians and yet it treated the tribes as though it was dealing with another nation. The Constitution expressed the powers of the government as follows: "To regulate commerce with foreign nations and among the several states, and with the Indian Nations." There are several hundred treaties which have been made with the Indian and all with the aim that the Indian right to the land must cease. The present method now is to "terminate" the Indian reservations and thus what land is left will eventually leave Indian hands also.

Tribe

An Indian tribe is a large or small group of individuals who are bound together in a permanent body, having a unified purpose. Much the same as our states, bound together in a nation. This division can go still further to clans or smaller divisions of the larger tribe.

Tsoshi

The Yuchi name for sofki (q.v.), a corn meal food mixture.

Tuckahoe

This is a plant used by the Indians for food, known also as floating arum, Virginia Wake-robin, Virginia truffle. This was a name given to a type of fungus eaten by the Indians.

Also given to a root which they made in a type of bread. The term is also used in the South for a "poor white."

Tuckaseegee

This was a name used for two Cherokee villages, one located near Webster in Jackson County, North Carolina, and the other located along the Brasstown Creek near Hiwassee River in Towns County, Georgia.

Tucson

This is the Papago word for black area or base, which refers to the volcanic rock in the area of Tucson, Arizona. The area was first mentioned by the Spanish in 1699 when Father Kino visited the region and established a mission there in 1699. Tucson, Arizona, see Papago.

Tueadasso

This was a former village of the Onondaga located near what is now Jamesville, New York.

Tuff

A term used to describe that matter from a volcano known as volcanic ash.

Tukabatchi

This was a former town of the Upper Creeks which was located along the western side of the Tallapoosa River in Elmore County, Alabama, the present site of Talasse. It was at this village that Tecumseh met when he tried to organize resistance against the United States.

Tukinobi

This is the site of a former pueblo of the Hopi, located on a mesa known as East Mesa, near Tusayan in the northeastern part of Arizona.

Tukpafka

This former Upper Creek village was located along the

Chattahoochee River in Georgia in 1777. The name means "tinder" as used for fire making.

Tula

This village of a possible Caddoan derivation was located by De Soto in 1542 as being on the Arkansas River in Arkansas.

Tulibee

The name of this fish found in the Great Lakes is derived from the Chippewa and Cree dialects, meaning water mouth; this applied to the species of whitefish caught in the Great Lakes whose flesh had a rather flat or watery taste.

Tulkepaia

This group of Yuman and Apache people lived in the desert areas of western Arizona. In 1873 they were placed on a reservation. They spoke the Yavapai dialects.

Tulpa

Tulpa, see terrapin.

Tuluka

This village of the Patwin was formerly located in Pope Valley in Napa County, California. Around 1838 the Spaniards removed the tribe to a mission at Sonoma, where all but three of the tribe died of smallpox.

Tumac

This was the most western settlement of the Maricopa, located along the Gila River in the southwestern part of Arizona.

Tumpfeis

The Virginia Indian term used to describe an old woman.

Tump line

This was a strap which was placed around the forehead and extended over the back, used by the New England

Indians for carrying a pack, also called a burden strap or pack strap.

Tung
This was the former sun clan of the Tewa pueblo of Hano in northeastern Arizona.

Tunica
This distinct linguistic family lived along the lower part of the Mississippi. They were friendly with the French. They lived mainly by agriculture. In about 1706 they were driven from their villages by the Chickasaw.

Turebe
Turebe, see terrapin.

Turkey
See monanaw.

Turtle
See commotins.

Turtle Delawares
Turtle Delawares, see Unami.

Tuscarora
These people lived in several areas of North Carolina around 1709. One of their main towns was located at Newbern, North Carolina. Many of the Tuscarora were removed to New York State.

Tuscarora
An Iroquois reservation under the jurisdiction of the State of New York, with the state holding the lands in trust.

Tuskegee
From the Creek word for warrior, this was a small village of the Upper Creeks located in Elmore County, Alabama.

425

Tutelo

This was one of the southeastern tribes of the Sioux who formerly lived in Virginia and North Carolina. They were first mentioned by Captain John Smith in 1609. They were in constant war with the Powhatan Indians of Virginia.

Tuthill

Tuthill, New York, see Shawangunk.

Tuttafcuk

The Virginia Indian word for a crab.

Tututni

This Athapascan tribe lived along the Rogue River in Oregon. In 1856 the tribe was removed to a reservation as prisoners of war.

Tuzigoot National Monument

This partially restored pueblo was active in the 14th century, located near Clarkdale, Arizona, near U.S. highway 89.

Twana

A group of the Salish living along Hoods Canal, Washington. Sometimes called Skokomish.

Twilling

In the Indian weaving, this is the design which is made when the woof threads are carried over one and under two of the warp threads. This produces a diagonal design on the surface of the object.

Tyasoliwa

This name was used in the early days of settlement for the name of a pueblo of the Jemez, location unknown.

Typology

A term used by the archaeologist to describe the system of arrangement of individuals of an area according to type.

Tzekinne

These are the descendants of the Apache and Pimas who formerly lived in the cliffs of Sobaipuri. They were driven out by the Apache from Aravaipa Canyon in the southeastern part of Arizona.

U

Uainuints

In 1873 this band of the Paiutes lived near St. George in the southwestern part of Utah. The name means the diggers, a name given to these people because they dug roots of plants for food or practiced agriculture.

Uchean

This was a linguistic family limited to one tribe, the Yuchi.

Ucita

In 1539 this was the first Indian village visited by De Soto in Florida. It was located along Tampa Bay. The Indians fled from the village at the approach of the Spaniards, who arrived in what were, to the Indians, large ships with sails, and the Spanish themselves were dressed in armor.

Uinta

This section of the Utes formerly lived in the northeastern part of Utah. They are presently under the Uintah-Ouray Agency in Utah. See Indian Reservations.

Ujuiap

This was one of the tribes that came to the San Antonio Mission in San Antonio, Texas, and became Christians. They came between 1741 and about 1755. They belonged, it was thought, to the Tonkawan.

Umatilla

This former tribe of the Shahaptian lived along the Columbia River in Oregon. In 1855 they signed a treaty with the United States and were placed on a reservation at the

Umatilla Agency in Pendleton, Oregon. See Indian Reservations.

Umpqua

An Athapascan group which lived along the Umpqua River in Oregon.

Unaduti

This was a former chief of the Cherokee who was born about March 18, 1826, near what is now Cleveland, Tennessee. He was the son of Reverend Jesse Bushyhead, a Baptist minister. In 1849 he went west in the gold rush and stayed there until 1868, when he returned to the reservation. He died February 4, 1898. He was also known by the translation of his Indian name "bushyhead."

Unalachtigo

This was the southernmost part of the Delawares, who had three main divisions. This tribe, known as "those who live near the sea," lived along the Delaware River and down on the coast of New Jersey.

Unami

Also known as the turtle tribe of the Delawares, this was one of the three divisions of the Delawares who lived in Pennsylvania and in New Jersey.

Unanauhan

This was a former village of the Tuscarora, located in the northeastern part of North Carolina in 1700.

Una Vida

This ruin was located near the Pueblo Bonito in Chaco Canyon in northwestern New Mexico. It was known by the Navajo as Saydegil, meaning the house on the side of the rock.

Uncas

During King Philip's War in 1675, this chief of the Mohegan fought on the side of the English. He also fought against the Pequot and the Narraganset. He died around 1682. A monument was erected for him in Norwich, Connecticut, in 1847. A monument was also erected to him by Mrs. Edward Clark at Cooperstown, New York. His name meant "the fox who circles."

Unkapanukuint
This was a small tribe of the Paiutes who lived near what is now Cedar City in southwestern Utah.

Upper Cowlitz
A name used to designate those people who lived along the upper reaches of the Cowlitz River in Washington.

Upper Creeks
This was a division of the Creeks who lived along the Coosa and Tallapoosa Rivers in the northeastern part of Alabama. See Lower Creeks.

Upper Mdewakanton
This was the northern division of the Mdewakanton Sioux who lived in Minnesota.

Upper Sandusky
Upper Sandusky, Ohio, see Tarhe.

Upper Yanktonai
This was one of the divisions of the Sioux, so called because they lived farther up along the Missouri River than the other division known as the Hunkpapa.

U-ray
Also spelled Ou-ray and Ouray. See Ouray.

Ustoma
This was a former village of the Maidu, located near the present city of Nevada City, California.

Utchowig
In 1608 this was a village of the Erie, located along the Susquehanna River in Pennsylvania.

Ute

This was a large and important division of the Shoshonean tribes who formerly lived in what is now Colorado, Utah and extending down into New Mexico. They were a very warlike people. They did not practice agriculture. Most of the Ute live on the Consolidated Ute Agency at Ignacio, Colorado.

Utenstank

In 1608 this was a village of the Powhatan, located along the north shore of the Mattapony River in Caroline County, Virginia.

Utsehta

This was one of the divisions of the Osage, known as the "lowlanders."

Uttamussac

In 1608 this Powhatan village was active along the shores of the Pamunkey River in Virginia.

Uturituc

This former village of the Pimas was located near the present Sacaton in Arizona. It was visited by the Spanish explorers in 1775.

Uva

This was a small tribe of Chumashan people who lived in the Tulare basin of California. In 1851 they lost a battle with the Spanish and other hostile Indians, and so they held a small piece of land along the Kern River and gave the rest of their land to the United States.

Uxbridge

Uxbridge, Massachusetts, a village of the Praying Indians, see Wacuntug.

V

Vagerpe

This was a small village of the Costanoan who formerly were connected with the Mission at San Francisco, known as the Dolores Mission.

Vallecillo

In 1540 this pueblo or village was visited by Coronado. The Opata people who lived here roamed the north parts of the desert in Arizona.

Valleytown

This Cherokee village was located near the present town of the same name in Cherokee County, North Carolina. See Setsi.

Vanca

This tribe of the Coahuiltecan were met by the Spanish explorers in 1691 in the area around what is now Hondo, Texas.

Varves

These are glacial deposits, found in pairs, the upper layer of clay, the lower layer of sand. These varves are deposited each summer by the melting of the glacier. By counting the layers it is possible to date the area.

Vasisa

This was one of the towns of the Apalachee located in what is now Jefferson County, Florida. It was destroyed by the English in 1704.

432

Venango

This was a former settlement of the Senecas, located in Venango County, Pennsylvania, around 1752.

Vermilion

This was one of the tribes of the Kickapoo who formerly lived along the Wabash River in Indiana.

Vesperic Indians

This was a term proposed by Schoolcraft, to designate the entire Indian tribes of the exact geographical area of the United States. That is exactly what this dictionary covers.

Village du Puant

This former village of the Winnebago was located in Tippecanoe County, Indiana. It was abandoned around 1819.

Virginia Indian Language

Recorded by Strachey, known to belong to the Algonquian linguistic stock. Also known as a dialect of the Delaware Indians.

Virginia maple

See pickewh.

Vppeinfaman

This is the glue or gum that is used by the Virginia Indians to fasten their arrowheads on the shaft.

Vppocano

The Virginia Indian term for the tobacco pipe.

Vshuccohomen

The Powhatan word for the grinding of corn into cornmeal.

Vtchepetaiuwk

The Virginia Indian term for curled hair.

Vtchepwoiffonna
The Virginia Indian word for the east.

Vttapantam
The Virginia Indian name for the deer.

Vttocais
The Virginia Indian term for leather.

W

Waban

This chief of the Nipmucs is said to have been the first Massachusetts chief to become a Christian. He was born about 1604. He was a friend of the whites; however, in 1675, he went to warn the officials of the uprising which was to be called King Philip's War (1675). They did not listen to him, he was jailed and he died about a year later (1676).

Wabanaquot

This was the name of a chief of the Chippewa who was born about 1830. He became chief through the death of his father, who was made a chief by the federal government. In 1871 he became a Christian Indian. The state of Minnesota erected a monument over his grave, which is supposed to have been the only monument erected to an Indian in Minnesota. His name meant "White Cloud."

Wabash

This name was used by La Salle in 1682 to designate one or possibly more tribes that he met in Indiana and Illinois. The name collectively means bright or gleaming, which referred to the limestone bottom of the river along its upper reaches.

Wabasha

Wabasha, Minnesota, see Tamaha.

Wabokieshiek

Also known as the Prophet. He was born about 1794 in an area now known as Prophetstown, Illinois. He was an advisor to Black Hawk and was directly blamed for the

Black Hawk War, which he assured Black Hawk would be a fine venture. In 1832 he was taken prisoner to Jefferson Barracks, Missouri, in irons. After several pleas and moving about he died in Kansas on a reservation about 1841. Two paintings were done of the Prophet, one by George Catlin and the other by R. M. Sully.

Waccamaw
One of the small tribes of South Carolina who formerly lived along the Lower Peedee River. It is thought that late in the 1890's they became a part of the Catawba tribes of South Carolina.

Waco
By 1830 the last residents of the village of the Tawakoni were gone. This tribe lived at the present site of Waco, Texas. The Waco Indians were removed to Oklahoma, as provided in a treaty of 1872.

Wacuntug
This was a village of the Praying Indians (q.v.), formerly of the Nipmucs in 1674, the village was located near what is now Uxbridge, Massachusetts.

Wading River
Wading River, Long Island, New York.

Wafford
This Cherokee, known as James D. Wafford, was born near what is now Clarksville, Georgia, in 1806. As a boy he attended mission school at Valleytown. In 1891 he became an employee for the Bureau of Ethnology, where he was a valuable aid. He died about 1896 on his reservation.

Waganakisi
This was an old and important settlement of the Ottawa, located at the present site of Harbor Springs, Michigan. The village was active between 1743 and 1825, when a mission was established there.

Waha

This was the former cloud clan of the Jemez pueblo located in New Mexico.

Wahpeton

This was one of the seven divisions of the Dakotas who formerly lived in an area around Mille Lac, Minnesota, in the 1680's.

Waiilatpuan

This is a small linguistic family of the Cayuse and the Molala, who formerly lived in Washington and Oregon along the Umatilla and the Wallawalla Rivers.

Walapai

This tribe of the Yumans lived in an area in Arizona and along the Colorado River in the desert areas. They are related to the Havasupai (q.v.).

Walhalla

See Oconee.

Wallawalla

This tribe of Shahaptian lived along what are now known as the Columbia and Snake Rivers in Washington and Oregon. They were visited in 1805 by Lewis and Clark. The name means "little river."

Walnut

See afsinimins.

Walnut Canyon National Monument

This is a small group of pueblo ruins located about 10 miles east of Flagstaff, Arizona, near U.S. Highway 66.

Walpi

This is one of the six Hopi villages located in northeastern Arizona. The first village of the Walpi was built around 1628 and was later moved to a higher site on the mesa, a spot known now as Kisakobi.

Wameqtikosiu
See race.

Wamesit
This was a former village site of the Pennacook who lived along the Merrimac River near Concord, Massachusetts. In 1686 they sold their lands and moved to Canada.

Wampanoag
A confederacy on the shore of Narragansett Bay. One of their chiefs was Massasoit.

Wampum
The Algonquian word, meaning white, used to describe the beads or strings of beads made of shell. The word was so long in Indian (wampompeag) that it was shortened by the whites to wampum. The beads were made from the hard clam and the whelk, found along the coast. The beads were about a ¼ of an inch long and were either purple or white. Wampum became a medium of exchange between the Indian and the settler. Belts made from wampum were used to convey ideas when they were strung together, such things as peace or war could be arranged with a wampum belt. As early as 1640 the settlers made counterfeit wampum.

Waneta
This was a chief of the Yanktonai Sioux who fought for the English in the War of 1812. After 1820 he supported the Americans. He died about 1848.

Wanigan
This was the Abnaki name for a trap or device used to hold something. The name was also used in the lumbering days for a flat boat used to follow the board rafts down the river, a kind of office and cook house.

Wapello
This was one of the chiefs of the Fox. He was born at

438

Prairie du Chien, Wisconsin, about 1787. He agreed to abide by the treaty of 1804 and be "removed" with his tribe to a reservation in Iowa. He died near the present city of Otummwa, Iowa, on March 15, 1842.

Wapiti

This is the name, meaning white rump, the Shawnee gave to the American elk. This is the largest deer in America, with the exception of the moose.

Wappinger

This was one of the groups of the Algonquians who lived along the Hudson River in New York from Poughkeepsie to New York City. They fought the Dutch from 1640 until 1645.

Wareham

Wareham, Massachusetts, see Wawayontat.

Warren

Warren, Ohio, see Salt Lick.

Wasco

A Chinook tribe living along the Columbia River near The Dalles, Oregon.

Washa

This small band of the Muskhogeans lived around what is now New Orleans, Louisiana, around 1699. By 1805 they became almost extinct as a people.

Washakie

A chief of the Shoshoni. He was born about 1804. He became chief of his tribe in Wyoming, and when he was about 70 some of the younger men of the tribe tried to get rid of him as a chief. He disappeared, and after almost two months he appeared at the council meeting with six scalps that he had taken, thus he squelched any ideas that he was too old to be a chief. He became a friend of the early settlers and did much to help them in their trek west. He died February 20, 1900, and was buried with military honors at Fort Washakie, Wyoming.

Washo
A tribe of the Hokan group, living on the Truckee River, Nevada.

Watap
From the Chippewa, it denotes the roots of the pine, spruce and tamarack which were used to sew the seams on the birch bark canoe.

Water
See suckquahan, suckquohana.

Wateree
This is one of the early Siouan tribes of South Carolina; they lived near what is now Camden, South Carolina, and other sites in the Carolinas.

Watopachnato
This was one of the divisions of the Assiniboin (q.v.) who lived on the plains from Missouri to Yellowstone. They were visited by Lewis and Clark in 1804.

Waugullewatl
This was a former village of the Hupa, located along the Trinity River in California.

Wauregan
A Mohegan term for something showy or fine, good. Also a town in Windham County, Connecticut.

Wautacone
See race.

Wawayontat
This was a former village of Praying Indians (q.v.),

active around 1674. Located at the present site of Wareham in Plymouth County, Massachusetts.

Waxhaw

This small tribe lived in North and South Carolina, and were related to the Sugeree and the Catawba. This tribe practiced head flattening. Around 1715 the Waxhaw were so reduced by the war with the Yamasee, that they combined with the Catawba.

Waxhaw

Waxhaw, North Carolina, see Sugeree.

Wayabishkiwad

See race.

Wayon

This South Carolina chief was a friend of the French. His village was near Port Royal in South Carolina.

Weanoc

In 1608 this tribe of the Powhatan lived along the James River in Charles City County, Virginia.

Weataug

This was a former village of the Mahican who lived near the present cities of Litchfield and Salisbury, Connecticut, around 1740.

Webster

Webster, North Carolina, see Tuckaseegee. Also see Tennessee.

Wechquetank

This was the name of a former village of Moravian Indians who lived northwest of Bethlehem, Pennsylvania. It was settled in 1760, and in 1763 they were driven out by the whites who burned their village.

Wecquaesgeek

This was a tribe that lived in Connecticut and New York, and were members of the Wappingers. In 1643 they fought with the Dutch and it was not until 1644 that peace finally came. One of their villages was located near what is now Greenwich and Norwalk, Connecticut. Another village was located at Dobbs Ferry, New York.

Wecuppom

In 1608 this village of the Powhatan was active along the banks of the Rappahannock in Richmond County, Virginia.

Weinshauks

In 1636 this village of the Pequots was located along the Mystic River near the present city of Groton, Connecticut.

Weitspekan Family

A linguistic family consisting only of the Yurok tribe.

Welsh Indians

The Welsh Indians are so called because they are supposed to have been "discovered" around 1170 by a Welsh prince, they are supposed to have lived in the Carolinas. The story has been kept alive by the people of Wales, especially in the early days, because they wanted to prove a claim to the new world and so offset the Spanish claims.

Wenrohronon

This term was used for those people who lived near a pool in Allegheny County, New York, near the present town of Cuba, New York. The word is Iroquoian for skum or film which is floating. The name was given to this pool which had its surface covered with a yellowish film, an oil-like substance. The Senecas had a high regard for this pool. It was the source of a cure-all of the time known as Seneca Oil.

Westchester

Westchester, New York, see John W. Quinney.

442

Westenhuck

This was a former village of the Mahican, located near what is now Great Barrington, Massachusetts. This was the site of the main town of the Mahican. In 1736 these people were removed to a reservation.

Westhampton

Westhampton, Long Island, New York, see Patchoag.

Westo

This is the name applied to those Indians who formerly lived along the Savannah River and along the coast of South Carolina. Not much was heard about them after 1681.

Wethersfield

Wethersfield, Connecticut, see Pyquaug.

Wewenoc

This was a former Abnaki tribe who lived along the coast of Maine. In 1749 they signed a treaty with the English and were moved to Canada.

Whiggiggin

This word is derived from the Algonquian and Abnaki dialects and is used mainly in the New England states to signify a written agreement, particularly a hunting permit.

Whilkut

This was a small division of the Hupa who formerly lived along the Redwood Creek in northern California. After 1870 they were removed to a reservation in California.

White Cap

The White Cap Indians were so called because they were under a chief known as White Cap. They were a small band of the Sioux and lived in Minnesota.

White Cloud

White Cloud, see Wabanaquot.

White dog

This was an annual ceremony of the Iroquois. This was a ceremony of the new year, aimed at re-newing life in all things.

White Eyes

This was the name of a former chief of the Delawares who lived near what is now Zanesville, Ohio, around 1776. He tried to keep the Delawares neutral in wars with the whites. In 1778 he was forced to lead his tribe in battle, he said that he would lead them and that he would be the first to fall so that he would avoid seeing their utter destruction. He died of smallpox, however, in 1778, before he had to lead his warriors.

White Indians

This name has been used in various parts of the country to describe a race of Indians who were white, had beards and who dressed like Europeans. This is on a par with the "Welsh Indians" (q.v.). They are also supposed to be from the lost colony on Roanoke Island in 1587.

White Mountain Apache

These people were so named because they lived in the Sierra Blanca Mountains. The name was later used to describe those Apaches who were placed on the reservation at Fort Apache at Whiteriver, Arizona.

White Race

See Race.

White Swan

This Crow scout served under General Custer at the battle of the Little Bighorn. In 1876 he received a severe wound in this battle with the Sioux which made him a cripple until his death in 1905. He is buried at the National Cemetery at the Custer battlefield in Montana.

444

White Woman's Town

This was the name given to a village of the Delawares, so called because the chief of the village married a white girl who had been taken prisoner; her maiden name was Mary Harris. She married Eagle Feather. Eagle Feather also had another white wife named Newcomer (q.v.).

Whittier

Whittier, North Carolina, see Stikayi.

Whizzer

See bullroarer.

Wiatakali

This was a former town of the Choctaws, located in Neshoba County, Mississippi. The name meant hanging above, so called because of the brush roof which was erected over the Choctaw council meeting area.

Wichita

These people who belonged to the Pawnee linguistically and to the Caddoan confederacy were first met by the Spanish explorer, Coronado, in 1541 in the area now known as Kansas. The meaning of the name has been lost.

Wickiup

This name is sometimes confused with tipi and wigwam (q.v.). This is the name for the mat covered houses of the Indians who lived in the Arizona, Nevada areas, such as the Apache and Paiute. The meaning has been lost but in several other languages it means a dwelling or house.

Wigwam

This word was borrowed from the Abnaki language and changed by the settlers of Massachusetts. The word was wetu or witu, also spelled wetuom and gradually was changed to wekuwomut and then in 1666 it was spelled wigwam and came into common use in books. The word is used to describe a house or dwelling of the Algonquian tribes of the northeastern part of the United States. The house itself is made from sticks and bark, made in a dome shape, with a hole in the top to let out the smoke. The wigwam differs from the tipi (q.v.) and the wickiup (q.v.).

Wigwassing
A term used by the New England settlers to describe the Indian when he went hunting for eels at night with a torch light; it means that he illuminates it, such as the fish at night.

Wild celery
See the Navajo word, haza'aleehtsoh.

Wild plum
See the Navajo, didzeh.

Wild Rice
Wild rice is found in the Great Lakes region and was a most important food in the early days. The rice is gathered by hand even today. A canoe is floated through the rice, which grows in shallow water, and the Indian bends the grain heads over into the canoe and hits it with a stick, thus collecting the rough grain in the canoe. The Menominee of Wisconsin gather most of the wild rice harvest.

Wild walnut
See the Navajo word, ha'altsedih.

Willewah
In 1805 Lewis and Clark met these Nez Percés who were then living in Oregon. After the Nez Percés War of 1877 they were placed on a reservation at Nespelem, Washington.

Williams
Eleazar Williams was born near Lake George, New York, about 1788. He was a son of a Christianized Indian, one of 13 children, all members of the Catholic Church. He went

446

to live with a minister named Williams. He became a well-known authority in many fields and held many high offices. He did, however, have many schemes. Toward the end of his life he claimed to be the Lost Dauphin of France. He died near Hogansburg, New York, on August 28, 1858. A painting of Eleazar Williams is in the collections of the State Historical Society at Madison, Wisconsin.

Windsor

Windsor, New York, see Shawiangto.

Winema

Also known as Toby Riddle, this was a woman chief of the Modocs. She was born about 1842 and married a miner from Kentucky named Frank Riddle. She became an interpreter for the government.

Wing

Austin E. Wing, a son of Negwagon (q.v.).

Wingan

The Virginia Indian term for good.

Winnebago

The Winnebago were first met by Nicollet in 1634 at Green Bay, Wisconsin. The name means dirty water or, in Chippewa, winipyägohag or the people of the filthy water. They also lived along the Fox and Wisconsin Rivers. In a treaty signed at Prairie du Chien in 1832, they gave all of their land in return for a reservation on the west side of the Mississippi and along the Iowa River. The dialect of the Winnebago is Siouan. They are woodland or forest people.

Winnemucca

This woman was a Paiute who was born in Nevada around 1844. Her full name was Sarah Winnemucca Hopkins. She became an interpreter and also taught an Indian school at Vancouver Barracks in Washington. She was able to secure lands for an Indian school which she established near Lovelock, Nevada. She died in Monida, Montana, on October 16, 1891.

Winona

This was the village of the Mdewakanton Sioux, the present site of Winona, Minnesota. The name means "first born," if it's a girl. See Tamaha.

Wintun

A division of the Copehan family, living around Mt. Shasta, California.

Winyaw

A small tribe that became extinct around 1715. They lived along the lower Pedee in South Carolina. They fought against the English in 1715.

Wiowah

Virginia Indian term for husband.

Wipho

This was a former settlement of the Hopi located northeast of the present Walpi pueblo in northeastern Arizona.

Wisconsins

This name was used to designate several groups of Indians who lived along the Wisconsin River, such as the Fox, Sauk and others.

Wishosk

This small tribe lived along the coast of northern California. After 1850 most of this tribe was killed by the settlers and they became wanderers and lived without support from the government.

Wishram

A Chinook tribe, also called the Tlakluit. They lived along the Columbia River, near The Dalles, in Washington.

Withlako

This was a former village of the Seminoles, meaning great lake or water. It was located in Hernando County, Florida. It was destroyed by the Americans in 1836.

Woapsit

See race.

Woccon

This was a small tribe that formerly lived in the eastern part of North Carolina, related to the Catawbas. They fought in the Tuscarora War of 1711 to 1713 and became extinct as a result of that war.

Wolf

See naantam.

Woman

See the Powhatan word, cucheneppo.

Woman's breast

See otaue.

Woman with child

See powevwh.

Woock

This is the Powhatan Indian word for the roe of the sturgeon.

Woodbury

Woodbury, Connecticut, see Pomperaug.

Wooteka

This was a former village of the Seminoles who lived around Apalachee bay in the western part of Florida.

Woqini

See Roman Nose.

Worcester

Worcester, Massachusetts, see Pakachoog.

Wovoka

This was the name of the Paiute medicine man who originated the Ghost Dance. He was born in Nevada about 1856. He was also known as Jack Wilson because as a boy he was taken in by a rancher by that name.

Wuckan

This was one of the seven villages of the Winnebago. Located on Lake Poygan in Wisconsin. They were active about 1806.

Wupatki National Park

This large group of pueblos which was occupied around 1100 to 1300 by the Anasazi peoples, is located about 45 miles from Flagstaff, Arizona, east of U.S. Highway 89.

Wutapiu

This was one of the main divisions of the Cheyenne, meaning the eaters.

Wyandotte

This is the name of a tribe of Iroquois, originally known as Hurons. It is also the name of a type of chicken which was named in Worcester, Massachusetts, in 1883. This type of chicken is said to have come from the mating of a Cochin hen and a Sebright cock.

Wyantenuc

This was the site of a large Indian gathering in Litchfield County, Connecticut, in 1675.

Wyoming

This name means "upon the great plains" in the Delaware dialect. The name has also been said to mean "field of blood." It is not known who suggested the name of the state.

450

Wysox

The Wysox may have been members of the Delawares or Munsee. They lived in Bradford County, Pennsylvania.

Wzokhilain

A Christianized Abnaki, see Osunkhirhine.

X

Xagua
This was the name used for a former village of the Chumashan who lived in what is now Ventura County, California. This village was active in 1542.

Xaiméla
This pueblo of the Piro was visited by Oñate in 1598, located near the Rio Grande in New Mexico.

Xalibu
The Micmac word for the American reindeer or caribou. The Micmac word means "scratching or shoveling," due to the habit of the animal of pawing the snow to get food which is covered by snow.

Xamunambe
This was the name of a village located along the South Carolina coast, visited by Ayllon in 1520.

Xarame
This was a tribe of the Coahuiltecan who came to the mssions in and around San Antonio, Texas, about 1699. The first Indian baptism at the San Antonio mission was a Xarame child.

Xinesi
This was the name given to the head of the ceremonies or what we would call a religious leader. This term was used by the Hasinai of east Texas.

Xisca
This was a former village of the Costanoan who lived near the mission of San Juan Bautista in California.

Xoxi

This was one of the villages located along the coast of the Carolinas which was visited by Ayllon in 1520.

Xutis

This unidentified pueblo was mentioned by Oñate as a pueblo that he visited in 1598.

Y

Yacum
This was a band or tribe that combined with the Cocopa who lived in the valleys between the mountains and the coast of California. They were active around 1850.

Yagua
This was a former village of the Calusa, located along the southwest coast of Florida. Active around 1570.

Yahalgi
This was the wolf clan of the Creeks.

Yahuskin
This former tribe of the Shoshonean lived in Oregon. In 1864 they ceded their land to the government in a treaty of Klamath Lake. They were then placed on a reservation. About 1898 they were officially called Paiutes and so lost their identity.

Yah yah algeh
See race.

Yaka
These are the former corn clans of the Keresan pueblos of New Mexico. These clans were of different colors, red, blue, brown, etc.

Yakima
This family of the Shahaptian lived along the Columbia River in Washington. In 1806 they were visited by Lewis and Clark. In 1855 they ceded their lands to the government and were removed to a reservation. Under this treaty

several different tribes were incorporated under the name of Yakima. The name means the "runaway." The Yakima name for themselves meant the people of the gap or the narrow place in the river.

Yakonan
This linguistic family lived in an area of western Oregon along the Umpqua and Yaquina Rivers.

Yamacraw
This village of the Creeks was located along the southern bank of the Savannah River, near what is now Savannah, Georgia, in 1730.

Yamasee
This tribe formerly lived along the coast of Georgia and down through Florida. About 1570 the Spanish tried to bring those who came to their missions to the West Indies as slave labor. The Yamasee revolted and in 1687 they left Florida and traveled to South Carolina to live under the English Rule. They were treated rather poorly by the English traders and fought against the English. They were very adept with the canoe and the term for a certain canoe stroke came into being, known as the Yamasee stroke.

Yampa
This was a division of the Utes who lived in the eastern part of Utah, they were later included under the White River Utes and the name Yampa was not used from then on. Yampa is also the name of a plant whose roots were used by the Indians of Oregon (Carum gairdneri).

Yana
This linguistic family of tribes lived in Shasta and Tehama Counties in California. In 1864 the prospectors and miners in the area attacked some 3,000 of the Yana and all but about 50 were killed in a few days. In a few years they became extinct as a tribe.

Yanegua

A former chief of the Cherokee who lived in the late 1700's, he was one of the signers of a treaty in 1798 and in 1805. He was also known as Big Bear.

Yangtsaa

This was the former coyote clan of the Jemez and Pecos pueblos in New Mexico.

Yankton

This was one of the seven main divisions of the Dakotas. They lived along the Missouri River in Iowa and the Dakotas. They belonged to the Siouan linguistic family. The name means the end village.

Yanktonai

This important tribe of the Dakotas lived in Minnesota and the Dakotas to the Red and Missouri Rivers. In the War of 1812 they fought against the United States. They were moved to reservations, especially to the Fort Peck Agency at Poplar, Montana.

Yatasi

This was a former tribe of the Caddo Confederacy who lived along the Red River in Louisiana. They became friends of the French against the Spanish influence. After wars and smallpox, which hit the tribes around 1805, they were reduced in number to less than thirty. What was left of the tribe was placed on a reservation in Oklahoma.

Yatokya

This was the sun clan of the people of the Zuñi pueblo in New Mexico.

Yavapai

This was a former Yuman tribe who lived in the arid areas of western Arizona along the Salt and the Rio Verde Rivers. They were known as the people of the sun. They were also known as the Mohave Apache. In 1875 they were placed on the reservation at San Carlos, Arizona, but later were given land near the Rio Verde at the site of old Camp McDowell.

Yazoo
A small tribe who lived along the lower Yazoo River in Mississippi. In 1729 they attacked the French fort on the river and destroyed it. The French had built the fort to guard the river travel. The meaning of Yazoo is unknown.

Ye
This was the former lizard clan of the pueblos of San Ildefonso and San Juan of New Mexico, belonging to the Tewa.

Yellow Thunder
This chief of the Winnebago was born about 1774; there was also an Indian village named after him in Wisconsin. He lived in an area around Green Bay, Wisconsin. On November 1, 1837, he signed a treaty which provided for the removal of his tribe to reservations to the west. The removal was to take place in eight months, however, the tribe thought that it was to be in eight years. In 1840 troops were sent to force the tribes to move and Chief Yellow Thunder was put in chains. After this removal was settled, Yellow Thunder returned and secured a homestead on the west side of the Wisconsin River about seven miles north of Portage, Wisconsin. He died in February, 1874. A portrait of him done by S. D. Coates is in the collections of the State Historical Society at Madison, Wisconsin. A monument was erected in his honor near Baraboo, Wisconsin.

Yesterday
See ofayoh.

Yguases
This was a tribe that Cabeza de Vaca lived with in 1527. He said that they were very poor and were frequently out of

457

food, which they gathered wild, they did little or no planting. They became extinct at a very early date.

Yohacan

The Virginia Indian term for a house.

Yoholomicco

This former chief of the Creeks who lived in Georgia and Arkansas was born about 1790. He fought with General Jackson against the Creeks in 1813. He was a signer of a treaty with the whites which ceded the lands to the government. He agreed to the removal of his people to lands west of the Mississippi, but he died on the way west in Arkansas about 1838.

Yojuane

This was one of the Tonkawan tribes of Texas, who are frequently mentioned by the early Spanish explorers. See Tonkawa.

Yokut

See Mariposan family.

Yonaguska

This was a prominent chief of the Cherokee. He lived in an area near what is now Bryson City, North Carolina. He was a strong leader and at about 60 years of age he became a prophet and led his people in a drive against drinking and removal to other lands. He was extremely suspicious of missionaries. At one time, after being read a part of a Bible that a missionary had given him he said, "It's a good book, but it's strange that the white people are not better, having had it so long." He died in April, 1839. He was also known as Drowning Bear.

Yoroonwago

This was a former village of the Seneca located near what is now Corydon in Warren County, Pennsylvania. The village was active around 1779.

You

See kear.

Yowani

This was a former town of the Choctaws, located near the present town of Shubuta in Clarke County, Mississippi. The village was active around 1764. During the removal they were placed in Texas and Louisiana.

Yscanis

This was one of the tribes of the Wichita confederacy who lived mainly in east Texas around 1684. Because of the pressure of warfare from the Comanches they moved down into Texas, around San Antonio, for protection.

Yuchi

This tribe lived along the Atlantic coast states in the south, Georgia and the Carolinas in particular. They were an early part of the Westo peoples. They had cultivated fields which were located near a stream and their houses were of the bark type (wigwam, q.v.). They made much pottery.

Yuki

The Yuki was a small linguistic family who lived in the northern part of California. They were more warlike than most of the California tribes. During the gold rush days they had much trouble with the prospectors; up until that time, very little was known of these people. Their name means the "enemy."

Yuloni

This was a former division of the Miwok who lived along Sutter's Creek in what is now Amador, California.

Yuma

One of the chief tribes of the Yuman family, living along the Colorado River in southern Arizona and California.

Yuman

This was the name used for those people who lived in the southwestern part of the United States and along the lower part of California and around the Gulf of California. This linguistic family had what could be classed as the lowest culture of any of the people in the United States. They made rafts constructed of bundles of grass tied together to cross the water and made no canoes. The land where they lived had a great deal to do with the poor living conditions that they had. They wore little or no clothing.

Yungyu

This was the former cactus clan of the Chua or snake phratry of the Hopi of Arizona.

Yurok

It was around 1850 that the Yuroks had contact with the whites, and in 1855 they were placed on a reservation in California along the Klamath River, near their former locations. However, the government finally discontinued this reservation and the tribe became self-supporting.

Z

Zaclom
This was a former village of the Chumashan which was connected with the mission at San Francisco in California.

Zaco
A former village of the Chumashan, located on Miguel Island, California, active about 1542.

Zanckone
The early Virginia Indian term meaning to sneeze.

Zanesville
Zanesville, Ohio, see White Eyes.

Zhanichi
This was a former village of the Kansa tribe who lived along the Kansas River in Kansas, the village was active around 1820.

Zia
A pueblo. See Sia.

Zuñi
This is the name of a well-known pueblo, located in Valencia County, Arizona. The name Zuñi is an adaptation of the Spanish from the Keresan, of which the meaning has been lost. This is supposed to be one of the lost seven cities of Cíbola for which the early Spanish explorers were searching. The first Zuñi mission was established in 1629. The

Zuñi of today is known for his fine works of art in silver and painting.

Zuñi Pueblo

The modern Zuñi pueblo is located about forty miles south of Gallup, New Mexico. It has limited tourist accommodations.